MICHAEL KEATING

TO THE LAST DROP

Canada and the World's Water Crisis

Macmillan of Canada
A Division of Canada Publishing Corporation
Toronto, Ontario, Canada

CANADIAN CATALOGUING IN PUBLICATION DATA

Keating, Michael, date.
  To the last drop

Includes index.
ISBN 0-7715-9704-5

1. Water-supply—Canada. 2. Water—Pollution—Canada. 3. Water quality—Canada. 4. Man—Influence on nature. I. Title.

HD1696.C2K43 1986   333.91'2   C86-093812-3

All inquiries regarding the motion picture or other dramatic rights for this book should be addressed to the author's representative, The Colbert Agency Inc., 303 Davenport Road, Toronto, Canada, M5R 1K5. Representations as to the disposition of these rights are strictly prohibited without express written consent and will be vigorously pursued to the full extent of the law.

EDITED BY Maggie MacDonald
DESIGNED BY Brant Cowie/Artplus

Macmillan of Canada
A Division of Canada Publishing Corporation

PRINTED IN CANADA

For Nicole

CONTENTS

ACKNOWLEDGMENTS

A book of this scope is the work not of one person but of many and the list below, based on my recollection at the time of writing, is, at best, a partial record of the many people who have helped me over many years.

Among individuals who have been very helpful are Douglas Hallett, Frank Quinn and Henry Regier who provided information on key issues and made helpful comments on the manuscript. In addition Thomas Brydges, Charles Caccia, Donald Chant, Katherine Davies, Richard Findlay, Ross Hall, Gerry Harris, Margherita Howe, Jeanne Jabanoski, James Kingham, Alex Manson, Robert Slater and John Vallentyne have contributed greatly to my understanding of water issues.

Several environment groups, particularly Pollution Probe, the Canadian Coalition on Acid Rain, the Canadian Environmental Law Association and the Canadian Environmental Law Research Foundation, have provided much help in identifying key issues.

Many people in the International Joint Commission, Environment Canada and Ontario Ministry of the Environment have been particularly helpful over the years in providing voluminous data and interpretation to go with it.

I would like to note the writings of Sandra Postel for the Worldwatch Institute, of Harold Foster and Derrick Sewell who wrote *Water, The Emerging Crisis in Canada* in 1981 and the Inquiry on Federal Water Policy which published *Currents of Change* in 1985.

The Globe and Mail deserves a special mention because it is there that I wrote the series on water issues and the many other environment stories which laid the groundwork for this book. The publisher and editors have encouraged my environment writing and provided the lengthy leave of absence necessary to complete the manuscript.

I offer special thanks to Ontario Arts Council for its generous financial support.

It was The Colbert Agency, which first proposed the book, and Macmillan of Canada, which was close behind with the same idea, who together got the project off the ground.

And most importantly I thank my wife for the patience and support so essential in seeing this book to completion.

Preface

Every now and then one comes across a work that is as prophetic as it is profound, combining scholarship with vision, albeit a foreboding one. Michael Keating's *To the Last Drop* is not just another warning of the "doomsday" variety. It is a clear and unmistakable call to action to the leaders of Canada and the managers of its patrimony to address with a new sense of urgency the state and fate of this critical resource.

Paradoxically, the volume seems an anomaly, at least in the case of Canada. After all Canada, in addition to its other blessings, is a water-rich country, not some semi-arid region where the shortage of water is a way of life and its exploitation and management a major national preoccupation. Still, Keating's message is clear: it could happen here. But the message doesn't end there. In effect the author is speaking to the rest of the world.

In our lifetime, with a rapidly expanding population and an equally rapid acceleration of industrialization with an insatiable appetite for water, this resource will undoubtedly assume strategic significance. In this connection also, the question is especially important to the Third World, where priorities will at some point have to include effective water management policies, since no development plan can hope to succeed without a readily available and predictable supply of water. This is a concern of the United Nations Environment Program, for whom Keating's very thoughtful message provides a welcome support. But perhaps Keating's most significant contribution is in the timeliness of the work, coming as it does in the second half of the Water Decade, one of the most far-reaching decisions of the United Nations Water Conference held at Mar del Plata, Argentina. That conference, it will be recalled, not only sought to make water a priority issue on the global agenda, but also alerted governments to a changing resource equation: water is likely to become increasingly an object of competition, even a new source of conflict, especially among the 70 per cent of the world population that is without reliable supplies of safe drinking water or adequate sanitation. But while it would be unrealistic to expect that the goals of the Decade, namely safe and adequate drinking water supply and sanitation for all people, could be achieved by 1990 or 2010, there can be no doubt that water should never again be allowed to revert to a low order of priority or an undervalued resource. Hence we have a new responsibility for the care and management of a resource that is vital to human development and well-being.

Keating has not only given the reasons why threats to our water resources should be treated with a sense of urgency, but he has also provided a coherent framework for thinking about the subject anew. One can only hope that the introduction of this volume will enlarge public enlightenment and stimulate the kind of public debate that will lead to the adoption of sound water management policies in North America and elsewhere.

Surely this book must be included among the most significant long-term contributions to the goals and objectives of the world's Water Decade.

NOEL BROWN
Director
United Nations Environment Program
New York, April, 1986

INTRODUCTION

The lone canoeist glides across a wild, northern lake. Behind the sleek hull, ripples spread out in silver Vs until they lap the granite shoreline. Below, the water is clear and cool, so typical of a Canadian shield lake. The canoeist dips a cup and drinks deeply of this liquid that has never seen a tap, let alone a water treatment plant. Just past the tree line, a short portage away, lies another lake and beyond that thousands more. It is part of the endless system of waterways which have shaped the history of our country since the first inhabitants travelled it by canoe.

For Canada, or any other nation, water is the element which binds us together both as individuals and as a society. It dictates where there can be life and where there is desert. Water is responsible for the birth of civilizations, population growth and the production of everything from food to nuclear weapons and spaceships. Water, harnessed for human use, is one of the oldest tools we have, whether it is used to float a canoe across a great river, send a caravel to new continents, create electricity for our modern, industrial age or help to make computer chips.

But water is more than just another commodity like coal, oil or minerals, which are shipped across the country or around the world to sell to the highest bidder. Water is the lifeblood of Canada's environment and is the striking point over such diverse issues as pollution and food production. In Canada we look north to see a blue and green wilderness of rocks, trees and endless lakes, rivers and beaver ponds. It is so vast that it has fostered a myth that we can never run out of water, even in a world which is outstripping its natural resources. This dangerous myth must be put in perspective.

We have long taken such pleasures for granted. Now our waters are under attack from many fronts.   (MICHAEL KEATING)

Even in Canada, which has so many lakes they have not all been counted, the assumption that there is clean, abundant water for everyone is turning into an illusion. Millions of people are bumping up against the hard statistics of flow meters and toxic chemical analyses. Already there are real or impending water shortages in British Columbia's Okanagan Valley, the southern Prairies and parts of southern Ontario inland from the Great Lakes. Cities are simply outgrowing their local water supplies and farmers are demanding more and more water to irrigate crops as a hedge against drought. The nation's water is under attack by pollution, resulting in poisoned wells, fish sprouting grotesque cancers and acid rain corroding huge parts of the environment. In a growing number of places we have water that is unfit for drinking and sometimes even for swimming.

Our problems pale by comparison with those emerging in other parts of the world. Just to our south the United States is wrestling with pollution issues so widespread that they are hard to define, while large tracts of western U.S. farmlands have outright water shortages. The pollution represents the legacy of decades of careless handling of toxic chemicals. The shortages reflect a wanton overuse of small western rivers and the pumping out, in a few decades, of underground water sources which were laid down over millennia.

This picture is magnified around the world, as one local or regional water supply after another reels beneath the twin blows of pollution and over-consumption. The world's population, already nudging five billion, is virtually certain to reach more than six billion by the end of the century. In its 1985 State of the Environment report the United Nations Environment Program said that population growth does not have to mean a worse life but: "In a large number of countries, notably in Africa, rapid growth of population over the last decade has been accompanied by a steady decline. . .in the quality of life as measured by indicators such as per capita availability of food and nutrition, drinking water and sanitation." As more rural nations industrialize and try to grow more food, both activities which are highly water intensive, regional shortages will increase. International water experts say that a number of nations will outgrow their water supplies over the next couple of decades while others will suffer limited but damaging droughts.

Already an increasing number of rivers around the world are overused. On the Canadian Prairies some rivers run so shallow in dry years that farmers have to let their crops wither rather than withdraw more irrigation water. For years not a drop of the Colorado River, the major river in the U.S. southwest, has reached the Gulf of California. In the southern part of the Soviet Union so much water is taken from some rivers that the Aral and Caspian seas are receding. Underground water resources are being used up in key food-producing regions of the United States, China and India. In parts of the world humans have destroyed the water balance of local ecosystems to the point that they have actually created deserts. The problems are most visible across Africa's vast Sahel region, where drought has brought starvation to millions and sand dunes of the advancing Sahara Desert are stalking and consuming villages.

Pollution is like a form of desertification and its spreading cancer is undermining the quality of the water which must be shared by ever more people. The World Health Organization recently set new guidelines for tolerable pollution levels in drinking water and then conceded that some regions will not be able to enforce them stringently if they are to have any drinking water at all. We have created modern versions of the mythical River Styx, whose poisonous waters marked the dividing line between the land of the living and the underworld of the dead. Long reaches of the Mississippi and the Rhine are probably not fit to drink, the United Nations says. There are serious doubts about the safety of water from the Niagara and St. Clair rivers.

We are just beginning to understand how air pollution affects our water. Acid rain is only part of a toxic rain falling around the planet. Millions of tonnes a year of other pollutants fall from the sky mixed in rain, snow, sleet and fog, or as tiny droplets of gas or dry dust. These hazardous chemicals and metals destroy our lakes, get into our drinking water and become part of the very food we eat. And looming in the future like the plot from a science fiction movie is the threat of air pollution changing the world's climate and its water balance. Scientists say that a chemical blanket now forming overhead will raise global temperatures over the next several decades. They call it the greenhouse effect because, like the interior of a greenhouse, everything beneath this atmospheric layer will get warmer. Many areas will also get drier, including the grainbelts of western Canada and the United States, which are already borderline semi-desert regions, prone to periodic droughts.

Sustained drought in the west could be the ultimate test of Canada-U.S. relations. Already that traditionally good relationship has been strained by the fact that about half the acid rain destroying the eastern Canadian environment comes from the United States. The situation is not helped by the fact that U.S. chemical factories and their old dumps, like Love Canal, leak into the Niagara River, threatening the drinking water of nearly seven million Canadians downstream. A bi-national study revealed that the United States is also consuming more than seven times as much water from the shared Great Lakes as Canada. In turn Canadian acid rain is attacking the northeastern states and we are the main polluters of the St. Clair River.

The alarming question between the two nations is the demand for water in the dry U.S. west and southwest, an area of growing population and dwindling water called the Sun Belt. For more than two decades both Canadian and U.S. engineers have proposed giant canals to divert Canada's northern lakes and rivers south to bail out dry U.S. areas. So far most Canadian politicians and the public have rejected water transfers, showing little desire to export this last and most valuable resource.

North America, like many parts of the world, faces a host of water problems. For many years the problems were assumed to be limited to industrial areas but with toxic rain and development in more and more areas there is no place which is free of pollution or the possibility of development. (BERNARD BENNELL)

Canada, the United States and the world are not running out of water. But we are seeing the last frontiers of untapped water in one part of the globe after another. As we head towards the twenty-first century we are caught in a fundamental bind. Our modern industrial society is geared to using up natural resources and polluting the environment. It is on a pathway which cannot be followed indefinitely. We have to start making major decisions about how we are going to live in our environment and we had better start now.

The aim of this book is to explore these problems in detail, to inform people about the issues and to arouse awareness. Only a well-informed populace can force the governments responsible for the laws and the private interests responsible for water consumption and pollution to control their thirst and to stop the fouling of our nest.

Many of the chapters are framed as questions because we do not yet have all the answers. Either the research has not been done or we as a society have not yet grappled with the issues.

We are heading into complex and controversial times over water issues. Here are facts, figures and some alternatives to enable you to participate in the debates over the future of your water.

MICHAEL KEATING
Toronto, March, 1986

CHAPTER ONE

WATER: THE MYTH OF THE BOTTOMLESS WELL

To THE ASTRONAUTS Earth is the blue planet. Three-quarters of it is covered with water and it seems inconceivable that there could be water shortages, least of all in Canada. In a nation that holds more than one-seventh of the world's freshwater lakes and one-half of one per cent of the world's population, we have smugly assumed that the tap could never run dry. But for half the world's population clean, plentiful water is just a dream. In many areas people walk for hours across dry plains just to find a muddy waterhole. Others drink from rivers which are contaminated with chemicals or life-threatening diseases. Even in Canada hundreds of thousands of people drink water piped from somewhere else because their local sources are overtaxed or polluted.

To understand our water problems you first have to understand the water cycle, and the astronaut's view from above the clouds can be misleading. There are 1.35 billion cubic kilometres of water on our world, just as there have been for most of the 4.6-billion-year lifespan of this planet but more than 97 per cent of that is salt seas. It is great for fish, seals and sailors but it is undrinkable. That still seems to leave plenty of fresh water but 29 million cubic kilometres of it are frozen solid, in glaciers and polar icecaps which cover Greenland and Antarctica with 3 to 4 kilometres of ice. Another 8 million cubic kilometres of precious fresh water lie underground in the spaces between grains of sand and pieces of gravel and only a fraction of that can be tapped by wells.

In fact only about $1/100$ of 1 per cent of the planet's water is readily available as fresh water. It is in the lakes and rivers to which we turn for our daily two litres of water to sustain life itself. It is in the topsoil

1

where it provides moisture for plant life—the base of much of our food chain—and it is in the sky, forming clouds which will fall as rain and snow to replenish our lakes and rivers.

—(Nature's water wheel, the fresh-water cycle driven by sunlight and gravity, is what keeps us alive. Sunlight evaporates water from the surface of the ground, from oceans, lakes, reservoirs, rivers and streams, even from plant leaves. The water in the air moves invisibly until it condenses into droplets to form clouds. When moist air hits mountains or cold air masses water droplets become larger and fall to earth. Gravity drives the water downhill through the rivers and lakes, towards the oceans in a never-ending cycle. Some of the precipitation seeps into the soil to become what is called ground water—the type that is drawn out by wells.)

— (It is this water cycle which replenishes our rivers, keeps our lakes from drying up and provides a constant supply of water to our crops) This moving water supplies our needs for drinking and industry as it falls, runs off to the sea and is evaporated back into the sky to fall again.

The fact that we have a water cycle which supports life as we know it is because we are 150 million kilometres from the sun, giving us just the right amount of warmth to keep our water in motion. If we were closer to the sun than 134 million kilometres our moisture would be boiled away and we would be like Venus, with the surface temperature of a self-cleaning oven. If Earth were more than 166 million kilometres from the sun it would be frozen solid in a permanent ice age, like Mars.

Where the water goes after it falls on Earth is governed by the shape of the land and what is on it. In hilly country the runoff is fast, so fast that dangerous floods may occur after rainstorms or during the spring thaw, and rivers carve sharply defined valleys. Where the land is gentler, so is the flow, and on the prairies, for example, rivers meander across the countryside, quietly seeking out the path of least resistance. Rivers feed the lakes, most of them the result of 2 billion years of volcanic eruptions, shifts in the earth's crust and glacial advances and retreats. In northern latitudes, such as Canada, most lakes were carved out by glaciers, the last of which retreated about 10 000 years ago. As the glaciers receded their meltwaters carved channels, many of them now dry valleys or whose rivers are just shadows of their former selves. The water also filled up our lakes. The glaciers were up to 3.5 kilometres thick and their immense weight literally pressed down the earth, which is still rebounding ever so slowly. As a result the shorelines of lakes are still slowly rising.

Plant cover is the second factor that decides how water behaves once it hits the ground and starts running. Trees, grasses and cattails all slow the runoff and capture some of the water for their own uses. Without vegetation, raindrops hit the ground like bullets, exploding the surface of the soil into loose particles, which can be washed away as the water rushes to nearby rivers.

How much water is there and how much do we need? Every year nature's water wheel delivers about 110 300 cubic kilometres of water to the continents, much of it distilled from the surface of the oceans. This is enough rain and snow to cover Canada to a depth of 12 metres. Two-thirds of that is evaporated back into the sky but this leaves what seems like a generous 38 800 cubic kilometres of fresh water. It is twice the amount of the water in the Great Lakes, surely enough to give every human being a daily ration. However, the life-giving rains do not fall evenly on the planet. Canadians, with a big land and a small population, are the most generously endowed of any people with a river flow of 130 000 cubic metres of water per person each year. By comparison the global average supply is 8 300 cubic metres per year and in a dry country like Egypt it is only about 90 cubic metres. For comparison: one cubic metre is 1 000 litres and will fill seven average bathtubs.

But even those water supply figures can be misleading. More than half the water in the rivers runs off quickly to the oceans and globally only about 3 000 cubic metres per person are considered a stable supply. It is sobering to note that while the global average demand for water is more than 800 cubic metres, the United States uses 2 300 cubic metres of water per person per year and Canadians rank second with a demand of 1 500. Simple mathematics show that as soon as the year 2000, if the world economy develops on the U.S. model, there will not be enough water in the world's rivers for everyone, given the population growth on the planet.

The driving force behind our problems with water, as with all other natural resources, is the combination of a growing per capita demand in a mechanized world and a population explosion that staggers the imagination. At the end of the last ice age, about 10 000 years ago, the world's population was an estimated 4 million. By 1986 it was 4.9 billion, more than double what it was at the end of the Second World

War, and it is still growing by 78 million per year. At this rate it will reach 6.12 billion by the end of the century and 8.2 billion by 2025. It will not stabilize until sometime between a century from now, when it could be as low as about 8 billion, and the twenty-second century, when it could level off at between 10 and 14 billion.

Thomas Malthus, the English political economist, predicted in 1798 that population growth would sooner or later outstrip the world's resources. In 1976 a member of the Club of Rome said that the world's supply of fresh water could support an industrialized population of only 8 billion. In 1980 the "Global 2000" report to U.S. President Jimmy Carter warned of increasing strains on the planet's natural resources and increasing pollution. It predicted growing regional water shortages as supplies become more erratic. A Canadian version of the "Global 2000" report said that this country will face increasing pressure on our water and other resources to generate food, energy, forest products and minerals for the rest of the world. It predicted that Canada will likely face demands to supply water to the southwestern United States and parts of Mexico, which will have very low water supplies by the turn of the century.

(The effect of the population explosion on water supplies is further magnified by an increasing demand for more and more water per person.)The world's population was about 1.5 billion in 1900 and since then has increased threefold. At the same time water demand has risen seven times. Where does it all go?)

(The biggest user is irrigation, at close to 70 per cent, followed by industry at 23 per cent. Only 7 per cent goes for domestic use.)"We are facing unprecedented pressures on the environment and resource basis of development and we are entering a period when those pressures will increase at rates never before seen in history," says James MacNeill, a Canadian environment expert and the secretary-general to the United Nations World Commission on Environment and Development. "The pressures on the planet's environment and resources today are nothing compared to what they will be over the next 20 years, when the world economy could double again, and over the next 30–40 years, when a whole extra world of people and their demands will be imposed on the present one."

—(Already the strain is beginning to show, as a growing number of regions fail to meet demand. As people pump wells harder, denude the land with more grazing animals, cut the forests and drain wetlands, the natural regulators of water are removed. This will mean irregular water supplies, with more floods and droughts. Towns and cities that have always had enough water are already facing shortages, as population growth upstream reduces the amount of water flowing past their doorsteps. As populations grow, so do their needs for food, housing and consumer goods. Irrigated land already produces a large part of the world's food and with the ever-growing demand for more food there will be greater pressure to irrigate more land. And industries will expand to provide the goods people demand.)

A number of major watercourses are, or soon will be, fully exploited, including such rivers as the Nile, the Tigris, the Syr Darya and Amu Darya in the Soviet Union, the Chu in northern Vietnam and many rivers in Australia, India, Mexico and Africa. In parts of North America, particularly the U.S. Great Plains region, rivers such as the Colorado are already taxed to their limits and underground water is being pumped up faster than it can be replaced.

Half the world has little or no access to safe drinking water and even fewer people have sanitation to protect them from waterborne diseases, which the World Health Organization estimates cause 80 per cent of the illness on the earth. At any one time 1.6 billion people are affected by such diseases. Developing rural nations face some of the greatest problems as they struggle to industrialize and to grow more food, both activities which are highly water intensive. At the same time millions of rural dwellers flock to already overcrowded cities, in many cases moving to areas where drinking water is already scarce. In 1974 only one-third of the world lived in urban areas but by 2000 about half the population will live in towns and cities, creating as many as 21 mega-cities with populations over 10 million each.

The growing scarcity of water may provoke severe political consequences. In 1984 Earthscan, a London-based organization, published a report suggesting that environmental degradation and conflict over deteriorating natural resources underlie much of the world's political tension. Nations have been fighting over shared river basins for centuries, Earthscan said, and a dispute over the Indus River was an element in the 1965 war between India and Pakistan. The study noted that 214 river basins, including some in tense areas of Africa and the Middle East, are shared by two or more countries.)

Even good neighbors like Canada and the U.S. are squabbling over such water issues as who is polluting the Great Lakes and creating the acid rain in eastern North America and who will pay the billions of dollars to clean up the mess. For at least 20 years there have been periodic calls to export Canadian water to the United States, provoking political debate and a recent pact between Great Lakes states and provinces to prevent such diversions. In Europe a whole continent is wrestling with the problem of acid rain, which has killed thousands of lakes in Scandinavia and is partially if not totally behind widespread forest destruction.

The world water equation is, of course, at the base of the world food supply, as has been proven so tragically in Africa where two decades of drought have caused terrible famine. It became a world-wide issue by the mid-1980s, when two dozen nations faced disaster. The Swedish Red Cross Society says droughts killed about 230 000 people in the 1970s and affected 244 million.

The population explosion multiplies the amount of pollution, deforestation and wetland drainage that causes such problems as unsafe drinking water, drought and desertification. The problems started when the first human settlements fouled their water with human sewage and garbage. This degradation has accelerated dramatically with industrialization, especially in this century, which saw the creation of giant cities and huge industries.

At first glance some of the other environmental issues, such as cutting down forests and draining swamps, seem unrelated to water supply. But such indirect action upsets the water balance. Plant life is an essential part of the hydrologic cycle, something that many people are just starting to realize. Trees, bushes and grasses capture part of the rainfall and spring snow melts, preventing, or at least reducing, the danger of devastating floods. They slowly release water to streams and rivers during the rest of the year, a system that is crucial during dry weather.

By the process of transpiration, plants release moisture from their leaves into the air, raising the humidity and helping to form clouds, which, in turn, release rain to return the water back to earth. We are creating deserts by denuding the land—removing the plant life which keeps it not only green but moist. Every year about 110 000 square kilometres, an area twice the size of Nova Scotia, are cut out of the world's tropical rainforests. In addition a large chunk of temperate forests across the rest of the world falls to the chain saw, bulldozer blade and mechanical tree harvester for a total forest loss of 150 000–200 000 square kilometres a year. Only a tiny fraction is replanted. Once denuded of protective cover, soil which was built up over millennia is exposed to the full force of pounding rains and the land becomes deeply furrowed with erosion gullies.

It is the tropical forests which are most in danger, according to a three-volume report, *Tropical Forests: A Call for Action*, issued in 1985 by the World Resources Institute. The report said that 40 per cent of the world's tropical forests have already been cleared or damaged and that in many developing countries most of the remainder will disappear within two or three decades if present trends continue. The pressure on the forests comes not just from lumber companies. About two billion people, nearly half the world's population, depend on fuel wood for a major part of their cooking and heating. Many of them clear forests to create new farmland in a technique called slash and burn, the way people in most of eastern North America and Europe formerly cleared their own farmland. When the cutting is on hills, rains wash away the soil and cause effects hundreds of kilometres downstream. Deforestation in the Himalayas sends vast amounts of silt downstream into India, Pakistan and Bangladesh, where it clogs dams and irrigation systems, costing billions of dollars a year. More than 400 million people downstream from the Himalayas are hostage to the deforestation practices of 46 million hillside dwellers. At least half the global population is affected by the way watersheds are treated upstream because while 10 per cent of the world lives on hillsides, another 40 per cent lives downstream.

Soil erosion is reaching epic proportions, with estimates of 23 billion tonnes of soil lost each year from croplands. So far we have eroded the fertility of cropland on an area of the globe twice the size of Canada. The downstream effects of soil erosion include: the filling up of rivers, harbors and dams with silt; reducing navigation and the production of hydro-electricity; the destruction of fish habitat; and water pollution, both by dirt and by herbicides and pesticides bound to soil particles.

Even when we try to harness water rather than let it run off rapidly to the sea, our failure to understand water systems can negate our efforts. In the case of many irrigation projects too much water is put on the land and allowed to lie there, making the soil waterlogged and drowning crops. In other cases the excess water is not drained away, so it has time to dissolve natural salts out of the soil and float them to the surface of the land. When the water evaporates in the sunshine it leaves behind a crust of salt which renders the land sterile.

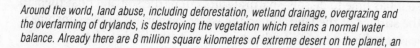

Around the world, land abuse, including deforestation, wetland drainage, overgrazing and the overfarming of drylands, is destroying the vegetation which retains a normal water balance. Already there are 8 million square kilometres of extreme desert on the planet, an

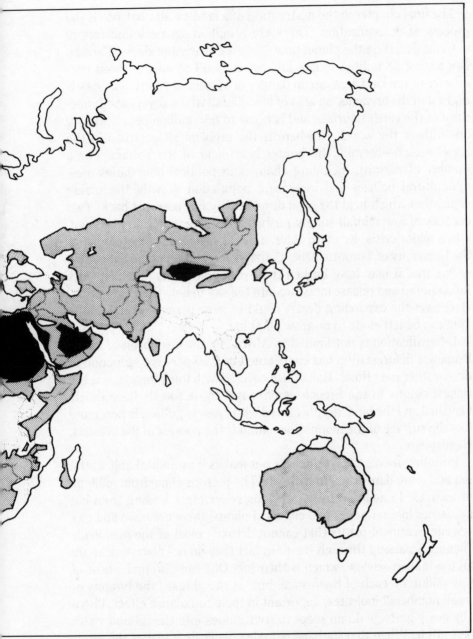

area nearly the size of Canada. But almost 38 million square kilometres more, in 63 nations, is in danger of becoming unproductive desert. This means one-quarter of the world is in danger of desertification.   (BERNARD BENNELL)

The final chapter in the destruction of a land's water balance is the process of desertification. There are 8 million square kilometres of extreme desert on the planet now—an area nearly the size of Canada. But almost 38 million square kilometres in 63 countries, about one-quarter of the land area, are in danger of becoming desert. The risk is highest in the drylands, an area of low rainfall which covers about one-third of the earth's surface and is home to 850 million people, nearly one-fifth of the world. Nowhere is the problem clearer than in the Sahel region—literally the border beachland of the Sahara. For a number of reasons, including changes in political boundaries, new agricultural policies and increasing population growth, the sparse vegetation which held the sand dunes at bay has been cut back. Two decades of low rainfall simply pushed a bad situation over the edge, into a major crisis. Kenneth Hare, a world-renowned climatologist at the University of Toronto, believes that deforestation in the Sahel is so severe that it may have broken the hydrologic cycle, in which trees hold rainfall and release moisture into the sky to help form clouds. Dr. Hare says the expanding desert could become permanent unless the land can be left alone to re-grow plant life.

Desertification is not limited to Africa. On the Caribbean island of Dominica deforestation has contributed to a 50-per-cent reduction in dry-weather river flows. Haiti, once covered with thick forests, was the richest colony in the French empire. But those forests have nearly vanished and the land, deeply carved with erosion gullies, is now more like the surface of the moon. The nation is the poorest in the Western Hemisphere.

Pollution leaves the water there but makes it as undrinkable as the sea and more dangerous to bathe in. The poisons come from millions of sources. In addition to the obvious sewer pipes leading from big industries like refineries and chemical plants, there are town and city sewage treatment plants that cannot detoxify most of the man-made chemicals passing through them. In fact they do not always clean up all the human sewage, which is their job. One can also find a host of tiny polluters, each of them small but, as the phrase "the tyranny of small numbers" indicates, important in their cumulative effect. Virtually every garbage dump seeps nasty residues into the ground water beneath it. When that garbage is toxic chemicals it makes the water unsafe to drink, often without people realizing it. Farmers spray and spread millions of tonnes of pesticides and fertilizers on their land every year and a substantial part of that chemical mix finds its way into the rivers and lakes from which we drink. Home gardeners add their share of chemicals to the land and we all flush nasty materials down the drain. Although each person's contribution is small, the action of millions of individuals adds up to a lot of pollution.

In a major assessment of the state of Canada's well water, the federal environment department found reports of pollution from Prince Edward Island to British Columbia. "Contamination of ground water...with pesticides and other organic and inorganic chemicals is becoming a major, nationwide problem. Organic chemicals have been detected and wells have been closed in all regions of the country." The report continued: "We are in great danger of contaminating our ground water irreversibly with carcinogens and other toxic pollutants from our practices of waste disposal, application of pesticides and from other industrial, agricultural and residential activities. And if we don't act soon to protect it we may lose this important source of drinking water forever." In the United States 17 per cent of small municipal well water sources and 28 per cent of large underground sources are contaminated with traces of organic chemicals.

Despite the growing list of danger signs, we are allowing more pollution. For example the Alberta government decided to permit a heavy oil plant to pollute the nearly pristine Beaver River to what the government thinks is an acceptable level. Around the Great Lakes a number of industries do not even meet existing pollution regulations and across the country much of the waste is not even treated before it is dumped into lakes and rivers.

Where does Canada fit in the world water equation? Our share of the world's water is generous by any measure. For example, the Great Lakes, shared with the United States, hold 22 800 cubic kilometres or about 18 per cent of the lake water on Earth. Canada has millions of other lakes, rivers and streams covering some 770 000 square kilometres or nearly 8 per cent of the country. The figure rises to almost 20 per cent when you include wetlands such as marshes, swamps and the famous northern muskeg. Canada has, or shares with the United States, seven of the world's largest lakes, and 45 lakes with areas larger than 1 000 square kilometres.

But those lakes are a gift of glacial recession from 10 000 years ago. For the first 8 000 years after the glaciers melted the lake levels gradually dwindled as the massive source of water drained to the oceans, then they stabilized at the current levels about 2 000 years ago. In the case of the Great Lakes, for example, current levels reflect the amount of rain and snow that runs into the lakes every year from thousands of tributary streams and rivers, and that finally makes its way to the St. Lawrence River—a journey that can take more than two centuries for a drop of water starting in Lake Superior.

The annual flow through is only about 1 per cent of the Great Lakes volume and any attempt to use more than that can actually drop lake levels. In fact any substantial using up of that runoff also lowers the levels of the connecting channels, the St. Marys, St. Clair, Detroit and Niagara rivers. All that is really there for our use is the the flowing water which drops each year as rain and snow to flow again to the sea. Already the Great Lakes have dropped about five centimetres (the width of three fingers) because of dredging the connecting rivers and because of industrial development, settlement and farm irrigation around the lakes. It does not seem like much but it cuts the amount of hydro power generated at Niagara Falls and shaves the amount of clearance for big ships travelling the seaway and putting into Great Lakes ports. In the future, lake levels are predicted to keep dropping, possibly by dramatic amounts, as the population of the lakes basin, now at 37 million, is predicted to double over the next 50 years. Inland, in parts of southern Ontario, there are already water shortages in a number of towns and cities. As they outgrow their local rivers and wells they must snake pipelines out to the Great Lakes. In western Canada the problems are already more serious. During dry years some rivers in the southern Prairies even now do not have enough water for everybody who has settled this semi-desert land.

The second measure of a nation's water wealth, and the one used by most planners, is the volume of river flow. Eight billion tonnes of water falls as rain or snow on Canada every year. Parts of the west coast, where the mountains comb rain from the ocean clouds, get more than 3 metres of precipitation, enough to produce temperate rain forests holding some of the continent's biggest trees. But some Prairie regions get only about 300–400 millimetres and less than one-tenth of that makes it to the rivers, creating semi-desert conditions. As little as 100 mm of rain and snow fall on the high Arctic, making it a frozen desert. On average Canada's rivers discharge about 105 000 cubic metres of water every second, which is about 9 per cent of the world's renewable water supply and is enough to fill the nation's bathtubs every seven seconds. This is a generous 360 000 litres per person per day though in certain parts of the country, notably the dry Prairie regions, people have less than one-tenth that amount. It is a fact of life that while more than half the water in our rivers flows north, 90 per cent of our population lives within 250 kilometres of the U.S. border. And most of the water in the south flows through the Great Lakes and down the St. Lawrence or runs off the westerly slopes of the Coast Mountains and into the Pacific. Even statistics suggesting that lots of water remains can be misleading when one looks at the tremendous variability of river flow, especially in the dry Prairies. For example, even in dry years rivers in eastern Canada keep at least two-thirds of their average flow but in the Prairies the figure tumbles to one-third.

Canadians also use a lot of water, more than anyone in the world except U.S. citizens. Our cities, farms, mines, factories, and especially our power plants, suck up 40.7 cubic kilometres of water a year. That works out to 4 650 litres per person a day, though in fact the average household share of that is around 500 litres per day, enough to keep a Sahel dweller alive for more than half a year. Even within Canada the demand varies from 614 litres a head in Quebec to 358 in drier Manitoba.

Across Canada there are rumbles of discontent about not only the quantity but the quality of our water. A federal survey found that although two-thirds of Canadians have sewers to their homes, less than half the nation treats its sewage before it is dumped into lakes and rivers. The problem is most acute in remote areas, especially among native people where many have a standard of drinking water and sewage treatment systems well below the national average and even below World Health Organization guidelines.

In parts of the north one can still see rivers running free and relatively pure, much as they were throughout the land four centuries ago, before Europeans arrived. But even in these remote areas there are growing conflicts between mining and hydro-electric developers and native groups, fishermen and environmentalists. Spills from oil and uranium works have already caused damage in northern lakes and rivers while power dams have upset water levels and with them the lifestyle of northerners. Even Nahanni National Park Reserve in the Northwest Territories, named a World Heritage Site for its wild beauty and its waterfall twice the height of Niagara, is threatened by mining wastes in tributary rivers. There is potential for major hydro-electric development in the Yukon and Northwest Territories, which would change river flows. And there is concern that Alberta and British Columbia will proceed with their own power dam construction plans, changing river flows that reach the Northwest Territories. In a number of spots old mines pose a threat, as their abandoned piles of rock dug from underground expose toxic metals to the environment and release sulphur to react with air, moisture and microbes to form sulphuric acid. In British Columbia and the Yukon, gold mining has created a heated debate as dirt dumped into the rivers after the gold is removed fouls the spawning areas of salmon and grayling trout.

British Columbia has a tremendous river flow but most of it races down the westerly slopes of the Coast Mountains to the Pacific Ocean. The Okanagan Valley, an intermontane region, is so dry that there was talk of bringing water in from the north several years ago. Hydro dams have long been a major issue in the province because they flood valleys and block migration routes for salmon. The dam-building issue was defused in the early 1980s by the recession and a drop in the appetite for more power. But in late 1985 B.C. Premier William Bennett promised more hydro dams so that hydro power could be sold to the

In some remote wilderness areas one can still drink the water pure and fresh from big, fast-flowing rivers, but no lake or river water should be drunk untreated unless you know from local people that it is safe.   (MICHAEL KEATING)

populous U.S. west coast. Another big British Columbia industry, logging, is fouling salmon rivers with its wastes, both from wood dumped into the river and from shoreline erosion caused by the removal of trees.

In the dry, southern Prairies some rivers cannot supply everyone who is there now during dry years. The Milk and St. Mary rivers along the U.S. border, parts of the North and South Saskatchewan and the Red-Assiniboine river systems are facing or risk water shortages. The lack of water in these and other small rivers will limit plans for more irrigated farms and industrial development, such as chemical production and the flooding of old oil wells to float remaining petroleum to the surface. For years some Albertans have been demanding diversions of northern rivers to the dry southlands so irrigation of farmland can continue. This upsets northerners, who say the loss of water will disrupt their environment, economy and lifestyles. Prairie waters are often borderline for drinking because of naturally dissolved materials they contain and because of algal growth which fouls shallow lakes. Regina and Moose Jaw held the title for the country's worst-tasting drinking water for years until a $15-million advanced water treatment plant was opened in June, 1985. The granular activated carbon filters remove most of the foul-tasting and foul-smelling material.

In eastern Canada water pollution is the major threat, endangering drinking water, making swimming unhealthy, killing fish or giving them cancer or making them hazardous to eat. If the pollution gets too bad the drinking water of the one-third of Canadians living in the Great Lakes basin could become unsafe to drink without special water purification systems costing hundreds of millions of dollars. Already countless people are buying bottled water or special home filters. Consumption—taking water out of the lakes and putting it into manufactured goods, food and people or evaporating it into the sky— is a growing issue. Ontario faces widespread pollution problems from industries, cities and old, leaking dumps. In south-central Ontario urban growth is outstripping local water supplies, forcing the province to pipe in water to a growing number of towns and cities. In towns like Stouffville and Perkinsfield leaking chemical dumps made wells unsafe and people were supplied with bottled water and then connected to pipelines from other towns. By the late 1970s Quebec had channelled great northern rivers through some of the world's biggest powerhouses but only treated 6 per cent of its sewage, although that is changing. Montreal, the second-largest city in the country, has long dumped its sewage raw into the St. Lawrence River, as does Quebec City. The province has now embarked on a $7-billion program to catch up work that should have been started decades ago, to build sewers, clean up industry and reduce agricultural pollution. It also faces the problem of cleaning up old, leaking chemical dumps, the ghosts of past pollution activities.

The recent federal water inquiry found that the Atlantic provinces need money to build and maintain expensive water and sewage treatment systems. In New Brunswick and Nova Scotia there has been controversy over the effects on the drinking water when chemicals are sprayed on forests to kill bugs. Both provinces also face localized problems of wastes, leaking from old dumps and mines to threaten drinking water. For example Waverley, 20 kilometres north of Halifax, has been put on piped water because wells were contaminated with arsenic from an old gold mine. Nova Scotia has seen acid rain, mainly from central North America, start to destroy its salmon rivers. Prince Edward Island draws virtually all its drinking water from wells and now finds that Aldicarb, a pesticide sprayed on its famous potato crops to kill nematodes, is seeping through the earth and into its underground water supply.

Canada's native peoples have traditionally gained little from major water projects, especially the hydro-electric dams in the north, and usually they lost a lot. Those living downstream were simply ignored by the planners and in some cases they found out about the projects when water levels suddenly started changing. Native groups say that traditional fisheries have been destroyed and water travel disrupted and sometimes they were even forced off their lands by suddenly changing water levels.

An Alberta Indian association complained to the federal water inquiry that white southerners are carving up natural resources with the arrogant assumption that non-human forms of life are expendable. The Athabasca Chipewyan Indian Band depends on hunting, fishing, trapping and the wild rice harvest, all of which rely on a natural flow of water. In 1967 British Columbia finished the 183-metre-high Bennett Dam on the Peace River and since then it has affected the level of Lake Athabasca far downstream. Natives fear not only another proposed dam on the Peace at a location called Site C, but Alberta's interest in building yet another dam on the same river system, this one on the Slave River near the Northwest Territories border. Not far to the south, other Indians fear the effects of pollution, especially after an oil spill from an oil sands plant at Fort McMurray closed the fishery on Lake Athabasca in the summer of 1983, forcing people to eat tainted fish or buy more expensive imported food. In Quebec, native people read about the James Bay project and took the dam builders to court for compensation before their rivers were changed. In 1975 they won a $225-million settlement plus guarantees of hunting, fishing and trapping rights from the province and the developers of the gigantic James Bay power project in return for the diversion of some of their rivers and the flooding of some of their lands.

Canada's water problems pale when compared to those of the United States, which has 10 times the population and, excluding Alaska, half the river flow. The United States must confront a growing series of water crises including widespread pollution, the over-use of some rivers, like the Colorado, and the depletion of irreplaceable underground water reserves. Pollution is a threat from millions of tonnes of waste in tens of thousands of dumps spotted across the nation, like running sores. This dangerous combination is decreasing the amount of water available for each citizen even as the population expands. Names like Love Canal and Times Beach are going into history books among the world's worst pollution cases. A number of commentators have made the point that while the massive U.S. defence budget is oriented towards external enemies, there is an internal battle to protect water supplies and spending on that front is not keeping up with the demand.

In 1978 the U.S. Water Resources Council, in the Second National Water Assessment, estimated that by the year 2000, 17 of 106 regions in the country would no longer have enough water from their lakes, rivers and streams for all the growing needs. Even the humid eastern seaboard is faced with periodic drought emergencies, such as the one in the 1960s which spawned the New York slogan: "Save water, shower with a friend." That giant city sits on the banks of the Hudson River, yet no longer considers the polluted water safe to drink, except during water shortages. It draws fresh water from far away in the Catskill Mountains but this exposes the city to recurring shortages during dry years, such as in 1985, when water was again rationed and even Hudson River water was used. A sign in a New York City hotel room mutely pleads: "Conserve precious water. Please limit water usage. Secure all faucets when not in use. Save water. Save Energy."

In the western U.S. there are critical water supply problems extending across major regions. Huge tracts of rich farmland are irrigated with water from underground reserves, which are being pumped down far faster than nature's scanty rainfall can replenish them. This is called overdrafting or mining, and it means that sooner or later you run out of water. There is major overdrafting of ground water in the High Plains region of the central U.S., from Texas north into Kansas, and to the west in states like Arizona and California. Former Utah governor Scott Matheson said people in a 9 000-square-kilometre region in the western states, an area twice the size of Prince Edward Island, have now pumped out half of their underground water reserves. The best-known problem is that of the Ogallala Aquifer, a huge bed of water-filled sand and gravel which lies beneath eight western states from Texas to Nebraska. It supplies well water for one-fifth of the irrigated crop land in the country. But 70 000 wells are draining this source of water, laid down over centuries, at the rate of 34.5 cubic kilometres a year—twice the flow of the Colorado River. There are predictions that if the overdraft continues it will finish in a massive collapse of irrigation agriculture and the area will go back to much poorer dryland farming and grazing. Already irrigation is declining by large amounts in parts of the United States, owing to lack of water and the increasing cost of energy to pump from ever-deeper levels.

The world water picture is one of growing regional crises. Hundreds of cities will have trouble providing fresh water and coping with their sewage, particularly in areas of explosive urban growth, such as Asia and Latin America. Many nations have inadequate water resources for basic needs and industrial development now but they face the problem of a swelling population which wants to emulate the water-using society of North America. Water tables are falling in southern India, northern China and Mexico. As a result cities and rural areas alike are sinking as they pump out the water beneath them. In coastal areas the problem is compounded as salt water in land beneath the oceans moves in to replace the fresh water pumped from underground, making wells unusable. This is a problem in Israel and Arab gulf states, as well as in some U.S. communities on all three seacoasts.

Mexico, the world's second-largest city and among its fastest-growing, is an example of a mega-city in trouble. It struggles to supply water to over 17 million people clustered on a 2 300-metre-high plateau. The city, built on a filled-in lake bed, has sunk 10 metres in 70 years as underground water is pumped out, but even this water is not enough. Now Mexico is planning to reach down 1 000 metres and out

150–200 kilometres for more water. The population of Beijing has shot up from 2 million in 1949 to over 9 million now and household demand could grow fivefold by the year 2000, even though the city is already short of water. Its underground water withdrawals exceed natural recharge rates by 25 per cent and parts of the city are sinking. Ground-water overdrafting is a serious problem in several northern Chinese provinces and water tables are dropping by as much as 1 to 4 metres a year. As a result the country is planning to build a major water diversion to bring water from the more humid south.

After a hard-won battle to become self-sufficient in food, India, with more than 700 million people, now risks losing cropland because of growing water scarcity. B.B. Bohra, one of India's top civil servants, said in 1985 that "environmental protection is for us a matter of nothing less than survival." Deforestation is a critical problem. India, which covers 3.2 million square kilometres of a sub-continent, has forests left on only about one-tenth of its land and at the present rate of cutting they will be gone by about the year 2000. The Himalaya chain is in danger of becoming so barren it could resemble "the mountains of the moon," said a leading U.S. environmental scientist. In the north, rain is carrying away an estimated 11 billion tonnes of topsoil and in the southern state of Tamil Nadu, well overpumping has lowered the water table by 25 to 30 metres in 10 years. Unless it can stop the water loss, India risks sliding into the same sort of drought crisis which is gripping parts of Africa.

The Soviet Central Asian Republics are withdrawing so much water from local rivers for irrigation that there is not enough flow to maintain normal water levels in the three inland seas—the Aral, Azov and Caspian—and their levels are dropping. As a result the Soviet Union is planning limited water diversions from its north-flowing rivers to slake the thirst of its dry southlands.

Over the next few years the whole world will have to come to grips not just with the already well-documented issues such as pollution and overuse of rivers and wells, but with the more subtle ones such as hidden consumption of lakes by a thousand small sources, climate change and long-range air pollution, which can destroy the life in wilderness lakes and rivers.

We are finding that there is more than just acid rain attacking our environment from the air. There are thousands of chemicals in what has become a toxic rain. Fish in remote wilderness lakes are being polluted by toxins carried hundreds, even thousands of kilometres by the winds. Chemicals flow from the smokestacks of incinerators, factories and power plants, from exhaust pipes, spray guns and even aerosol cans, to form great, invisible rivers of pollution in the skies. Even carbon dioxide, which has always been portrayed as a colorless, odorless and virtually harmless gas, is turning into a villain. Spewing from hundreds of millions of fires around the world, including every internal combustion engine and every furnace, it is collecting in the sky to form an invisible heat shield. This acts like a greenhouse, letting in the sun's heat but slowing the natural escape of Earth's excess heat into space. As heat builds up it will raise global temperatures, playing havoc with rainfall, crops, shipping, drinking water and the entire biosphere in which we have evolved.

And in many of our debates about water we spend most of the time talking about the direct effects on humans. But the federal water inquiry reminded us that "in Canada we are only beginning to appreciate the magnitude of water needs for the support of the ecosystem. We do not have very reliable estimates of instream requirements." What we do know is that even in this huge land the real wilderness is shrinking. According to Parks Canada's wild rivers survey, 86 of Canada's 178 major rivers have been dammed for hydro-electric power, flood control or irrigation. The demand for our rivers is not abating. A mining company wants one river to generate power, an oil company wants another river to receive the company's wastes and farmers need a third to divert for irrigation.

What we have to do in this and every other country is to draw a clear line on how much more of our water we want to allot to commerce and industry and how much we will save in a more or less natural state. Then we have to decide how we are going to live within those limitations.

CHAPTER TWO

WHO'S KILLING OUR LAKES AND RIVERS?

"The reality is that Canada, though a small country, pollutes to its ability."—THE CANADIAN COALITION ON ACID RAIN.

SINCE THE DAWN OF human history we have thrown things away when we were finished with them. For the first few million years of our existence it did not matter very much, because the foods, clothing and tools we made, used and discarded usually decayed back into nature. But as civilizations grew, so did pollution. Waterborne diseases were the scourge of cities around the world until the nineteenth century when we discovered bacteria and, subsequently, methods of killing them by disinfecting drinking water. These diseases still pose a serious threat to one-half the world's population, which lacks ready access to clean water.

Now we have created a new and more insidious threat to our health: the toxic synthetic chemical. Using temperatures, pressures and chemical combinations not found in nature we have forged, then unloosed, dangerous genies. Harnessed for our use, chemicals have provided much of our comfortable lifestyle, from synthetic clothing, to pesticides which produce scab-free apples, to rocket fuels, silicon computer chips and weed-free lawns. But let loose in the environment these chemicals have turned against us. They have made some waters unsafe for drinking, or even swimming, rendered millions of fish unsafe to eat and killed whole species of wildlife in large areas. There is a steady deterioration of water quality around the world, due to increased pollution and increasing land use around once pristine lakes and rivers and atop underground water sources called aquifers. Complex chemicals are being dumped into the water or onto the ground, where they are seeping into underground water supplies, turning wells into sources of danger.) Pollution which we often cannot see, smell or even taste is attacking our water supplies and "could destroy economies," says Brent Blackwelder of the Environmental Policy Institute in Washington.

How did it all start? It began with the concept, still dearly held in some circles, that the solution to pollution is dilution, a phrase that is becoming an epitaph for our once-clean waters. It simply means that if you dump a small enough amount of a substance into a large enough lake or river it seems to go away and become harmless. The practice works reasonably well when the wastes are natural—such as discarded food, dead animals and even human wastes—assuming you do not try to drink the water until microbes in the environment decay the wastes into simpler organic matter. However, this process broke down as soon as towns and villages started discharging large amounts of raw sewage into the same sources from which they drew drinking water. As a result humans have been plagued with waterborne diseases for millennia. The problem got suddenly worse with the industrial age and the discovery of how to concentrate large amounts of toxic metals and how to fabricate synthetic chemicals never found in nature. These products joined the ever-growing stream of human waste and turned into a flood tide after the Second World War, when the chemical explosion coincided with the population explosion.

Douglas Hallett, for years a senior scientific advisor to Environment Canada, says the problem was caused by an engineering approach which held that anything can be diluted to a safe point. This is true in the sense that toxins can be diluted to levels where they do not make anyone keel over, but this approach fails to address two problems. The first is that even small amounts of chemicals can be hazardous in ways that are not immediately obvious—for example they may promote a cancer which does not appear for decades. And secondly many persistent toxins are absorbed by any animal or person using the water and are stored in body fat, resulting in a growing load of toxins in our bodies.

The dilution fallacy is finally being addressed in official circles. In December, 1985, Ontario Environment Minister James Bradley announced that instead of just dilution ratios, companies would also be assigned maximum amounts of hazardous chemicals which they could dump into the water every year, thus putting a cap on the amount of pollution. Mr. Bradley said the new system will first be used on the St. Clair River but he wants to extend it across the province. By the year 2000 he wants to have lowered the limits to the point that no persistent toxins will be discharged any more.

Pesticides are the leading edge of a series of modern pollution scares which by now have begun to overlap each other so quickly that they are becoming a grey blur of facts, figures and fears. By the 1950s scientists were starting to speak out against the growing number of pesticides and their increasing, often indiscriminate use. In 1962 Rachel Carson, in her famous book, *Silent Spring*, galvanized an already nervous public into the beginnings of serious environmental concern and action. By then the biological effects of pesticides on wildlife had become severe enough that birds were sterilized and were even falling dead from the skies. Another major warning signal came in 1970 when scientists discovered dangerous levels of mercury—a heavy metal which can cause nerve damage—in fish from a number of northern Ontario lakes and rivers. The knowledge of toxic chemicals grew quickly in the 1970s as more and more were found in fish and wildlife: polychlorinated biphenyls (PCBs)—a widely-used electrical insulating fluid—the insecticides Mirex, Lindane, Aldrin, Endrin, Chlordane, Heptachlor and a shopping list of other poisons turned up in one fish sample after another. This led to extensive warnings about the hazards of eating fish, especially from the Great Lakes, which were becoming a giant holding tank of pollutants.

By now pollution is so extensive that we tend to forget that "normal" pollution is zero and we start looking for "safe" or at least "acceptable" levels of environmental degradation, often without defining very well for whom and what they are acceptable. Pollution is a complex mix of chemical and metal compounds. Some, such as insecticides, are designed to act as poisons, and others, including industrial and household chemicals, just happen to be poisons. We each have our personal images of chemical horrors, most of them garnered through the news media: mercury making fish unsafe to eat, Love Canal leaking toxins into basements or the poisonous gas leak at Bhopal, India, which killed the equivalent of a small town. Even though many toxins start their travels into the environment in the air or on land, water is aptly named the universal solvent and just about everything ends up in our lakes and rivers sooner or later. To understand the problem you have to know the players. First, some basic types of pollution.

CHEMICALS AND METALS

This is the first thing that most people mention when they speak of pollution. It is these hazardous compounds which are usually the villains in poisoning the food chain. There are millions of chemicals, and we only understand the toxic effects of a handful. A number of them will be dealt with later in detail.

RADIOACTIVE SUBSTANCES

About half a century of uranium mining and milling has extracted millions of tonnes of uranium ore from mines in British Columbia, Saskatchewan, Ontario, Quebec, New Brunswick and Nova Scotia. Radioactive wastes are in the muds of some northern Saskatchewan lakes, the Serpent River on the north shore of Lake Huron and in Port Hope's harbor on Lake Ontario. In the Serpent River uranium levels in the water were high enough to force installation of special water treatment equipment to protect people living downstream. In addition to radium there are acids leaching from 80 million tonnes of uranium mine tailings piled near the town of Elliot Lake in northern Ontario. Those acids killed off fish downstream. There also have been spills of radioactive materials from nuclear generating stations into Lakes Huron and Ontario and from waste dumps for the uranium processing industry. More than two decades of large-scale nuclear power production in Ontario has created high-level radioactive wastes for which there is no approved disposal method. The wastes lie in water basins in the nuclear power plants, emitting an eerie blue glow, as they await safe disposal. Now researchers are drilling into solid rock in the Precambrian Shield to see if deep underground storage of the wastes, possibly encapsulated in a form of corrosion-resistant glass, will prevent them from entering our water supply over the centuries, even millennia, it will take for the radiation to disappear.

DISEASE-PRODUCING MICRO-ORGANISMS

The oldest waterborne enemies, microscopic diseases in forms such as bacteria and viruses, are still with us, causing sickness and even widespread death in many parts of the world where the water is purified inadequately if at all. Typhoid fever, cholera, infectious hepatitis, bacillary and amoebic dysenteries and many varieties of gastrointestinal disease can all be transmitted by water. The main sources of these diseases are poorly treated human sewage and animal waste, mainly from farms. Typhoid fever and cholera no longer stalk

A sign of the times. A government employee testing for pollution is the only person on this beach, where human sewage is mainly responsible for unsafe swimming conditions.
(ONTARIO MINISTRY OF THE ENVIRONMENT)

North America the way they and other waterborne diseases do in many less developed nations. But some water experts warn that purification systems in a number of North American towns and cities are poorly run and people are exposed to the risk of intestinal infections from their tap water.

NUTRIENTS

Chemicals like phosphorus and nitrogen are fertilizers and thus basic elements of plant production. Farmers and gardeners add them to the soil to enhance plant growth. Phosphorus was also a major additive to laundry detergents and is still used in some cleaning agents. And phosphorus is part of human and animal wastes and thus of sewage discharges. When large amounts of these chemicals began pouring into lakes and rivers in recent decades they over-fertilized normal algal growth, turning once-clear waters murky green with excessive plant life.

Oxygen Starvation

Biochemical oxygen demand (BOD) is a term that few laymen run across. It simply refers to the effects of organic material that humans dump into the water, upsetting the bacterial and therefore the oxygen balance in the water. Organic matter—sewage, animal manure, industrial waste, even wood chips and sawdust from pulp and paper mills—is attacked by bacteria in the water which start digesting it. The bacteria proliferate, consuming the oxygen which is naturally dissolved in the water. This robs fish and other aquatic life of the oxygen they need and if the pollution gets bad enough the oxygen loss literally suffocates the fish.

Sediments

Around the world billions of tonnes of priceless topsoil, formed over centuries of slow plant decay, are being washed into rivers, reservoirs, lakes and the oceans as human development dramatically accelerates the natural process of erosion. But there is a double loss here, for the suspended silt particles cloud the water, making it unfit for many species of fish, especially trout and salmon. To make matters worse, the fertilizers and pesticides bind to soil particles and are carried off farm fields and into lakes and rivers, where they threaten aquatic life and drinking water.

Heat

Waste heat, mainly from huge coal-burning and nuclear power plants, is generally considered a pollutant although it can have a mixed effect. The warm water gushing from the discharge pipes into a cool lake can increase the productivity of some fish species, but kill other species or increase their susceptibility to parasites and disease. In addition the intakes drawing cooling water into the plants kill large numbers of fish simply by crushing them against screens or grinding them through the water pumps.

But it is the chemical threat which keeps rearing its ugly head in one newspaper story and government report after another. The situation has stymied governments around the world. For years they stood by while industry went its inventive way, and now the people who are supposed to protect us with regulations are playing a giant game of catch-up as they try to understand the risks which have been created.

The task is stupendous. There are more than 7 million known

chemicals and the majority of studies refer to 60 000 in common use, presenting hazards which are poorly understood. Roughly 1 000 new chemicals are created every year. Even that list is deceiving because a single chemical can have hundreds of variants, each behaving differently in the environment and presenting a different level of risk. And many thousands of other virtually unknown chemicals are created as intermediates during the manufacture of chemical products. They often end up as wastes but no one knows how hazardous they are. When different waste chemicals are dumped together they can react and create new substances.

Pollutants include heavy metals, inorganic chemicals like cyanide, organic chemicals like PCBs, pesticides and herbicides, and radionuclides, mainly produced by the nuclear fuel cycle for atomic power plants. Hazardous substances include such everyday items as gasoline, which contains several carcinogens and neurotoxins, ranging from ethylene dibromide to benzene and lead. The nastiest chemicals tend to be the halogenated organics, which are derivatives of oil or natural gas treated under high temperature and pressure with halogens: chlorine, fluorine, bromine and iodine. Most of the problem chemicals, such as the pesticide DDT and industrial chemicals such as PCBs, are chlorinated organics, a combination which is both toxic to life and very slow to break down in the environment. This persistence means the hazard lingers, often for decades, and progressively accumulates in the food chain in which humans are the top predator. About 12.5 million tonnes of chlorine are produced each year in the United States alone. Some of it is combined with petroleum products to produce insect and weed killers and a large amount is used directly to kill bacteria in drinking water. Unfortunately the chlorine that kills the bugs also reacts with naturally occurring plant material in the water to form toxic compounds, called trihalomethanes, in chlorinated tap water.

Many of the problem chemicals we are just finding in our environment have been there for years. Trihalomethanes are a good example, because we have been chlorinating tap water for most of this century. But the problems were only discovered during the past couple of decades and the list has grown explosively since the late 1970s. The driving force behind these discoveries is a sophisticated piece of equipment called the gas chromatograph-mass spectrometer, or GCMS for short. This chunk of hardware, with a price tag as long as its name—several hundred thousand dollars a copy—is to the discovery of toxic chemicals what the microscope was to the discovery of disease-causing bacteria in the last century. The cataloguing of most chemicals in the environment had to await such high-tech help because of the dilution factor. In the water a very toxic substance may be so dilute that there is only one molecule for every million molecules of water, or roughly a drop of pollution in a barrel of water. In fact a modern GCMS is capable of detecting parts per billion, trillion and quadrillion. That is getting so tiny that even the experts have trouble coming up with comparisons which make any sense to the average person, who just wants to know what is in the water. Among the comparisons offered so far is that one part per trillion is like a grain of salt in an Olympic-sized swimming pool and one part per quadrillion like one second in 32 million years. Technicians now boast that they can detect almost any chemical in the computer memory of a GCMS by sniffing almost anywhere in the environment. If this is hyperbole now, it will likely become fact as the machines become ever more sensitive. The spate of discoveries has been so rapid in recent years that the toxin-of-the-day syndrome appeared.

Discovery is just half the equation. It prompts the question: "Is that enough to hurt you?" In a few cases we know that certain chemicals are toxic in tiny amounts, because people have died or become ill from them. But in other cases we assume they will hurt us because they hurt laboratory test animals or because they are similar to chemicals known to be a danger. In many cases no one knows how much risk there is but scientists emphasize that you cannot dismiss something just because it is small. While one part per trillion may seem too small to worry about, scientists point out that it is also the amount of vitamin B^{12} that we need every day just to stay alive.

Health and environment agencies are struggling to make sense of a rapidly growing list of suspect chemicals found in our fish and water. For example, in just over a decade in Canada we have come from considering mercury virtually the sole contaminant of concern in the water, to listing 1 081 substances in the Great Lakes ecosystem, including real, suspected and possible hazards. In an attempt to confront the situation and at least start to act, environment officials have begun to carve up the chemicals into lists, putting the known "bad actors" at the top and ranking the others accordingly. The U.S. Environmental Protection Agency has created a list of 129 Priority Pollutants, which is not comprehensive but includes chemicals known to cause serious environmental problems. The list is particularly useful in helping environment agencies to decide which old dumpsites pose a risk to surrounding waters. In addition the EPA has a list of 403 chemicals which pose a hazard in case of spills.

A group of Great Lakes scientists has made an even more dramatic attempt to zero in on the problems posed by the long list of pollutants in our environment. Rather than treat each of the 1 081 substances found in the wildlife, water or muds of the Great Lakes as an equal risk, they selected 197 that were considered serious toxins. Then they created a list called the Dirty Dozen, which identifies the worst of the poisons in the lakes and the life around them. Douglas Hallett, an expert on Great Lakes pollution, says the list is more comprehensive than it seems. If you clean up the polluters discharging the Dirty Dozen, he says, you will also stop most of the other contaminants because they usually come from the same sources and will be captured by the same pollution controls. The hit list of nasty chemicals will fluctuate, depending on what is discovered by the chemical sniffers being unleashed in the hunt for pollution. The list being used by the Canada-U.S. International Joint Commission on boundary waters in 1985 included 11 substances: PCBs, Mirex, Hexachlorobenzene, Dieldrin, DDT, dioxins, furans, polycyclic aromatic hydrocarbons, lead, mercury and Toxaphene. To that list Dr. Hallett adds radionuclides, chlorinated phenols and polychlorinated styrenes. He is also concerned about cadmium, selenium, organotins and polychlorinated diphenyl ethers.

The pollution of our waters comes from so many sources that it is like death by a million tiny knife cuts. Among the polluters are big and little factories, city sewers draining millions of homes and industries, old dumps, farms, accidental spills, sewage sludge spread on the ground and a host of air pollutants including acid rain. There are the use of pesticides and fertilizers by farmers and gardeners, the incomplete treatment of wastes by industrial and municipal sewers, abandoned mine tailings, coal and ash piles at thermal power stations, leaking underground storage tanks for chemicals such as gasoline and the constant runoff of such wastes as highway de-icing salts and pollutants that spew onto the roads from automobile exhaust pipes. Some pollutants break down once they are in the environment but others, such as PCBs, are very persistent and remain dangerous for a long time.

Pollution is often put into two categories: point and non-point sources. The point sources are literally fixed points on the map, big,

A classic example of how far we still have to go to stop the pollution which is destroying our lakes and rivers.   (ONTARIO MINISTRY OF THE ENVIRONMENT)

messy and easy to identify. They include large industries, major city sewer discharge pipes and big smokestacks belching chemicals which fall back into the lakes. The term non-point source was coined to identify all those other sources which have not been catalogued or are too small to count. Among them are such diffuse problems as the runoff of pesticides and fertilizers from farm fields, fallout from the smokestacks and vent pipes of millions of small industries and even homes and the use of small amounts of hazardous chemicals by a large number of people. The release of hazardous substances is a mixture of the deliberate and the accidental. It includes industries knowing exactly what they are making and what they are dumping down sewer pipes into the river and how much money it is saving them not to properly treat their wastes. In some cases industries dump chemicals into municipal sewers knowing that sewage treatment plants designed to break down household sewage can do little, if anything, to render their wastes harmless. Some of the industrial waste goes straight out the sewage discharge pipe, forming who knows what combinations on the way, as chlorine is added in the sewage plant to kill bacteria. Other wastes, including chemicals and particularly heavy metals, become part of the sewage sludge and pose a new hazard when that sludge is used as fertilizer or is burned in incinerators and the chemicals are released from smokestacks. There is negligence when polluters fail to take reasonable precautions to control wastes which later leak from storage lagoons and pits in the ground. And there are accidents such as mishandling of chemicals, valves left open and road and rail crashes involving tankers.

Who are the main culprits? "Industrial pollution remains the greatest single threat to water quality in Canada," states the federal water inquiry in its 1985 report, *Currents of Change.* In the last couple of decades tighter pollution controls have reined in some of the worst abuses but industry continues to pump out vast and dangerous amounts of pollution. About 100 major factories discharge their untreated or partially treated wastes into the Great Lakes, including pulp and paper, iron, steel, coking, lead and petrochemical industries. About half of these are not even meeting government pollution controls, which, as the name says, control pollution but do not eliminate it. Some wastewaters are so polluted that they are hard to analyze for toxic chemicals. The Ontario Waste Management Corporation says that more than 16 000 large and small industries in that province alone produce hazardous wastes. At the head of the list lies the petroleum and chemical sector with its vast array of products, including oil and gasoline, plastics, pesticides, fertilizers, paints, inks, acids, alkalis, synthetic resins, dyes and a host of other materials. The petroleum refining industry has only met government-imposed pollution targets since 1980 and continues to release many tonnes of phenols, sulphides, ammonia, oil, grease and suspended solids every year. The federal water inquiry noted that the petrochemical industry is a problem industry because its wastes are inadequately treated, partly due to the inconsistent enforcement of regulations. Pollution control is difficult because the toxins vary so widely and so little is known about them, largely because of industrial secrecy.

The forest products industries, including logging and the pulp and paper plants, rank high on the list of polluters. For years those plants have been notorious for fouling rivers with wood and chemical waste. Despite hundreds of millions of dollars spend by business and government on pollution controls and new less-polluting equipment, the industry as a whole still does not meet government standards. Between 1971, when new federal anti-pollution regulations were introduced, and 1982, pulp and paper production increased 20 per cent to 65 000 tonnes per day and the industry reduced the discharge of suspended solids by two-thirds to about 970 tonnes a day. This is still well over the compliance level of 655 tonnes for the country's 123 mills, some of which do not even have compliance schedules. A 1975 report on the 20 mills in Ontario said that discharges from one were lethal to fish and 10 others were moderately lethal. The study predicted that compliance was not likely before 1989. One major improvement has been the virtual elimination of mercury discharges since 1970. The forestry sector also uses a number of hazardous chemicals such as the wood preservative pentachlorophenol, which is applied to logs to keep them from rotting in the woods. It sprays insecticides over huge areas to kill bugs which eat foliage and it sprays herbicides to kill trees which compete for growing spaces with the seedlings of commercial tree species. Some of the most bitter environment battles in recent years have been fought over the use of such sprays. Even the physical act of logging upsets the water cycle as land is laid bare by huge machines and rain sweeps dirt into rivers, blinding fish and fouling their nesting areas. For example, in January, 1979, federal fishery officials tried to prevent logging on the steep slopes of Riley Creek in the Queen Charlotte Islands but the provincial government allowed logging to continue. By June large-scale slope failure had occurred and salmon spawning beds were destroyed.

Another hazardous industry is the metals field, ranging from the mines to the smelters and finally to the plants and shops where metals are made into products. Mines extract huge amounts of rock to get small amounts of metal and the waste rock is dumped in piles called tailings. Some metal is left in the rock and that can be leached out gradually and can drain into nearby watercourses. In addition dangerous substances like arsenic and cyanide are sometimes used to extract metal from rock, and they too are in the waste residues. And many ore-bearing rocks also contain sulphur, which, when exposed above-ground, is attacked by microbes which convert it to sulphuric acid in the presence of water. The drainage of such acids alone has been enough to kill fish. Once ores are fed into the giant furnaces of smelters an air pollution problem begins. The nickel and copper smelting industry is Canada's largest producer of acid rain, since its chimneys spew vast amounts of sulphur dioxide into the air where it turns into sulphuric acid. The iron and steel industries produce a number of pollutants including PAHs. The metal finishing industry, which involves the forming, plating, assembly and cleaning of metals, produces such pollution as cadmium, chromium, cyanide, copper, lead, nickel and zinc. A 1983 Canadian survey found that only 60 per cent of this industry's wastes was being adequately treated. In 1985 Metro Toronto prosecuted a number of metal finishing companies for dumping hazardous wastes into the sewers. Not only were the wastes a hazard to aquatic life and drinking water but they threatened the health of sewage treatment plant workers and could destroy the microbes used in the plants to break down sewage.

While farming seems one of the few natural occupations left in the world, a number of environment experts see it as one of the worst contributors to pollution. Dr. Hallett, who also operates a farm with his wife, thinks that agriculture is the biggest polluter when one counts the indirect effects. By this he means that most of the pesticides that we worry about, and some their harmful byproducts, such as dioxins, are the result of pressures to use chemicals for protection against insects and weeds. The resulting pollution comes not only from huge amounts of pesticides and fertilizers that rain washes annually from farms into the rivers, but from the pesticide factories which discharge manufacturing wastes. In addition to chemical runoff there is a problem with the erosion of dirt into rivers from the cultivation of fields. Canada's Prairies alone lose about 160 million tonnes of soil a year from wind and 117 million tonnes from water erosion. Another form of farm pollution is livestock waste, which is becoming a severe problem in areas where large numbers of animals are packed into small feeder lots not far from urban centres where they will be slaughtered and sold for food. The pollution from many Quebec pork farms turns some rivers yellow.

Urban areas have for millennia been a major source of water pollution because people failed to cope with their own wastes. Even after the discovery of bacterial infection and the link to human sewage in the last century people were reluctant to eliminate the problem. Government officials reacted in the early 1900s by adding chlorine to drinking water to kill the bacteria. They did not start serious sewage treatment to try to eliminate the problem until several decades later and the battle is still going on. Sewers were built in Canada as long ago as the 1860s but sewage treatment did not become common until after the Second World War. Despite the $1.1 billion spent in Canada each year just to build sewers, half the population discharges its sewage untreated and only one-tenth of the sewage east of Ontario is treated before being discharged into the nearest body of water. Quebec, the second-largest province, is the worst offender with sewage treatment for only 11 per cent of its 6.6 million residents, albeit an improvement from the 5 per cent treatment as recently as 1978. More than 2 million people in Montreal, the country's second-largest city, pour 2 billion litres of raw sewage into the St. Lawrence River every day. It is the only major city in North America to dump all its raw sewage into a river used by others for drinking water.

The results are to be expected. Water treatment plants downstream wage a constant war against bacteria and viruses and in the summer of 1984 all but two of the 49 beaches and public parks within a 70-kilometre radius of Montreal were closed to swimming. Only six have been open in recent years. Quebec has undertaken a $4.5 billion program to treat 85 to 90 per cent of its sewage by the early 1990s, with Montreal's gigantic sewage treatment plant to start operation even sooner. In addition Quebec's environment ministry estimates another $2 billion must be spent to reduce pollution from farms and industry.

The record for the cleanest province goes to Alberta, which has put 99.3 per cent of its municipalities on sewage treatment. Saskatchewan is close behind with 99 per cent. This is understandable, since Prairie towns and cities are lined up along rivers like beads on a string, with each one drinking the water discharged by its neighbors upstream. Despite the treatment there are still complaints downstream from cities like Calgary and Lethbridge, especially in dry years when there is little water in the rivers to dilute the remaining wastes. Even the septic tank, an old threat to drinking water when it is placed too close to wells or lakeshore water intakes, remains with us.

James MacLaren, the former head of one of Canada's major water and sewage engineering companies and a member of the inquiry on federal water policy, worries that the expansion of sewage treatment is not keeping pace with demand. Mr. MacLaren states that a large number of existing sewage treatment plants cannot keep up with urban growth and the amount of untreated sewage is building up in the environment. Sewage treatment is a difficult art at best because plants have to cope with unknown mixtures added by small industries and with the vagaries of rainstorms, which can suddenly add a huge flow of water from street runoff. In recent years it has become fashionable to spend large amounts of money separating storm sewers from sanitary sewers so that heavy rains will not overload treatment plants, causing them to discharge raw sewage. But this means that storm waters are not treated at all, leaving an unimpeded flow of pollutants to be washed off the roads and lawns, including lead, oil, animal feces, de-icing fluids, topsoil, fertilizers and pesticides. The typical storm sewer runoff from city streets is as polluted with heavy metals as is sanitary sewage, which is treated. Storm sewer wastes include organic matter which decays in the water, robbing aquatic life of oxygen. Now some municipalities are creating big holding tanks to catch storm sewer runoff so it can be put through sewage treatment plants when normal demand is light.

Dumpsites, known as landfills, are the new bogeymen of toxic waste. For untold generations humans have dumped their refuse into any handy pit in the ground and in recent years, as we filled up natural cavities around our cities, we took to gouging out big holes and filling them with garbage. When these pits were full we covered them up and forgot about them. But our memories were jolted when Love Canal, a chemical waste dump in Niagara Falls, New York, leaked its poisons out of the ground and into the backyards and basements of a whole subdivision. Suddenly buried chemical dumps, hundreds of thousands of them around the world, were viewed as toxic time bombs.

Many old dumps are a problem because they are in old sand and gravel quarries, used because they were free holes in the ground. Some people had the naive assumption that the coarse ground would filter out the wastes but in fact this porous material provides the fastest route to underground water short of a direct pipe. Solid clay is the safest type of ground since it is less permeable to water and will retard leakage for decades if not centuries. Canada has about 10 000 known dumps, mainly full of household garbage, but an unknown number of them will pose a high risk to nearby waters because they received hazardous industrial waste. There are as many as 2 000 dumps of concern in Ontario alone according to the Ontario Waste Management Corporation.

Another dumping problem is the underground injection of liquid wastes. In North America there are an estimated 100 000 wells for the disposal of chemical wastes, especially oil and gas field brines which were pumped out of the ground in the first place. In theory underground injection is very attractive—out of sight, out of mind. You sink a pipe a hundred to several hundred metres deep until you get below the local water table and find open areas in the underground strata. Then you start pumping. The problem is that the wastes do not always stay down. In some cases they seep back up along the sides of the injection pipe, either popping to the surface or, worse, taking a lateral detour along the way into someone's well water. Sometimes the injection pressures are so high that the underground rock formations crack, opening up pathways for seepage. And there is another type of underground problem, the leaking underground storage tank, LUST for short. In the United States there are about 3 500 000 underground storage tanks, about half for gasoline and half for heating oil. The U.S. Environmental Protection Agency estimates that 10–30 per cent of them are leaking and they are losing about 2 700 tonnes of petroleum a year. In Canada the estimates are about 100 000 tanks with an estimated 21–25 per cent of them leaking. Even a small amount of gasoline can render an underground water source unfit for human consumption.

Chemical spills are still another threat to the environment and our health. Between 1974 and 1983 Canada had 24 400 reported spills and leaks totalling 3.7 million tonnes of petroleum, chemicals and brines. In 1983 there were 1 000 spills reported in Ontario but many more were not reported. Spills can be highly dangerous to aquatic life, as shown by the 1984 spill from the E.B. Eddy Company into the Spanish River in northern Ontario, which wiped out all the fish downstream from Espanola to the North Channel of Lake Huron. Along the St. Clair River, where there are 13 major Canadian factories and chemical plants, there has been as many as one spill or overflow per plant per week.

Canada has its share of old dumps but the real problem is in the United States, with 10 times the population, less land area and a huge share of the world's chemical industry. A U.S. Environmental Protection Agency official says that there are 14 000 major waste producers and as many waste haulers, and 5 000 sites which treat, store or dispose of waste. No one seems sure of just how many old dumps are hazardous, though the E.P.A. has a list of 812 deemed as most hazardous to human health and 75 per cent are known, or suspected, to be polluting underground water. These are the sites on the Superfund list, which was created in 1980 and had $1.6 billion to start cleaning up the Love Canals all over the country. But even the E.P.A. estimates there will eventually be about 2 200 Superfund sites, while the General Accounting Office, a Congressional watchdog agency, puts the number at 4 000. An association of U.S. waste industry officials calculates that there are 7 100 sites and the U.S. Office of Technology Assessment estimates that there are more than 10 000 problem sites among the 621 000 known landfills—and an unknown number of abandoned dumps which may be discovered in the future.

The costs of clean-up keep escalating too. The E.P.A. estimates it will cost $11–28 billion over a decade, the General Accounting Office figures it will be $39 billion and the Office of Technology Assessment says that over 50 years a real clean-up will cost $100 billion to Superfund alone, plus several hundred billion dollars to the nation as a whole. By comparison, research for the Strategic Defence Initiative, know as Star Wars, is estimated to cost $26 billion. Money is not the only problem. The E.P.A. says there are not even enough trained toxic waste experts in the United States to cope with more than 2 200 sites on its list. In many cases the clean-up must be carried out by workers in sealed clothing, called moon suits because they resemble astronauts' clothing.

The damage counts are even more vague because people are just starting to measure what is happening. There is one estimate that there are between 4 500 and 22 000 square kilometres of contaminated aquifers in the United States, most of them near people. Already the damage from dumps and careless handling of chemicals has forced the evacuation and bulldozing of homes around Love Canal and the closing of the whole town of Times Beach, Missouri, which the U.S. government bought for $35 million. Thousands of other people have had their water contaminated.

The problem of non-point source pollution is creating a frustrating series of threats which are hard to find let alone control. An Ontario Environment Ministry report on the pollution of Metro Toronto's three main rivers—the Humber, the Don and Mimico Creek—said the water contained hazardous levels of bacteria in the river and high levels of toxic chemicals. This was despite $270 million poured into pollution control since 1954. Inspectors found 2 000 pipes dumping an unknown mixture of chemicals and bacteria into the rivers. This mix comes from illegal sanitary sewer connections, factory wastes and simple street runoff from a dense, industrialized population.

The diffuse sources of pollution are particularly a problem for the Great Lakes, with their huge expanses and many tributaries and sewer outlets. It has been estimated that the lakes receive hundreds of tonnes a year of metals and chemicals in airborne fallout, discharges from industrial and municipal sewers and runoff from the land.

While factories and dumps are obvious sources of dangerous wastes, almost every home has its own cache of hazardous chemicals: paints and paint thinners, insect sprays, anti-freeze, chlorine bleach, nail polish, oven cleaners, mildew removers, rust dissolvers and a dozen other household products, many labelled poison, corrosive or explosive. Some of them, such as toilet bowl cleaners and drain cleaners, are deliberately poured into the water system, often in far greater amounts than are really needed. When we are finished with old paints the wastes usually go down the drain. Partly-empty cans of insect sprays, mercury and cadmium batteries, mildly radioactive smoke detectors and hundreds of other materials go into municipal landfill dumps where they pose a long-term hazard of leakage. If the wastes go into municipal incinerators they pose an immediate air pollution problem. The green-lawn syndrome has been promoted with such vigor that homeowners spend large amounts of money dumping herbicides and fertilizers on their lawns to kill weeds. Part of that chemical load is washed off into the sewers and then to the lakes from which we drink.

Each consumer of these hazardous products is responsible for a share of the wastes which flow from the factories where they are made. Our individual contribution is minuscule, but with the population of North America around 260 million the combination of individual actions can have a tremendous effect. One study estimated that on average in the Great Lakes basin, agriculture released one tonne of pesticides per square kilometre; household consumption of pesticides, solvents and chemicals accounts for double that load to our environment.

In recent years we have discovered that large amounts of pollution are falling from the sky. Most industries have cleaned up the black smoke, which was once touted as a sign of prosperity, by installing precipitators which remove the soot particles or by burning cleaner fuels such as oil or natural gas, instead of coal. But the chimneys still release clear gases and in some cases these gases can be even more dangerous than the smoke we used to see. Sulphur dioxide and nitrogen oxides leading to sulphuric and nitric acid rain are invisible to the naked eye and can only be seen with special filters. The discovery of toxic chemicals in remote lakes has proven that such chemicals as PCBs and Toxaphene are carried far and wide by the winds.

Once we find out about pollution the natural question is, how much is there? It is a scandal that no one has yet produced such an inventory. We know neither how much hazardous material is going into our drinking water, nor how much is removed by present drinking-water treatment systems. This ignorance came back to haunt Canada in recent negotiations with the United States. After extensive joint studies showing that most of the Niagara River pollution was from the U.S. side and most of the water flowing into Lake Ontario was from that river, Canada accused the United States of being the major source of hazardous chemicals in the lake. The U.S. side retorted that it thought Ontario was the major polluter from its many industries around the lake and the Canadian side lacked the information to prove otherwise.

The best one can do is to try to assemble some figures and apply basic arithmetic. This does not give a precise estimate of direct pollution, because some of the chemicals listed will not be going directly into water. But it is fair to assume that sooner or later a substantial proportion will enter the water cycle through direct disposal, accidental spills, runoff from land, evaporation into the rain or leakage from disposal sites.

- Environment Canada says that about 75 million tonnes of chemicals are made each year in North America and this is increasing by about 7 per cent per annum.
- A Canada-U.S. study of pollution estimated that 45 million tonnes of toxic wastes are created each year in North America.
- Statistics Canada stopped collecting figures on the amount of pesticides sold in 1977 when the figure was 34 300 tonnes and growing rapidly. U.S. farmers alone use an estimated 500 000 or more tonnes of pesticides annually.
- A recent federal study estimated that 3.7 million tonnes of hazardous wastes are generated in Canada each year, with about half from Ontario and almost one-third from Quebec. Ontario industry, business and homes produce over 6.4 million tonnes a year of garbage, nearly three-quarters of a tonne for every man, woman and child. The Ontario Waste Management Corporation estimates that 1.5 million tonnes of industrial waste are created every year in this province by as

many as 16 000 large and small sources and about half that amount is disposed of improperly. This includes about 375 000 tonnes of wastes going through sewers into municipal treatment plants not designed to detoxify chemical waste. Manitoba's industry produces about 20 300 tonnes of hazardous waste per year. One-half goes into sewers and one-quarter is dumped into landfills while the rest is disposed of by other means. Across Canada there are huge amounts of mine wastes scattered on the ground, including about 100 million tonnes of uranium mine tailings.

• About 52 million tonnes a year of sulphur dioxide and nitrogen oxides, the precursors of acid rain, spew from North American smokestacks, chimneys and cars every year, with 7.7 million tonnes of that from Canadian sources. Canadian officials estimate that about 12 million tonnes fall on this country every year, showing a transfer from the United States. More than 30 million tonnes of a selected list of chemicals go into the air over North America annually. One Canadian scientist calculated that over 20 tonnes a year of seven toxic chemicals fall on the Great Lakes and its drainage basin of rivers and streams. Another estimated a fallout of 137 tonnes of eight pesticides. Since then research on just one of the chemicals, PCBs, estimates their fallout is over 29 tonnes a year. A study of an eighth substance, PAHs, calculated they had a fallout of from 130 to 480 tonnes a year, depending on the estimates.

• About 150 000 tonnes a year of potentially harmful substances are estimated as coming from direct industrial waste discharges into lakes and rivers. In addition pulp and paper plants release 450 000 tonnes of wood waste and phosphate fertilizer plants discharge about 900 000 tonnes of calcium sulphate, a substance that is not hazardous but can upset the balance of aquatic life.

• The International Joint Commission estimates that about 12 000 tonnes a year of phosphorus still go into Lake Erie and about 9 000 tonnes into Lake Ontario. This degrades water quality.

• Canada's municipal sewers discharge an estimated 475 000 tonnes a year of organic materials, which break down and reduce oxygen in the water, and about 440 000 tonnes of suspended solids.

• An estimated 91 000 tonnes a year of toxic pollutants from 160 000 industries and businesses flow into U.S. sewage treatment plants and, at best, 62 per cent is neutralized.

The constant stream of pollution reports carries a series of ominous messages. They tell a story of growing risk to every living thing and dismal failure by governments to deliver on promises of a clean environment. They also tell of a failure by many industries to be good corporate citizens. Despite the claims of governments and industry that chemicals are being brought under control there are still toxic substances such as PCBs getting into the environment years after they were supposedly restricted to "closed-loop systems," engineering jargon for a sealed container which is not supposed to leak.

Peter Pearse of Vancouver, chairman of Canada's first national inquiry on water, says that environmental problems are not always the result of deliberate action. In some cases, he says, "nobody is being irrational; everyone is just following their own self-interest from day to day." Former federal environment minister Charles Caccia says that we are in this mess because "we prefer as a civilization, as a Western society, to react and cure rather than to anticipate and prevent. Second, we have accepted in our economic approach to industrial activity that it is alright to borrow clean and return dirty. Thirdly, we have contradicted ourselves in applying the principles of free enterprise. The private sector behaves in a manner not consistent with free enterprise ideas at all. If it did, private enterprise, which prides itself on being self-reliant, would not expect public sector subsidies to pay the cost of repairing the damage caused when industry returns dirty what it borrows clean."

For years it has been obvious that we are dealing with a deck loaded in favor of polluters. In virtually all cases industry is supposed to be self-policing and only recently have governments started to hire substantial numbers of real environmental police, trained and equipped to detect sophisticated pollution. Generally governments lacked the expensive equipment and highly trained work force to track down pollution. When they trained experts, private industry used higher salaries to hire many away. Most polluters were only caught after a sharp-eyed citizen spotted a blatant violation, such as fish belly-up in a river, or when a plant employee blew the whistle. Even when polluters were hauled into court most of the fines have been laughably small compared to the profits to be made, and were seen as little more than a licence fee to continue polluting. A study paper for the Canadian Law Reform Commission said, "Pollution usually arises out of business activities, either through carelessness or in an attempt to save or make money." The financial incentives to pollute will increase as disposal becomes more costly and even impossible to find.

While most pollution is white-collar crime by "honest" businesses, there is a dangerous infiltration of the waste hauling and disposal business by organized crime in the United States, with signs that it affects Canada. Big industries have paid disposal companies to get rid of waste in acceptable ways but the dangerous chemicals were simply poured into a ditch in the dark of the night, leading to the phrase "midnight dumper." In another technique, waste haulers open the valves of their trucks and drive down rainy roads, hoping the chemicals will not destroy the windshield wipers of drivers behind them. Hazardous wastes have been mixed with oil and sold as fuel in a number of cities. In Tillsonburg, Ontario, PCBs were found in oil used to undercoat cars. In recent years governments have started to crack down by requiring documentation, tracing chemical movements and passing laws which put more responsibility for safe disposal on the factory which ships its wastes.

Another factor which has hampered governments' effectiveness is the approach that many have taken to pollution control. Government officials often sit down with company officials and negotiate the amount of pollution reduction and a time schedule based on what the company says it can afford to pay. The idea of negotiating is not bad but it often puts the governments in the position of defending the deals—even the bad ones—when someone else challenges the risks that government negotiators have permitted on behalf of society. Sometimes environment departments—Ontario was a notorious case for years—even actually withheld or downplayed pollution reports. When the Liberal government took power in Ontario in 1985, the new environment minister, James Bradley, said he thought there was too cosy a relationship between government and industry in polluted areas such as the St. Clair River, Canada's Chemical Valley.

Government organization is also a handicap at times, especially when environmental responsibilities are shared among a dozen or more departments and agencies. For example at the federal level, environment, health, agriculture, economic development, fisheries, Indian and northern affairs and transport departments are all major players on environment issues. To make it even more complicated, environmental responsibilities are divided between federal, provincial and territorial governments, which then pass on some of the responsibilities to municipalities. Around the Great Lakes there are 11 federal, state and provincial governments, plus the International Joint Commission and scores of towns and cities, all playing a role. *Chemical and Engineering News*, a major U.S. publication, said of government

performance: "The poor judgment, downright ineptitude and conflict-
ing agendas [at different political levels] have increased the risks to the
public and environment." The only good point to come out of the
duplication of environment services is that sometimes one agency acts
as a watchdog on another and, if the public is really lucky, blows the
whistle on pollution cover-ups.

Governments are also sensitive about employment, and companies
have used outright blackmail in an effort to stave off environmental
regulations. They have threatened to close down plants and with them
one-industry towns if they are forced to install anti-pollution equipment. Only recently have governments recognized that one cannot
have a healthy economy without a healthy environment. Only recently
have they realized that most voters want both jobs and safe drinking
water and believe that we can afford both. Few companies have packed
and moved out when regulations were enforced firmly but fairly. In a
number of cases, such as acid rain and pulp and paper mills, governments have decided that tax dollars will be used to help the clean-up
since the public benefits from the industry, and the costs of controlling
pollution will be very high. There is also a fundamental problem of
chemical wastes being just that—waste. Environment Canada estimates that we need not even create 80 per cent of the toxic contamination that we now have to dispose of.

In other cases we have accepted some degree of pollution as a
necessary evil and pesticides are a prime example. The thesis from
pesticide promoters is that these chemicals are necessary to keep up
food production in a starving world but there are some dissenters to
this theory. According to Robert Metcalf's textbook, *Introduction to
Insect Pest Management,* farmers use more than twice as much
pesticide as they need and still get poor results. "We now suffer about
a 20 per cent crop loss to insects, the same as we did in 1900," says
Mr. Metcalf, of the University of Illinois. "We have won some individual battles along the way but we are losing the war." Pesticides have
killed off natural predators, causing some pests to flourish. In addition
the constant use of pesticides helps to breed insecticide-resistant pests
because those which survive and reproduce will pass on genes for
resistance to poisons. Mr. Metcalf says that more than 250 of the
world's crop pests are resistant to some type of insecticide and 20 are
resistant to all types of bug killers.

Former Ontario environment minister Keith Norton added his voice
to the chorus of people who want a change in pesticide usage when he

said in 1983 that governments must "control the extravagant use of chemicals" by farmers. However, environment ministers are usually junior to agriculture ministers and the status quo is slow to change.

In the final analysis who is responsible for the poisoning of our most important resource? It is right and proper to point accusing fingers at big industries and big cities which have failed to spend the money or mental effort necessary to control their pollution, and it is right to flail governments for turning a blind eye to much of the pollution. But the driving force behind the growth in pollution is the ravenous appetite of the consumer, who buys more and more synthetic products without questioning the side effects. And it will only be the outraged voices of consumers which will force governments and industries to change their dirty ways.

CHAPTER THREE

THE NASTY POLLUTANTS

SOME OF THE TOXINS in our water, such as DDT, PCBs and dioxin, have become well known by name because they turn up so frequently and have caused damage. Others have received less attention but are serious threats. Among some of the bad actors:

DIOXIN

This is the horror chemical of the 1980s. In fact dioxin is the name for a family of 75 related isomers, all of which behave differently and have different toxicity. The one most feared and most commonly referred to is 2,3,7,8-tetrachlorodibenzo-para-dioxin, known as TCDD. It is the most toxic synthetic chemical yet discovered—less than one-millionth of a gram of TCDD dioxin is enough to kill a guinea pig. In test animals it causes cancer, cell mutations, and birth defects, and kills embryos and suppresses the immune system, which protects the body against disease. Dioxin is so toxic that special, high-hazard laboratories have been built to protect researchers who are handling the substance. Dioxin is one of those oddball chemicals which is an accidental byproduct formed when certain substances, particularly those containing chlorine, are burned.

It broke into the headlines in November, 1980, with the announcement that TCDD had been discovered in herring gull eggs from around the Great Lakes, particularly from those in Lake Ontario. The source for Lake Ontario was identified as the Hooker Chemicals and Plastics Corporation (now called the Occidental Chemical Corporation) in Niagara Falls, New York. Other dioxin hot spots were identified in the Titabawassee River and Saginaw Bay in Lake Huron, downstream from the Dow Chemical Company factory in Midland, Michigan. Both

Sign at the edge of Love Canal chemical dump is a reminder of the legacy we have created by failing to adequately treat the residues of our chemical society.
(THE TORONTO DEPARTMENT OF PUBLIC HEALTH)

factories made large quantities of 2,4,5-TCP, a chemical used to make the potent herbicide 2,4,5-T and a germicide, hexachlorophene, once used in hospitals. TCDD dioxin is an accidental byproduct of 2,4,5-TCP production. The herbicide 2,4,5-T was widely used in North America, particularly as a brush killer, until 1980 when the U.S. government and several provinces severely restricted its use. At times it was mixed with another weed killer, 2,4-D, and this mixture, called Agent Orange by the U.S. military, became notorious after it was sprayed as a defoliant on the jungles of Vietnam. Recently a large number of Vietnam veterans and North American forestry workers who were exposed to 2,4,5-T have launched lawsuits alleging that the herbicide and its dioxin contamination harmed their health. Other forms of dioxin have turned up in some types of 2,4-D and in chlorinated phenols, a widely used wood preservative often sold as pentachlorophenol. The effects of dioxin on human health have not yet become clear because it is just one of thousands of chemicals we encounter, but dioxin was implicated in the sudden and massive reproductive failure of several waterbird populations on the lower Great Lakes in the late 1960s and early 1970s. Since then dioxin levels have declined and the bird populations are recovering.

In the last few years dioxins have been found in a large number of fish, particularly in Lake Ontario salmon and trout, in pike in Rainy River, in a chemical dump at Elmira in southern Ontario and in the mud in the bottom of the St. Clair River in Ontario's Chemical Valley, just to name a few places. Dioxin contamination in Times Beach, Missouri, led to the town being evacuated and closed by the U.S. government. In different parts of the world including southern Ontario, dioxin has been found in human tissues, even among people who apparently never worked directly with the chemical. Despite controls on the production of chemicals to reduce dioxins, they are still appearing in the environment. Among the sources are smokestacks, particularly those of incinerators where a wide variety of chemicals contained in city garbage is burned. And there are large amounts of dioxin in old chemical waste dumps.

FURANS

Furans are chemically similar to dioxins, and are another accidental byproduct of industry and incineration. Chlorinated furans have been found in PCBs and although the research is not yet clear, they may turn out to be the poisonous element that makes PCBs so hazardous.

POLYCYCLIC AROMATIC HYDROCARBONS (PAHS)

PAHs, like dioxins and furans, are another unwanted byproduct of combustion. They are primarily a result of the incomplete combustion of organic material, such as in the fossil fuels we burn in our homes, cars and industries and in virtually any fires, including naturally occurring forest fires. They are prevalent around coking operations associated with the production of iron and steel. They are also found in creosote. And, like dioxins and furans, they appear in a number of forms including benzo(a)pyrene, which has been targeted as one of the most dangerous variants. PAH particles are fine and will travel great distances in the air but they are most concentrated around urban areas. There are estimates of about 130 tonnes of just seven variants of PAHs falling on the Great Lakes every year. Some researchers, such as John Black of the Roswell Park Memorial Cancer Institute in Buffalo, found a high incidence of tumors in carp and goldfish hybrids in areas where there are high PAH levels in the bottom muds. Dr. Black also induced cancers by painting the skin of laboratory fish with PAHs.

POLYCHLORINATED BIPHENYLS (PCBS)

Along with the insecticide DDT, the industrial group of chemicals called PCBs is among the best-known set of initials in the field of toxic chemicals. PCBs are a family of 209 variants, and, as the name chlorine suggests, are another of the chlorinated organics which cause so many problems in the environment. They were invented in the late 1800s and produced industrially in North America from 1929 until 1978. PCBs remained stable under heat and chemical attack and were relatively cheap, making them an ideal substance for use in hostile industrial environments. As a result they went into insulating fluids in electrical transformers and capacitors all over the world. They were used in some industrial pipe systems for transferring heat from one area to another, they were used in cutting oils, hydraulic fluids and lubricating oils and they were added to plastic to make it pliable. In addition to these industrial uses they were put in such consumer goods as paints, printing inks, carbonless copy paper, sealants and adhesives.

PCBs were found in Great Lakes coho salmon in 1969 and by the early 1970s scientists studying PCBs became suspicious of their apparent toxic effects on animals. By 1971 a study found that mink

fed with such Great Lakes fish as coho salmon were suffering reproductive failures. Other studies indicated that PCBs cause cancer, a
high rate of reproductive failure, an increase in infection by diseases
and a wide range of other harmful effects in laboratory animals. PCBs
have a nasty habit of storing themselves tenaciously in body fat and
thus accumulating in the food chain. A PCB accident in Japan has
provided an example of what can happen to humans: infants exposed
to PCBs in their mothers' wombs were born small and often prema-
turely. As they grew they were retarded both mentally and physically,
with an average IQ of 70. Governments reacted to the PCB threat with
gradually tighter restrictions on the ways that this chemical could be
used. By now PCBs are only to be used in such sealed containers as
transformers, but this means that most of the 21 million litres of PCBs
in Canada still pose a risk of spills. The problem is that once PCBs are
spilled into the environment they are so stable that they will be with us
for generations. Although the United States has several incinerators
licensed to burn PCBs at extremely high temperatures, there is so far
no such destruction equipment approved in Canada. The reason is that
no one will accept an incinerator in their neighborhood.

PESTICIDES

Pesticides are the hired guns of the modern farmer, the gardener and
even the householder. We spray, dust, paint, fog and inject them in
vast quantities in what seems a never-ending battle against bugs, rats,
mice, worms, moulds and fungus and even some species of birds and
fish that we do not happen to like. We spray them over much of our
cropland and gardens to combat weeds, paint them on the bottoms of
boats to prevent slime from forming and even put them in wallpaper to
prevent moulds. Under the Pest Control Products Act, Canada has
registered 514 active pesticide ingredients for use in this country and
they are sold as mixtures in 5 123 pest control products. In the United
States there are about 1 400 active ingredients in 35 000 commercial
pesticides.

Unfortunately chemicals, like bullets, are dumb and do not know
whom they are supposed to attack and whom they should leave alone.
For several decades there has been a growing number of complaints
about the damage caused by pesticides. Their residues, which have
poorly understood effects on our health, are found in both our food
and our drinking water. The chemicals are tested for some health

effects before they go on the market but many were registered years ago, under simpler testing methods, now considered inadequate. In 1977 it was revealed that more than two hundred chemicals, mostly pesticides, had their safety tests falsified by the largest testing laboratory in North America. The Canadian and U.S. governments broke their own rules, which say chemicals should be proven safe before being allowed on the market. They left the suspect pesticides in use until several were proven to have failed safety tests or were withdrawn from the market by their manufacturers.

There is a heated debate about the use of pesticides, particularly in such vast quantities and with present standards. Anyone can walk into a hardware store or gardening shop and buy unlimited quantities of chemicals which present a hazard to human health and the environment. They are even sold in grocery stores. Large amounts of money are spent on publicity to convince people that they need to spread weed killers on their lawns and gardens. Some advertisements even show a man in a shirt with no gloves or protective gear spraying herbicides and insecticides into the same air he is breathing. It is a sign of the growing seriousness of the problem that in 1986 the U.S. Environmental Protection Agency said that pollution by pesticides was the most urgent of all the problems it faced.

DDT (dichlorodiphenyltrichloroethane) was the first and best known of the popular organochlorine insecticides. After the Second World War it dominated the market for years and it is still used in many countries around the world. Once touted as the way to save the planet from bugs, DDT was found to be killing off some species of wildlife (especially predator birds high up on the food chain), upsetting spawning behavior, causing reproductive failure in fish and threatening human health. The chemical became the first major target of pesticide controls and most uses were banned in Canada by 1969 and in the United States by 1972. It is therefore disturbing that DDT and its decay products such as DDE have still not disappeared from the environment. Researchers think that the DDT might be coming from old chemical industry dumps leaking into the river and may be blown on high altitude winds to Canada from Central and South American countries, where it is still used. Both of these conclusions are possible but some of the researchers discovered that DDT is a component of another insecticide, which is licensed for use in North America. While retesting old pesticides the U.S. Environmental Protection Agency found that Dicofol, which was licensed for use in the United States eight days after the ban on DDT became official, contains 9–15 per cent DDT. The chemical is sold under the name Kelthane and is recommended, in gardening columns among other sources, for killing mites on fruit trees and ornamental plants. About seven tonnes of Dicofol are used in Canada each year but two to three million tonnes are used in the United States. And Keith Rodgers, a senior Great Lakes researcher, was shocked when Quebec farmers told him in 1985 that they were still buying and using straight DDT.

The insecticide Toxaphene replaced DDT in many uses and remained on the market much longer. Two of the reasons are that it is a complex mixture of 177 variants and it is hard to identify in wildlife, so it was not confirmed as a problem chemical until recent years. Toxaphene was used on more than 170 agricultural products, primarily cotton but also on soybeans, peanuts and cattle. The greatest use has been on cotton crops in the southeastern and southern United States so it came as a surprise to find high Toxaphene levels in Great Lakes fish. The chemical has caused cancer and mutations in test animals and appears to affect hormonal levels in women. At one point scientists feared the levels would become high enough that they would seriously increase the hazard of eating Great Lakes fish but Toxaphene was controlled. Since little if any Toxaphene has been used around the Great Lakes, researchers are certain that the chemical was blown hundreds, even thousands, of kilometres to the lakes, making it a classic case of long-range contamination on a scale comparable to acid rain. Production of Toxaphene was banned in the United States in 1982, with people allowed to use up existing stockpiles until 1986.

Among the other pesticides which have created havoc with fisheries is Mirex, which was used as both an insecticide and a fire retardant. Mirex has been found to induce cancer in animals and is linked to birth defects in birds. Chlordane, Dieldrin and Aldrin were pesticides widely used in the Great Lakes region to control insects and rodents but they are now restricted. They accumulate in the food chain, are slow to decay, cause reproductive problems in animals and are suspected of inducing cancer in humans. Pentachlorophenol, a widely used wood preservative sold under such names as Pentox, has been found to be contaminated with members of the dioxin family and is therefore considered hazardous. Warnings about its use have been increased recently but millions of litres have already been used as a wood preservative.

Some of the chemicals are widespread while others are highly localized. For example Mirex was spilled into Lake Ontario, and so has become a chemical marker for wildlife from the lake. In fact the winning fish was once disqualified from a Lake Ontario salmon derby because it did not have enough Mirex in its tissues, and judges ruled that it must have come from another lake. There are some other ironies in the pollution casebooks. Tributyltin, a popular anti-fouling paint for boats, is so toxic that it is likely killing the fish beneath fishermen's boats. This compound is painted on many boats and some docks to prevent slimy marine growths from accumulating. The worst problems appear to be in harbors where boats are moored. In Toronto harbor tributyltin has been found at levels 10 times higher than those needed to kill young trout.

HEAVY METALS

Heavy metals is another term that has crept into the lexicon of toxicology. Mercury and lead, both neurotoxins which attack the human central nervous system, are the two prime examples, with the former a major polluter in fish, particularly in eastern Canada. In fact it was the announcement in 1970 that mercury had been found in fish from southwestern and northwestern Ontario which marked the beginning of the true discovery of poisons in Canada's waters.

Mercury, a naturally occurring metallic element, was not seen as an environmental contaminant that would pass up through the food chain, and as a result many thousands of tonnes were dumped or allowed to leak by chemical companies and other users. However, mercury accumulated in the mud at the bottoms of lakes and rivers, where it was converted by micro-organisms into methylmercury, which is toxic and accumulates in fish and anything which eats them. The two major hot spots were Lake St. Clair and the English-Wabigoon River system, which is northeast of Kenora. Upstream from Lake St. Clair the Dow Chemical Company of Canada was discharging mercury from a chlor-alkali mercury cell plant used for making chlorine. At Dryden it was the Reed Incorporated pulp mill which had a similar chlor-alkali plant.

Within weeks fishing was banned in both areas and many commercial fishermen lost their jobs. The Ontario government did not ban sport fishing but advised people not to eat their catch. Those most harmed were Indians along the English-Wabigoon River system, where between 9 to 11 tonnes of mercury lay strewn along the river bottom as far downstream as Clay Lake. The people beside the river lost a major source of low-cost food and their jobs as commercial fishermen and guides for sport fishermen. Some endangered their health when they continued to eat fish. In recent years the natural laying down of new sediments is burying the poison and gradually fishing restrictions are being relaxed, but there are still dangers. In the meantime intensive testing has turned up mercury in fish from other parts of Ontario and other provinces. For example, a 1983 Quebec Environment Ministry report said fish in parts of seven rivers—the Yamaska, Richelieu, Chateauguay, Ottawa, North, Assomption and St. Maurice—contained mercury above the acceptable level. Mercury levels in pike taken from many north central Manitoba lakes also exceeded safe limits. The levels were highest in the area of the Churchill River power diversion, where the damming of free-flowing waters has allowed natural mercury in the bedrock to be converted to methylmercury and to accumulate in the fish. A similar situation has developed behind some dams for the James Bay hydro project in Quebec.

The worst cases of mercury poisoning occurred not in Canada but in the town of Minamata on the Japanese island of Kyushu. Mercury discharged into the sea by a local chemical industry was concentrated in fish which were eaten by local residents. About 400 people died and 2 000 suffered neurological disorders, giving to mercury poisoning the name Minamata Disease. The symptoms include lack of coordination, the sensation of pins and needles, numbness of lips and mouth, constricted visual field, night blindness, tremor, deafness and diminished taste and smell.

Lead has been called a "pollution time bomb" because it is a heavy metal which attacks the nervous system, and because so much of it has escaped into the environment. Lead has been a gasoline additive for at least 50 years and so large amounts of the metal have spewed from the tailpipes of millions of motor vehicles, to land on the ground and later be washed into the rivers and lakes. Even lead-producing plants have been sources of pollution. The metal presents a hazard for aquatic life and for people who eat fish that are heavily contaminated with it. Since lead is very stable, the only way to get rid of it is to wait for nature to bury it with muds. Governments are also starting to restrict the amount of lead used in gasoline and to encourage the use of unleaded vehicles.

EUTROPHICATION

There is another type of pollution which is less toxic to humans but which still kills aquatic life and is even said to be killing lakes. The term eutrophication simply means the over-fertilization of waters, which causes an explosive growth of plant life.

The villains in the piece are phosphorus and nitrogen, two well-known fertilizers used by farmers and gardeners around the world. They are fine on land, where they help the growth of plants we need for eating and for feeding our livestock. But let loose in vast quantities in the water these fertilizers upset the ecological applecart. Even in small amounts they dramatically speed the growth of aquatic plant life, including algae, which spread across the surface in green, slimy mats. As this plant life dies it decays and this process uses up dissolved oxygen in water, literally suffocating fish. Even the clouding of water with excessive plant life can make it virtually impossible for some species of fish to see and thus to feed. In the 1960s and 1970s scientists alerted the public to the fact that eutrophication was turning the lakes into algal bowls of soupy, green water in a process which could only be stopped by pollution controls. The public was already incensed by foul-tasting drinking water, green slime on their boats, dead aquatic weeds rotting on the beaches and the decline of some fish species. People were saying that Lake Erie was dying. In fact parts of Lake Erie became dead zones where oxygen had virtually disappeared and fish could not live. Canada and the United States mounted one of the largest scientific investigations on water quality to date and came up with a landmark 1972 agreement to sharply reduce pollution and save the lakes.

The studies found that phosphorus was coming from human wastes, from fertilizers washing off farms, from animal wastes joining the flow and from phosphate detergents. These powerful detergents were introduced on a major scale in 1947 and like pesticides, their use blossomed. By 1969 the use of sodium triphosphate was over 1 million tonnes a year in the United States alone. There were literally soap-covered rivers across the continent as a result of non-biodegradable detergents. Eutrophication has even been a problem in the remote Arctic, where communities dumped untreated sewage in local rivers.

In an effort to stem the soapy tide Canada and the United States started reducing phosphates in detergents and building billions of dollars' worth of sewage treatment plants to catch both human wastes and some of the remaining soapsuds going down household drains. There have been dramatic improvements in Lake Erie and Lake Ontario but they are still receiving too much pollution to be called normal. An estimated 30 per cent of the phosphorus going into Lake Erie and 43 per cent of that going into Lake Ontario is from diffuse sources and water experts say only controls on farm runoff will reduce the pollution.

In the meantime eutrophication still threatens such inland waters as Lake Simcoe, where phosphorus pollution must be greatly reduced or fish species, such as lake trout and whitefish, will be eliminated. Rivers like the Trent, Rideau and Severn and harbors like Collingwood, Wheatley, Hamilton, the Bay of Quinte, Penetang Bay and Sturgeon Bay are also at risk from this process. The over-fertilization is also changing a large number of lakes and rivers in western Canada, where small water bodies have little capacity to dilute the sewage, fertilizer runoff and animal wastes. Already affected are such lake and river systems as the Okanagan in British Columbia and the Qu'Appelle in Saskatchewan. Regina and Moose Jaw draw their water from a shallow lake called Buffalo Pound, which is clogged with algae each summer. Decaying algae gave the drinking water such a bad taste and odor that it was dubbed the worst in the nation, before a special filtration system was installed in 1985.

CHAPTER FOUR

The Great Lakes: The World's Biggest Sewer

THEY ARE SO BIG that astronauts can see them from the moon. More ships pass through them than through the Panama Canal. They are the source of drinking water for 24 million people. They are home to uncounted millions of fish, birds, mammals, amphibians and reptiles. They are the five Great Lakes. And they are in serious trouble.

The early Jesuit missionaries called these lakes the Sweetwater Seas, for one could dip a cup into their waters and drink deeply while travelling their length by birchbark canoe. They are the largest reservoirs of drinkable water on the planet, holding 20 per cent of the fresh surface water on Earth and 80 per cent of that in North America.

In two centuries of settlement they have also become the world's biggest sewer. Canadians and Americans have thrown every pollutant in the book at them. Quick and dirty garbage disposal methods have laced their waters with phosphorus, pesticides, arsenic, mercury, PCBs and dioxin, to name just a few of the worst ones. About 60 000 chemicals and metals are used around the lakes and so far 1 081 have been detected in the lakes' ecosystem, including its water, muds, fish and waterfowl—and the humans around it. A few years ago senior members of the International Joint Commission, a Canada-U.S. watchdog agency in charge of boundary waters, said that if the pollution continued unabated, parts of the lakes would have to be written off as a source of drinking water or fish. Already their predictions are starting to come true. A lot of fish are too contaminated for commercial sale. Many residents of Niagara-on-the-Lake refuse to drink the outflow of the Niagara River and their counterparts along the St. Clair River feel the same way. Tens of thousands of other people have started drinking bottled water and there are even suggestions that water from relatively clean Georgian Bay should be piped to Toronto to replace that from Lake Ontario.

Visualize the lakes as a series of bowls, one above the other, connected by narrow channels: the Straits of Mackinac, the St. Marys, St. Clair, Detroit and Niagara rivers. The water plunges 183 metres from Lake Superior to the Atlantic in a trip that covers 3 800 kilometres and can take as long as 200 years just to clear Lake Superior, and another 50–75 years to get to the St. Lawrence River. Lake Superior is up to 400 metres deep—big enough and, during storms, mean enough to sink ships as large as the ore carrier *Edmund Fitzgerald.* By comparison Lake Erie is only 64 metres deep in one area and much shallower elsewhere, a condition which means that waves can be whipped up quickly. In total the lakes hold 246 trillion litres of water. The Great Lakes-St. Lawrence waterway penetrates nearly halfway into the continent, its waters cover 246 000 square kilometres of the earth and its tributary rivers drain a watershed of 1.75 million square kilometres of the continent's heartland. Like inland seas, the lakes moderate the climate over a vast region by soaking up the sun's heat and retaining it into the cold months to reduce the icy extremes found in Prairie winters. In the summer their cool waters are the source of refreshing breezes.

The first settlers around the Great Lakes arrived at least 9 000 years ago, not far behind the retreating glaciers. Archeological digs in Killarney Provincial Park on the north shore of Lake Huron show signs that the Plano people quarried fine-grained quartzite for tools. A major campsite, which then would have been on the shoreline, is now 100 metres above the lake, showing both how the lake levels have dropped as glacial meltwaters drained to the seas, and how the land is slowly rebounding from the crushing weight of the glaciers. In 1610 the French explorer Etienne Brûlé and a group of Huron Indians paddled into Georgian Bay, likely making Brûlé the first white man to see the Great Lakes. He was followed by explorers who found the semi-nomadic Iroquois and Algonquian tribes making clay pottery and copper tools, cultivating small plots of corn and catching the abundant fish in the lakes.

For some Europeans the lakes were a magnet to settlement and for others they were a pathway to the interior plains. They have been an exploration route, a source of food and drinking water, a major transportation corridor and a source of industrial water and cheap hydro-electricity for the fast-growing populations on both sides of the border. They provide recreation for millions of people whether they live in crowded cities or in the country. Since 1800 the number of people living around the five lakes has swollen from 300 000 to 37 million and, keeping pace with the world population, is expected to double in the next 40 years. By now one out of every three Canadians and one out of every seven U.S. citizens lives around and depends on the lakes. Actually, half of Canada lives in the Great Lakes basin, when one includes the tributary rivers and the St. Lawrence River.

When the first white settlers arrived along the shores of Lake Ontario over the next century, they were amazed by the bountiful Atlantic salmon which crowded into the mouths of rivers during spawning runs. By 1898 the salmon were extirpated from the lake, destroyed not so much by overfishing as by settlement. As loggers and farmers cleared the huge forests which once blanketed southern Ontario they exposed the raw soil to rains, and it was carried into the streams where it destroyed the salmon's spawning beds. Then the dams of sawmills and grist mills finished the job by blocking the fish migration routes up the streams and rivers. Fishing for other species remained one of the major early industries but greedy overfishing, destruction of spawning beds and predation by lamprey had severely reduced the catch by the 1940s. Pollution has further reduced the fishery by making some of the fish unfit for commercial sale. As a result recreational fishing is now more important than commercial fisheries because sport fishermen can do what they want with the fish while commercial sale is governed by pollution limits.

The lakes have become a great shipping corridor and for generations the long, low lake boats have carried iron ore for the giant steel mills and the related industries, like the automobile assembly plants, that have made the Great Lakes an industrial heartland for both countries. The boats also carry coal for giant thermal-electric power plants, and wheat, nickel, copper, bauxite, magnesium and dozens of other commodities. With the opening of the St. Lawrence Seaway in 1959, ocean-going freighters joined the cavalcade. By now the Sault Ste. Marie locks handle more tonnage per year than the Suez and Panama canals combined. Canada's Chemical Valley is located in Sarnia along the St. Clair River and one-quarter of U.S. chemical companies are in the Great Lakes region, with much of that along the Niagara River.

One-fifth of all U.S. industry is located in, and half of Canada's manufactured goods come from, the Great Lakes basin. About 200 towns and cities line the shores and many more are on tributary rivers. Canada's largest city, Toronto, sits on the north shore of Lake Ontario, and Montreal, the second-largest, is just downstream on the St. Lawrence River. Such other large cities as Quebec, Hamilton, Mississauga, Burlington, Windsor, Sarnia, Sault Ste. Marie and Thunder Bay are on the waterway. On the U.S. side lie such cities as Buffalo, Rochester, Detroit, Toledo, Chicago, Milwaukee and Cleveland.

Since the beginning of settlement we have behaved like slum landlords and used the lakes as a giant garbage can. We counted on dilution ratios to save us from poisoning ourselves with our own wastes. Now that garbage can is overflowing. We did not count on the supertoxicity of some compounds, their persistence in the environment and the fact that many chemicals accumulate up the food chain. We have been paying the price with problems in a number of areas around the lakes for three generations, but each time a bill comes in we ignore the true meaning of the warning and try to get by with a token remedy. By the last century the human population was big enough to start to poison the drinking water around cities with raw sewage, and disease rates for such fatal illnesses as cholera and typhoid fever were high. The pollution was serious enough that by 1909 Canada and the United States signed the Boundary Waters Treaty, a historic document presaging today's concern about pollution that respects no boundaries. The treaty said that "boundary waters and water flowing across the boundary shall not be polluted on either side to the injury of health or property on the other side." But one study after another by the International Joint Commission (I.J.C.), which was created to monitor the waters, has found continuing and often worsening pollution. In 1912 the I.J.C. investigated waterborne diseases and found widespread problems, particularly in rivers like the Niagara. By the 1950s it was obvious that not only the rivers but the lakes, particularly Lake Erie and Lake Ontario, were in serious trouble as raw sewage poured into their waters, threatening drinking water and forcing the closure of many public beaches.

Pesticides such as DDT were first found in Lake Erie in 1959, and in Lake Ontario and the St. Lawrence River four years later. But the issue of toxic chemicals was pushed aside by that of eutrophication when it appeared that the lower lakes, Lake Erie in particular, were choking to death on excessive plant growth caused by phosphorus pollution. In 1965 the I.J.C. recommended action to reduce phosphorus, by improving sewage treatment particularly. In 1972 Canada and the United States signed a historic Great Lakes Water Quality Agreement which concentrated on stopping phosphorus pollution. Since then the two nations have spent more than $8 billion on sewage treatment and in most areas have ordered reductions in the use of phosphorus in laundry detergents.

Meanwhile toxic chemicals were starting to rear their ugly heads as chemical production hit runaway speed in the economic boom of the 1960s. As industry produced the hundreds of millions of tonnes of metals and synthetics that gave a physical shape to those boom days, it also generated vast amounts of waste. Much of the waste created around the Great Lakes simply went into the water and was toxic enough to start killing things. Since 1966 there have been reproductive failures in fish-eating birds. The herring gulls, double-crested cormorants and common terns were among the most contaminated birds in the world and their population levels crashed. Studies of Lake Ontario herring gulls in 1975 found almost total reproductive failure, with many nests having no eggs and other having eggs which did not hatch. Adult gulls showed hormonal imbalances and had lost interest in defending their nests or incubating their eggs. The link with toxic chemicals did not become clear until years later, when sophisticated equipment was invented that could detect contaminants in wildlife.

Mercury was the tip of the toxic iceberg. It broke surface in 1970, provoking a total ban on commercial fishing in Lake St. Clair due to dangerous mercury levels. This was just the first of a shopping list of chemicals to be found at dangerous levels in Great Lakes fish. Warnings of PCBs in Lake Michigan trout came the next year, following studies showing that mink raised on such fish suffered reproductive problems. Dangerous levels of PCBs were found in trout from parts of Lakes Superior, Huron and Ontario. By now at least one species of fish from parts or all of each lake is unfit for human consumption. There are fish consumption warnings on the Great Lakes for: dioxin, DDT, PCB, Chlordane, Dieldrin, Aldrin, Endrin, Heptachlor, Lindane, Mirex, Kepone, mercury and Toxaphene.

In 1977 the environmental nightmare of the Love Canal toxic waste dump was "discovered." At first the problem seemed to be tragic, but limited to a neighborhood in Niagara Falls, New York. Then evidence started rolling in that Love Canal and a host of other chemical dumps in and around that city were leaking into the Niagara River and Lake

Ontario, affecting the drinking water of more than 7 million people downstream. In 1978 the news about the lakes worsened when the I.J.C.'s advisory Water Quality Board presented a list of 500 toxic or suspect substances in the air, water, land and living creatures of the Great Lakes basin. The next year dioxin was found in Great Lakes herring gulls, although the issue did not really take off until 1980, when a Canadian report said that it was seeping into Lake Ontario from Niagara Falls, New York. Since then what had been a nascent fear about the safety of drinking water has blossomed into near panic, first around Lake Ontario but later in other areas, such as the St. Clair and Detroit rivers. The concerns grew with every report of deformed birds, cancerous fish and toxic chemical discharges, many of which had been going on for years but were suddenly put under the scrutiny of an aroused public. Concern about the drinking water, particularly from Lake Ontario, has reached the point where many people are buying bottled drinking water and calling for advanced drinking-water treatment to remove chemicals. There have long been problems with bacterial pollution of swimming beaches because of raw sewage discharges and one recent study warned that people who waded or swam in the water at a number of southern Ontario beaches risked illness.

Now we are faced with the grim fact that the Great Lakes have turned into a giant waste dump. A joint report in late 1985 by the Royal Society of Canada and the U.S. National Research Council said that people living around the lakes are probably exposed to more toxic chemicals through their food and drinking water than any other population in North America. In the study a group of prominent scientists from the two countries voiced what a number of people were secretly afraid of—that the Great Lakes basin has become one of the most toxic regions of the continent. They said that the chemicals were not only in the drinking water and fish but were pervading the food chain. Chemicals are released from industrial chimneys and incinerator smokestacks, and evaporate off the surface of the lakes, to fall as toxic rain and be taken up by plants and animals. The research panel said that adults are at risk but it expressed particular concern about high levels of PCBs in women's breast milk. Henry Regier, the Canadian co-chairman of the study, said that "harmful effects on babies could be expected, based on previous studies that showed malformations of young and reproductive failures in fish, birds and mammals due to contaminants." The report drove home the point, better than any so far, that the Great Lakes are an ecosystem of plant and animal life and we humans are part of the system and share in its good and its bad sides.

In the future we face the problem not only of quality, but of diminishing quantity of the lakes themselves. The lakes have a natural fluctuation in level of more than 1.5 metres, depending on the rain and snowfall of previous years. But the long-term average level is starting to drop slightly as massive amounts of water are removed by cities, industries and agriculture and not returned. The I.J.C. has predicted that over the next few decades the lower lakes could drop by as much as 30 centimetres if consumption keeps growing at a high rate. This would result in shallower harbors, less power from hydro-electric turbines, less water to dilute toxic chemicals and a disruption of wildlife habitats. A 1975 study said that the two countries take 140 cubic metres of water per second from the lakes and do not return it. The United States takes seven times as much of that water as Canada and the I.J.C. recently recommended setting up a special binational team to prevent disputes over the sharing of these withdrawals, which could go as high as 880 cubic metres per second by 2035. The problem will likely be compounded by a global climate warming, which will result from certain types of air pollution. This climate change is predicted to further reduce the amount of water flowing through the lakes.

How have governments, which are supposed to protect us, reacted to the pollution problems? With the exception of the phosphorus problem, political responses have shown a general lack of comprehension of how ecosystems like the Great Lakes work. For example, 80 years ago the response to human sewage in the water was chlorination of drinking water to kill bacteria. Cleaning up the sewage to prevent the problems did not begin for several more decades and is still ongoing. Even the 1972 water quality agreement has achieved considerable success against only one substance, phosphorus. Real control of toxic contaminants has remained more of an idea than an achievement. Flushed with the success of the first agreement, the two nations signed a second in 1978, pledging to continue the phosphorus wars and rein in the hazardous chemicals. They agreed to a goal of zero discharge of persistent toxic substances but so far have only started to stuff the chemical genies back into their bottles. The governments have swiped at problems by passing laws to ban specific chemicals or by passing regulations to control pollution by industry, but have failed to pass laws which would really stop toxic chemicals.

This is not to say that nothing, except for phosphorus, has improved on the pollution front. For a number of reasons, including a plethora of national, provincial, state and local regulations and policy changes by industry, there has been a substantial decrease in some forms of pollution—particularly the obvious ones. There are fewer incidents such as the one in the 1960s, when more than 20 000 ducks were killed on a single day one winter after they landed on an oil-covered section of the Rouge River at Detroit. And the Cuyahoga River in Cleveland is no longer so larded with chemicals that the surface literally catches fire.

But the regulations are still spotty rather than comprehensive, and some industries simply have been allowed to continue to pollute. Recent reports list an estimated 400 000 tonnes a year of hazardous waste flowing into the Great Lakes from our sewers. The I.J.C. reported in 1985 that 18 per cent of the major industrial plants discharging into the Great Lakes were above permissible levels, according to 1983 data. There were 205 violations reported—and that was only where measurements were being taken. In addition there are no control levels for many toxic substances.

Canada has 302 municipalities, including 100 major ones, discharging pollution into the Great Lakes or its tributary rivers, and in 1983 there were 14 not meeting Environment Ontario requirements. There are also 11 000 industries discharging into the basin and of 99 significant industries, 43 were not in compliance. The United States has been trying to control chemical pollution caused by industries discharging toxic wastes into municipal sewage treatment plants that were not designed to cope with the materials. By January 1, 1985, there were 210 U.S. sewage treatment plants around the lakes that were supposed to have pre-treatment programs with local dischargers, but only 32 had approved programs.

Land runoff is a major problem because intensive farming and urbanization is denuding the land and speeding erosion. A major I.J.C. study reported that up to 11 million tonnes of sediments from agricultural, urban and forest lands reach the lakes each year. In addition to silting up harbors and clouding the drinking and swimming water, the dirt carries phosphorus, pesticides, heavy metals, asbestos, PCBs and other chlorinated organics into ditches, streams, rivers and finally the lakes. About half the 13 000 tonnes of phosphorus still going into Lake Erie each year is from farm runoff.

The lakes have been described as giant mixing bowls, spreading the pollution far and wide. But the worst area is closest to shore, where we swim, sail, fish and draw our drinking water. Researchers T.J. Simons and David Lean of the Canada Centre for Inland Waters in Burlington found that currents periodically send a "river" of pollution 5–10 kilometres wide sweeping along the shoreline. They studied Lake Ontario in particular but said the principle applies to any large body of water, from a lake to an ocean. What happens is that the effects of wind, of sun heating the water and the Earth's rotation set up currents along the shoreline. This means that pollution from one city is swept along the shoreline towards its neighbors. For example in the industrialized section called the Golden Horseshoe area, reaching from Hamilton to Oshawa, there are 31 municipal sewage treatment discharges and 49 industrial outfalls. Toronto alone has four sewage treatment plants and 41 other untreated storm sewer outlets. In addition the city's three main rivers are major sewers themselves, polluted with 14 chemicals, including PCBs, at up to 1 400 times the provincial objective for water quality. Along the same heavily settled stretch of Lake Ontario shoreline, there are 38 municipal drinking water intake pipes and 25 intakes for industries, including food processors.

Canada and the United States spend about $5 million a year each, just monitoring the state of the Great Lakes. They have spent about $11 billion in total on water quality improvements. What have we got for our money?

Lake Superior is the largest, deepest and cleanest of the lakes but even its distance from the big cities has not spared it from pollution. Here and there along its shores local industries, often pulp and paper mills, have created chemical hot spots, rendering fish unsafe for eating. Three Canadian pulp mills are listed as major polluters of organic chemicals and heavy metals, affecting the quality of fish. They are at Peninsula Harbor at Marathon, Jackfish Bay near Terrace Bay and Nipigon Bay near Red Rock. The Kaministiquia River delta and the surrounding waters at Thunder Bay are still polluted with mercury, toxic organic chemicals and sewage. In the northwest corner of the lake at Silver Bay, Minnesota, the Reserve Mining Company dumped 52 000 tonnes a day of taconite mining residues into the lake until 1980. The taconite, similar to asbestos fibres, has been found in the drinking water of several communities, including Duluth. At

Torch Lake, Michigan, on the south shore of Lake Superior, pollution which likely came from the now-closed copper mines is causing tumors in fish. More worrisome than these local hot spots is the airborne fallout of chemicals like PCBs and Toxaphene, which have pushed some fish in this big lake towards the danger limit for human consumption.

Lake Huron is second to Lake Superior in surface area and cleanliness but it is even more spotted with problems. Contamination levels in the fish are generally higher because of some seriously polluted areas such as Saginaw Bay, Michigan, which drains an area heavy in both chemical industry and farming. Other problem areas include polluted harbors like Collingwoood, which has lead and toxic organic chemicals in its mud, and the Midland Bay area, where phosphorus pollution is still causing eutrophication. Like its big brother to the north, Huron suffers from airborne fallout.

Lake Michigan, too, has heavy fallout but it has even more serious contamination from industry along its shoreline. It was Lake Michigan which tipped off scientists to PCB contamination nearly two decades ago, and trout and salmon from that lake have the second-highest levels of PCBs and DDT after Lake Ontario. They both exceed safe limits for commercial sale. In Green Bay the chemical pollution has been so bad that both fish and fish-eating birds suffered reproductive problems.

Lake Erie was aging so quickly in the 1960s and 1970s that some people wrote it off as a dead lake. Now Erie, like Mark Twain, might reply, "The reports of my death are greatly exaggerated." The lake is not normal but it is much healthier now than it was in the previous two decades, when massive algal blooms choked off oxygen to 65 per cent of the lake bottom. Phosphorus pollution was turning Erie soupy with plant life, so soupy that one researcher recalls that even a big ship could not create a normal, frothing wake as it ploughed through the murky waters. Many beaches were closed because of untreated sewage, dead fish and rotting algae washed in from the lake. A major clean-up effort by the two countries has resulted in improved fisheries and cleaner beaches. The annual amount of phosphorus entering Lake Erie has decreased by about 70 per cent since the 1972 agreement was signed.

Lake Ontario is last in line and catches any of the pollution that does not settle out or evaporate into the sky on the way downstream. This lake too has benefited from the phosphorus controls but the levels are still above the goals to protect its waters from deterioration. It suffers particularly from terrible chemical pollution, partly the result of industrialization around its shores but mainly from the huge U.S. chemical industry along the Niagara River. Among the worst chemicals in the lake is TCDD dioxin. There are an estimated 500 grams of dioxin in Lake Ontario (about the size of a pound of butter if it could be all collected into one deadly lump). That alone has been enough to make most of the large salmon and trout risky if not outright hazardous to eat, especially for pregnant and nursing mothers. As little as 10 times this amount of dioxin could make the lake completely unsafe for drinking. There is an estimated one tonne of dioxin in the chemical wastes lying in just one of the big chemical dumps along the shore of the Niagara River. After a decline in the levels of some key pollutants during the late 1970s, contamination in Lake Ontario has taken a disturbing turn for the worse. A 1985 report by Environment Canada found toxic chemicals in fish at levels up to 60 times those called for in the 1978 Canada-U.S. water quality agreement. In 1981 the amount of PCBs in lake trout was 35 times higher than the maximum acceptable level under that pact, but by 1983 the levels were 60 times above the limit.

After Lake Ontario the water—7 200 cubic metres of it every second—flows down the St. Lawrence River, bearing with it any toxic chemicals which have not been soaked up by the fish of Lake Ontario or sucked up by the drinking water intakes. From Lake Ontario downstream, the water offers its chemical wastes to 3 million Quebeckers and receives a massive load of waste from that province in return. The St. Lawrence has become a 1 200-kilometre-long cesspool tainted with poisons like lead, mercury, PCBs, DDT, Mirex and a host of other chemicals. The river's problems started two centuries ago and got worse year after year until now there are 60 major factories adding their pollution to the river. Largely using government documents, the environment group Société pour vaincre la Pollution calculated that 300 tonnes of pollution from Quebec industry goes into the river every day. Some Quebeckers are dubbing the St. Lawrence River the "Sixth Great Lake" and want it made part of the Great Lakes pollution-control plans.

The I.J.C. publishes a list of toxic hot spots around the Great Lakes, which it discreetly calls "areas of concern." Recently there were 39 of them in Canada and the United States but in 1985 the list grew to 42. In many of those areas the flow pollution has been reduced. But virtually all are living with the legacy of past pollution, in the form of contaminated sediments that will remain a threat for a very long time. In 38 of the areas the levels of organic chemicals or heavy metals exceed guidelines or objectives for the protection of human health, aquatic life or safe dredging of the bottom muds and their disposal in open waters.

The I.J.C. said that the effects on human health of the pollution in the Great Lakes have not yet been documented but that tumors are being found in some fish from all the lakes, with the heaviest concentration in the lower lakes. In 1985 the I.J.C. reported that there was significant but incomplete progress on phosphorus control, but little if any improvement in toxic contaminant clean-ups of highly polluted areas. In only a few areas were clean-up plans adequate or timely, and "in most cases there is little or no expectation of resolution." Fish consumption advisories, a sign of serious pollution, exist in 31 areas including, in Canada: Jackfish Bay, Nipigon Bay, Thunder Bay, Collingwood Harbor in Georgian Bay, Wheatley Harbor in Lake Erie, the Toronto waterfront, Hamilton Harbor, the St. Marys River, which connects Lake Superior and Lake Huron, the Detroit River and the Niagara River.

Industrial harbors are among the worst areas and Hamilton Harbor is one of the most polluted of those around the Great Lakes. The harbor is home to two of Canada's big steel companies and the mud is so rich in iron that it could probably be mined, some environment officials quip. But there is much more serious pollution there from chemicals such as PCBs, PAHs, phenols, cyanide, lead and mercury. The harbor also gets pollution from four sewage discharges and from a range of industries. Politicians have promised for years that they would swim in the harbor, but those who do always keep their heads above water and the practice is not recommended. Fish in parts of the harbor have been wiped out by pollution that has virtually eliminated oxygen in the water, and those fish living nearby have a high rate of tumors. According to the I.J.C. the poisoning is so bad that there does not appear to be any safe way to clean it up. Tonnes of chemicals and metals lie buried in its muds, seeping poisons into the surrounding water. But if anyone tried to dredge them out the immediate result would likely be the sudden release of large amounts of toxins as mud was pulled through the water. Unless a safe dredging technique is found we may have to leave the pollution where it is and hope that the natural laying down of sediments will bury the problem over time.

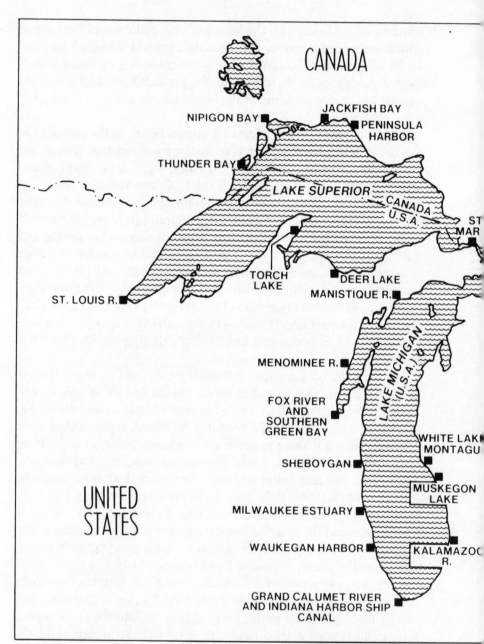

CANADA

JACKFISH BAY

NIPIGON BAY

PENINSULA
HARBOR

THUNDER BAY

LAKE SUPERIOR

CANADA
U.S.A.

ST
MAR

TORCH
LAKE

DEER LAKE

MANISTIQUE R.

ST. LOUIS R.

LAKE MICHIGAN
U.S.A.

MENOMINEE R.

FOX RIVER
AND
SOUTHERN
GREEN BAY

WHITE LAK
MONTAGU

SHEBOYGAN

MUSKEGON
LAKE

UNITED
STATES

MILWAUKEE ESTUARY

WAUKEGAN HARBOR

KALAMAZOO
R.

GRAND CALUMET RIVER
AND INDIANA HARBOR SHIP
CANAL

The Canada-U.S. International Joint Commission on boundary waters lists forty-two areas of continuing pollution, which ring the shores of the Great Lakes like running sores. Many of these areas have been listed as polluted for years, a sad testament to the inability of governments on both sides of the border to carry out their promises to eliminate pollution

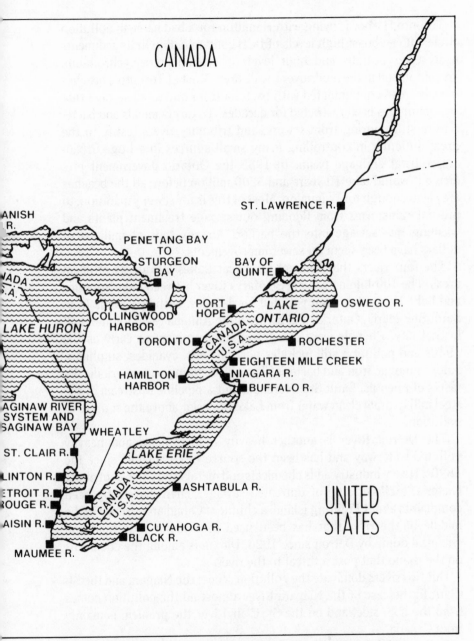

CANADA

ST. LAWRENCE R.

ANISH
R.

PENETANG BAY
TO
STURGEON
BAY

BAY OF
QUINTE

NADA
A.

PORT
HOPE

LAKE
ONTARIO

OSWEGO R.

COLLINGWOOD
HARBOR

LAKE HURON

TORONTO

CANADA
U.S.A.

ROCHESTER

EIGHTEEN MILE CREEK

HAMILTON
HARBOR

NIAGARA R.

BUFFALO R.

AGINAW RIVER
SYSTEM AND
SAGINAW BAY

WHEATLEY

ST. CLAIR R.

LAKE ERIE

LINTON R.

DETROIT R.

ROUGE R.

CANADA
U.S.A.

ASHTABULA R.

AISIN R.

CUYAHOGA R.

BLACK R.

MAUMEE R.

UNITED
STATES

from the world's greatest source of fresh water. Despite that failure there have been
some notable successes in controlling phosphorus pollution and in reducing pollution from
a number of cities and industries.   (BERNARD BENNELL)

Toronto Harbor is vying with Hamilton for a bad name in pollution circles. It can boast high levels of PCB contamination in its sediments near sewer outfalls and high levels of lead, mercury, chromium, arsenic and oil in the muds over a wide area. Most of Toronto's beaches have been so contaminated with bacteria from untreated sewage that swimming has been restricted for decades. Toxic chemicals and bacteria are still pouring from sewers, and tributary rivers testify to the great difficulty in controlling many small sources in a huge urban-agricultural drainage basin. In 1985 the Ontario government predicted it would take 10 years and $200 million before all the beaches are clean enough for swimming. Most of this is for sewer separation, to prevent rainstorms from flooding out sewage treatment plants and washing raw sewage into the harbor. Already tens of millions of dollars have been spent on sewer improvements.

The four rivers that connect the Great Lakes all rate as problem areas. The 100-kilometre-long St. Marys River between Lake Superior and Lake Huron has been polluted for decades, both by sewage from Sault Ste. Marie, Ontario, and by the huge Algoma Steel Limited mill in that city. Phenols were recognized as a problem as early as the 1940s and pollution still includes phenols, oils, cyanides, sulphides, zinc, ammonia, iron and bacteria. The city drinking water periodically tastes of phenols. Sault Ste. Marie has put a pipeline upstream of the steel mill to draw clean water from Lake Superior above the sources of pollution.

The Detroit River is another heavily industrialized and heavily polluted waterway and has been the source of complaints since the 1890s. Heavy industry adds chemicals and metals and cities contribute bacteria, a classic sign of untreated sewage. There have long been complaints about Fighting Island, a chunk of Canadian territory in the middle of the river that has been used as a major municipal and chemical dump by Detroit since 1926. Dioxin is among the chemicals on the island that pose a threat to the river.

But two rivers dominate the pollution scene: the Niagara and the St. Clair. In the case of the Niagara River almost all the pollution comes from the U.S. side, and on the St. Clair River the problem is mainly from Canada.

Pollution of the Niagara River, from old chemicals in Love Canal and its fellow dumps, plus the continuing new discharges from industry, have created a health problem and a diplomatic sore point between Canada and the United States. The old chemical dumps are buried beside the Niagara River, holding millions of tonnes of toxic chemicals, including the most dangerous ever made. They lie there like giant poison glands, squirting their toxins into the river. The four biggest, Love Canal, Hyde Park, S-Area and 102nd Street, contain 245 000 tonnes of chemical wastes, enough to fill 10 000 tanker trucks stretching bumper to bumper from Toronto to Niagara Falls. An unknown amount of those chemicals is seeping into the river, which provides 83 per cent of the water in Lake Ontario and so most of the drinking water for 4 million Ontarians, 3 million Quebeckers and about 1 million New York State residents. These four are just the flagships of 164 dumps within 5 kilometres of the U.S. side of the river, including 61 chemical dumps close to the water's edge, the graveyards for the wastes of nearly a century of chemical production. At least 28 dumps are known to be leaking into the river. More toxins come from 75 municipal and industrial sewer pipes and 50 storm sewers which pick up pollution from a number of sources. According to tests of the river water in 1985, at least nine tonnes a day, 3 285 tonnes a year, of toxic chemicals were measured flowing down the Niagara and into Lake Ontario.

How did the honeymoon capital of the world turn into one of its most hazardous regions? The answer lies in all that water, 5 700 cubic metres a second of it, rushing down from Lake Erie and hurling itself over Niagara Falls before finishing its 60-kilometre river journey to Lake Ontario. Lots of water and lots of electrical power generated by that rushing water started drawing major chemical and allied industries around the turn of the century, mainly on the U.S. side of the river. As industry churned out great quantities of chemicals, it produced huge amounts of wastes, including TCDD dioxin, the deadliest synthetic chemical known. Many of the chemicals in the dumps are unknown to any but a handful of engineers and when the wastes are mixed in the ground, even they do not know what chemical reactions will result. So while tourist operators in Niagara Falls, Ontario, were building public horror shows as part of the entertainment for the 20 million tourists who visit the area each year, the chemical industry was creating secret chambers of horrors across the river.

No one knows exactly how much waste was dumped in the ground and how much was poured straight into the Niagara River, but recent sediment cores drilled from the muds of Lake Ontario have turned up chemical pollution dating back to the first quarter of the century. Documents published a few years ago reveal that during the Second

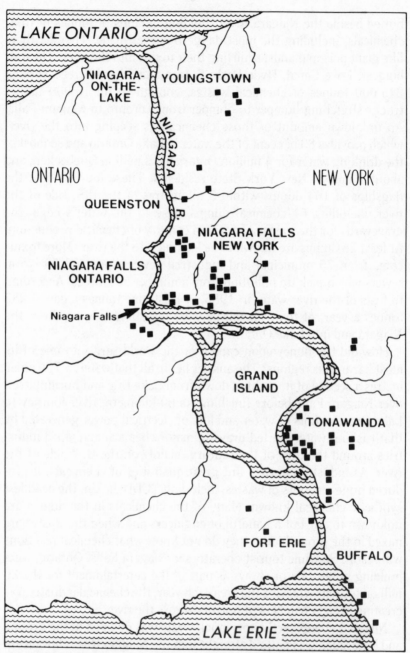

The number of hazardous waste dumpsites along the Niagara River graphically illustrates how serious is the problem facing us. Hundreds of thousands of tonnes of chemicals lie in landfills ranging from the world-famous Love Canal to unnamed and nearly forgotten pits.
(BERNARD BENNELL)

World War tens of millions of litres of military wastes, including cyanide, radioactive materials and the high explosive TNT, were dumped into sewers feeding into the Niagara River. The radioactive wastes came from the first stage of uranium processing for the U.S. government's Manhattan Project, which built the two atomic bombs dropped on Hiroshima and Nagasaki at the end of the war.

Though the full extent of its ailments is still being uncovered, the Niagara River was diagnosed as a sick river decades ago. The I.J.C. first reported on pollution in the Niagara in 1918, in one of its first studies. The problem then was bacteria, because almost no one treated their sewage. In 1950 the I.J.C. expressed serious concern over the amount of bacteria plus phenols, oil, iron, phosphorus, chloride and discoloration in the river. In 1976 researchers had identified 500 chemicals in the Niagara River and in its wildlife. Canadian wildlife experts say that during this period, pollution downstream became so bad that it caused a complete failure of herring gull reproduction on Lake Ontario. Some believe this was due to dioxin, a contaminant in the production of 2,4,5-T. The reasons for this burst of chemical activity are not yet clear but some scientists suspect that it was linked to heavy chemical production during the Vietnam War.

In November, 1984, Canada and the United States released the most comprehensive report yet on the state of the river, listing 261 chemicals of concern in the river water, its bottom muds and wildlife. The study by the Niagara River Toxics Committee said that many of the chemicals are known to harm human health, causing such problems as cancer and birth defects. The committee found 37 chemicals in the by-then-abandoned drinking water intake of Niagara-on-the-Lake at the mouth of the river, including 26 for which no safety guidelines exist. The report stated that 90 per cent of the pollution came from the U.S. side of the river. A more candid parallel report written by two Environment Canada specialists on the Niagara River said that even a partial inventory of U.S. dumps found 8 million tonnes of hazardous wastes near the river. If only one per cent of this leaked into the river it could threaten drinking water all the way to Quebec City. "The sobering reality is that, given the existence of these dumps, particularly those containing TCDD [dioxin], the potential for a contamination event that would irreversibly eliminate the ecosystem all the way down to the St. Lawrence and beyond cannot be dismissed." Even now, the report said, "the Niagara River and Lake Ontario are poisoned ecosystems in which all media, including people, contain varying amounts of biocides—chemicals produced specifically to kill biota [living things]."

In recent years much of the gross pollution, like substances that actually colored the river, has been stopped or reduced. But there are still such high levels of Niagara River chemicals in Lake Ontario fish that the big trout and salmon are contaminated. The river's pollution continues to violate the objectives set in the 1978 Canada-U.S. agreement to clean up the Great Lakes.

The Niagara River hot spot which leaps to mind as being the most polluted is Love Canal. Around the world it is synonymous with the legacy of chemical dumping that has come back to haunt us. It is a textbook example of how to turn a dangerous situation into a real catastrophe through bungling and ignorance. The dump, in the southern portion of Niagara Falls, New York, is a partially finished ship canal which was abandoned in 1894. Hooker Chemicals and Plastics Corporation (now the Occidental Chemical Corporation), one of the biggest chemical companies in the area, used the big hole in the ground as a dump for 19 000 tonnes of chemical wastes between 1942 and 1953. Then Hooker covered the pit with a layer of clay to prevent rainwater from seeping in, something that would have caused the chemicals to bubble out of the pit. In fact this type of dump, in dense clay soil, with a clay cap, is a waste disposal technique that was considered quite acceptable around the world until recently. Even now the site might be a much less serious problem if people had not tampered with the seals on this chemical tomb.

After closing the pit, Hooker sold the property to the Niagara Falls Board of Education in 1953 for a token one dollar, and warned that chemical wastes lay underground. Either the warnings (in an era before toxic wastes were well known) were not strong enough or the board of education was too eager to develop the land. First off it plunked down a school, partly on top of the poison pit, and in the process removed a portion of the protective clay cap. By 1960 the city had laid two sewer lines right through the canal, providing direct pathways for chemicals to escape the clay vault. In 1968 the state transportation department joined the demolition derby when it carved an expressway route through the southern end of Love Canal, exposing raw chemical wastes which Hooker trucked away. To compound the existing mistakes, hundreds of homes were built around the canal. The excavation of their basements and the installation of sewer and water lines and swimming pools into soil beside the canal set the stage for a real tragedy. The Pandora's box was unlocked after several years of heavy rain, seeping in through the many new openings, caused the canal to overflow its underground banks in 1976, unleashing chemical demons on the quiet, suburban neighborhood. Rainwater poured into the now-perforated bathtub of a disposal pit, floating chemicals up and onto the surface and carrying them into basements. There were 82 industrial chemicals identified immediately, including 11 suspected of causing cancer. One health department statement later said that people breathing the air in some parts of the neighborhood had a one-in-ten risk of contracting cancer each year.

At first people suffered the effects of the chemicals without fully realizing what was causing the problem or how serious it was. Children and animals were chemically burned while playing in puddles that had bubbled to the surface of the ground beside the school. Some visitors had the soles of their shoes corroded, and trees were partly dissolved. Smelly, black sludge began oozing uncontrollably through basement walls, choking and nauseating residents. Swimming pools popped out of backyards by the hydraulic pressure. Reports of excessive rates of disease began to circulate.

The lid came off in 1978, with a series of stories pointing to a health emergency around Love Canal. By that spring, state and federal health and environment agencies moved in, fencing off the canal itself and testing air and water samples. In August New York State declared a state of emergency, closed the school and evacuated pregnant women and infants. President Jimmy Carter termed it a federal disaster area, the first time a disaster created by human hands has won this title. The governments evacuated 255 families from what was called the "inner ring" of homes nearest the canal. Researchers found birth defects, high miscarriage rates, infections and rashes, nervous disorders, headaches, kidney and bladder problems. By early 1979 dioxin was found among the chemicals and there were evacuations over a wider area until about 850 families were finally moved away. Later the inner ring of homes was bulldozed into the ground. Since then an underground cement wall has been built around the canal in an effort to stop contamination from leaking into local waterways and the Niagara River, and a new clay cap was laid over the site. Grass was planted and driving by Love Canal during the summer you could mistake it for a city park—until you notice that most of the surrounding houses are boarded up.

After it filled up Love Canal, Hooker turned its attention to another dump called Hyde Park. This landfill, on the north side of Niagara Falls, was used until 1975 for the disposal of an estimated 72 000 tonnes of chemical wastes, including such poisons as PCBs and Mirex, in drums or in liquid form. Among the chemicals is an estimated 1 tonne of dioxin, probably the largest deposit in the world. One U.S. expert estimated that if that dioxin was evenly dispersed into the environment, theoretically there would be enough to kill everyone in western New York and southern Ontario. The dump sits atop the limestone Niagara Escarpment, 700 metres from the edge of the Niagara Gorge. Past the dump streams Bloody Run Creek, a natural watercourse, which wends towards the nearby gorge face, then tumbles into the Niagara River. For years that creek carried some Hyde Park chemicals directly from the dump to the river, until the dump was capped and drainage was controlled. But a more difficult problem remains. The limestone beneath the dump is not solid rock but is heavily fractured, and contamination has been seeping through thousands of fissures for years. Chemical wastes can be seen and smelled running down the gorge face and the levels of seepage of several chemicals increased 1 000 times between 1982 and 1985.

Third on the list is the S-Area dump, sitting on the property of Occidental's big Niagara Falls chemical plant and right next door to the drinking-water treatment plant for the city of 50 000. The dump was used from 1947 to 1975 for the disposal of 57 000 tonnes of chemical waste. Now it is a large mound topped with a lagoon holding other wastes. Chemicals have seeped out of the dump, moved laterally through the ground and entered the concrete water intake pipe for the city. This was discovered in 1978, forcing Niagara Falls to switch to an emergency water intake and to dump powdered activated carbon into the drinking water in an effort to remove chemicals. Ross Hume Hall, an expert on toxic chemicals from McMaster University, states that the types of chemicals known or suspected to be in the S-Area dump have caused cancer, birth defects and mutations, have adversely affected liver function and have changed the action of enzyme systems. Unlike nearby Love Canal, the S-Area was built on some of the worst possible ground: rubble and fill which was dumped on what used to be river bottom to create new land. This type of land is permeable and allows chemical seepage. In what some have dubbed "the spy boat caper," Canadian scientists pulled up beside the riverbank with a boatload of highly sophisticated equipment and detected chemicals coming into the water apparently right through the riverbank.

The 102nd Street dump is the least known of the big four because it is the last to be drawn into the glare of publicity by either an evacuation or a court action. It contains 123 000 tonnes of chemicals from Occidental and from the Olin Corporation, which, like Occidental, is part of a giant U.S. business conglomerate. The 102nd Street dump sits virtually on the bank of the river, only a short distance from Love Canal.

Another problem which rankled Canada for years was the Niagara Falls, New York, municipal sewage treatment plant, which discharged its partially treated wastes just below the Falls. The concern was not so much the domestic sewage as the fact that a number of major chemical industries pour their wastes into city sewers, and untreated material was ejected into the river through the sewer pipe. In 1978 the city installed a sophisticated filtration system in the sewage treatment plant to sharply reduce the chemical flow. It used activated carbon, somewhat like charcoal, to adsorb many organic chemicals. However, the filters literally collapsed after a few months. Instead of quickly repairing the beds of carbon the city, state and federal governments, which had all been involved in the project, got into a protracted legal wrangle with each other and with the contractor about where to lay the blame. While everyone downstream fumed, the governments did not start reconstruction until 1983 and the filter system was not operating until the summer of 1985.

On top of all the existing problems there was the case of the SCA pipeline. In some ways it was the straw which broke the back of Canadian patience. SCA Chemical Services Incorporated of Porter, New York, a suburban community near the mouth of the river, asked New York, in 1979, for permission to build an eight-kilometre-long pipeline from its waste treatment plant to the Niagara River. It wanted to discharge more than 378 million litres of water laced with such wastes as cyanide, arsenic, mercury and lead. Not only was the pipe going to add its load to the already overburdened Niagara River, it was going to do so three kilometres upstream from the water intake of Niagara-on-the-Lake, Ontario. Canadians were outraged and terrified for the future of their drinking water, and a three-year battle raged in courts, legislatures and the news media on both sides of the border. Even the U.S. co-chairman of the I.J.C. questioned how more wastes could be allowed in the river when it was already so polluted. At one point the pipeline was sabotaged, by someone who perforated it to stop its use. An agreement on discharge of treated waste was finally reached among the environment groups, the governments and SCA but only after Niagara-on-the-Lake had already switched to another source of drinking water.

In the last few years Niagara River pollution has emerged as a major sore point between Canada and the United States, with Canadian politicians virtually accusing the United States of poisoning Lake Ontario and failing to clean up the mess. The U.S. and New York governments did sue Hooker, Olin, and even Niagara Falls, New York, over the big-four dumps for an initial $1 billion but many people in both countries are unhappy with the results.

The Canadian position has been that as long as the dumps remain where they are they will pose a permanent threat to the Niagara River. Canadian technical experts point out that the chemicals will decompose slowly, if at all, while buried in the ground and will likely remain toxic for centuries. Canadian scientists and politicians have called for the dumps to be excavated, and either relocated far away from the river in a more secure landfill or, preferably, burned in a very high temperature waste disposal machine such as a rotary kiln. Even the binational Niagara River Task Force suggested that the United States should consider digging up and destroying the chemical dumps. The U.S. reply has been that this is impractical because such big dumps never have been dug up before, the exposed chemicals would endanger people in the area and no government could find an area to accept a new disposal or destruction site.

Although they sued Hooker, the U.S. and New York governments never dragged the chemical giant into a trial. Instead the lawyers dickered for years, usually behind closed doors, but with occasional sorties into a U.S. district court in Buffalo to seek direction or approval from a federal judge. By 1981 Hooker and the governments were proposing an out-of-court settlement over Hyde Park that would leave the dump where it was. Environment groups in both countries cried foul and Pollution Probe, the Canadian Environmental Law Association and Operation Clean Niagara joined forces with the Ecumenical Task Force of Niagara Falls, New York, to challenge the proposed agreement. The case created unexpected alliances between Environment Canada and the environment groups which were in effect representing Canada in a U.S. court. Ottawa decided not to join the legal battle because the U.S. government said that it would not negotiate through diplomatic channels with a government which was suing it. But Environment Canada did spend thousands of dollars on technical reports on the dumps, which it then handed over to the groups for their court case.

Despite the protests, Judge John T. Curtin endorsed the agreement in July, 1982, which leaves the dump in the ground but requires Occidental to try to stop it from leaking. This was a rebuff of Canadian evidence that it is virtually impossible to prevent leakage from dumps that are sitting on porous rock. Scientists say that the chemicals will keep leaking for centuries—a type of toxic time bomb which will threaten one generation after another. They warn the dumps will have to be monitored and the pumps to control leakage kept running for generations, at a huge cost and a perpetual risk.

Canadian environmentalists and government officials reacted with

One of the world's great landmarks has been turned into a world pollution capital by chemical industries around Niagara Falls. (ONTARIO MINISTRY OF THE ENVIRONMENT)

shock and horror to the decision to leave the dump in the ground. Environment Minister John Roberts called the decision "insensitive to environmental concerns," and Toby Vigod of the Canadian Environmental Law Association said it "flies in the face of scientific evidence." The S-Area case was a repeat performance of Hyde Park. This settlement, too, calls for the chemicals to be left in the ground and for pumps to be installed in an attempt to stop underground water from carrying them away from the dump. The Canadian position is that some of the chemicals that are heavier than water will seep through cracks in the rock, possibly moving under the Niagara River towards Ontario.

Over the past few years Canada has sent several stiff diplomatic notes of complaint to Washington over the U.S. handling of the Niagara River's pollution. In 1980 Mr. Roberts got so incensed that he considered suing the U.S. polluters in their own courts, though he did not pursue the idea. At one point a frustrated Mr. Roberts said that if the United States ignored Canada's pleas to stop the pollution there was nothing he could do, "short of sending the Mounties in to raid Washington." During an I.J.C. meeting in 1983, Mr. Roberts' successor, Charles Caccia, also attacked U.S. tardiness in cleaning up the river, saying, "Canadians and Americans are worried about the safety of their water supplies and are losing patience over the slowness of the clean-up efforts." He said U.S. work to date had been "agonizingly slow." In 1984 Ontario Environment Minister Andrew Brandt added his voice to the chorus by complaining that in a list of more than 500 major toxic dumps the United States planned to clean up, the Niagara sites rated no higher than 136th—and that was for Love Canal. What this illustrates is that the worst chemical dumps for Canada are in the United States, but these dumps along the Niagara River are not the worst ones with which the United States has to contend.

There is a latent suspicion among some people that despite U.S. denials to the contrary, Canadians are not being counted as important victims of the Niagara dumps. This feeling was not allayed when during the Hyde Park negotiations, Thomas Truitt, a lawyer representing Hooker, said the company would not remove the chemicals, "to satisfy certain parochial Canadian interests." Mr. Truitt threatened to pull out of negotiations with the U.S. and New York governments if Occidental was forced to remove the chemicals. The final settlement is expected to cost Occidental up to $16 million.

No one says that cleaning up the dumps to Canada's satisfaction would be cheap. Estimates of the cost range from as low as $160 million to over $1 billion. However, the alternatives are also pricey. Mr. Caccia points out that if the dumps leak enough poisons into the river, people around Lake Ontario will have to install advanced drinking water treatment that will cost $68 million a year. James Kingham, the senior federal environment official on the Great Lakes issue, estimates that to monitor the dumps to prevent leakage it will cost $8 million a year.

Complaints against the U.S. and New York governments are not unique to Canada. Joan Gipp, a Lewiston, New York, town councillor, said in 1980 that "New York State's known for at least four years that Bloody Run Creek has been leaking dioxin and Mirex plus a number of other toxic chemicals into the Niagara River and it's done nothing" to clean up the mess. By now a lot of information has been published about the dangers of Niagara's pollution, but a few years ago speaking publicly about the risks of toxic chemicals was considered anathema in some official circles. Dr. Beverly Paigen, one of the top biochemists at the Roswell Park Memorial Cancer Institute in Buffalo, said she was harassed by the governments for three years because she raised the spectre of serious health effects at Love Canal. Her mail was opened, her taxes were audited and government grant money evaporated. Dr. Paigen said her crime was that "I spoke out on the Love Canal chemical dump before it was acceptable to do so. I was saying that people in that area were sick when the [New York State] health department was saying they weren't." Another scientist who reported that people from Love Canal had an abnormally high number of broken chromosomes was also criticized widely. (Chromosomes carry the body's genetic code and breaks could lead to changes in future generations.)

As a result of years of warnings about the dangers of leaking Niagara dumps, Canadians have been growing fearful for their drinking water supplies from Lake Ontario. "We can have environmental devastation of world proportions," if the toxic dumps suddenly unleash a slug of chemicals, warned the former Ontario environment minister, Andrew Brandt. He said Ontario would rapidly have to build expensive new water treatment systems, of a design which the province is still testing. "We don't have 40 to 50 years to clean it up," said federal Environment Minister Thomas McMillan after he made the mandatory pilgrimage to inspect the Niagara dumps in late 1985. "With the Hyde Park dump we may not have five years. You only need a bucketful of dioxin to render Lake Ontario useless for drinking water."

With the exception of Love Canal, where people received very high doses of toxic chemicals, it has been hard to evaluate the effects of Niagara River's poisons on its people. But a federal study found death rates from cancer were five per cent higher than expected on Ontario's side of the river, and a U.S. study found similar results on that side of the border. Many residents of Niagara-on-the-Lake, the picturesque tourist town which lies at the mouth of the river, did their own risk evaluation. They became so afraid of the chemicals flowing into the drinking water intake that they forced provincial and local governments to supply them with water from another source. They started getting water from St. Catharines via a 15-kilometre, $3.25-million pipeline in July, 1982. Niagara Falls and Fort Erie still draw from the river but are upstream from most of the chemical discharges.

The St. Clair River is Canada's answer to the Niagara River and The Blob is vying with Love Canal for notoriety. Until late 1985 the chemical pollution of this river, which drains Lake Huron into Lake St. Clair, was the sleeping dog of Great Lakes toxic issues. The dog had bitten once, in 1970, when researchers discovered that mercury leaking from Dow Chemical Canada Incorporated at Sarnia had polluted fish all the way down to the western end of Lake Erie. In April, 1970, there was a total ban on all commercial fishing in Lake St. Clair due to mercury contamination in all species of fish. Since then the mercury losses have stopped, the heavy metal is slowly being buried by new muds and mercury levels in the fish are declining to less dangerous levels.

The St. Clair region created a brief flurry of headlines in 1981 when the provincial environment ministry reported 84 chemicals in the river, including 17 in drinking water, as far downstream as Windsor and Amherstburg. In laboratory tests some of those chemicals, when concentrated as they might be by the process of bioaccumulation in the body, damaged genetic material in cells. Things settled down for a few more years until all hell broke loose in the fall of 1985, with the discovery of The Blob in the river at Sarnia. In September divers from Environment Canada found an oily blob of chemicals on the bottom of the river, just offshore from a Dow sewer. Among other things the chemical patch contained dioxins, furans and more than a dozen other chemicals including perchloroethylene and carbon tetrachloride, two dry cleaning fluids, and hexachlorobenzene, all of which can cause cancer. Similar oily sludges had been found on a three-kilometre stretch of the river bottom as far back as 1984, but this one dwarfed them. Shortly after the story broke, a dispute erupted between Dow and the federal government over the parentage of The Blob and its cousins.

During the summer Dow spilled 11 000 litres of perchloroethylene dry cleaning fluid into the river and the company claimed The Blob consisted of this chemical plus a lot of old contaminants that it had soaked up from the river bottom. Some Environment Canada researchers were not convinced, and they speculated that the pollution was coming through the bottom of the river from some of the 16 deep injection wells and a salt cavern, which had been used for years for the disposal of hazardous wastes. If they are proven right, Canada has an environmental disaster on its hands which could make the Niagara River pale by comparison.

First, to set the scene. The St. Clair River south from Sarnia is Canada's Chemical Valley, and in many ways a match for the U.S. industry along the Niagara River. A lineup of 13 petrochemical, glass fibre and plastics factories stretches more than 10 kilometres along the banks of the river. It is the who's who of Canada's chemical and petrochemical industry and traditionally has been a symbol of the country's industrial strength: the image of the valley's towers and tanks decorates our $10 banknote. The giant factories produce gasoline, kerosene, diesel fuel, jet fuel, home heating oil, stove oil, lubricating oil, propane, butane, waxes, asphalt, polyethylene, benzene, toluene, xylene, synthetic rubber, latex, styrene, propylene glycol (anti-freeze), chlorine, caustic soda, tetraethyl lead (a gasoline additive) and a host of other chemicals.

Chemical companies have spent millions of dollars on pollution controls and in fact the St. Clair, though still filthy, is much better than it was a few years ago. However, the river is still laced with PCBs, mercury, cadmium, lead and other heavy metals, bacteria that make swimming unsafe in some areas, and phenols, which make fish unpalatable. Companies still discharge several tonnes a day of pollution into the river in the 1.7 billion litres of water they pass through their factories for cooling, mixing and discharging wastes. For example, Dow released 3.23 tonnes per day of pollutants through 10 sewers in August, 1985. In addition there are large numbers of chemical spills. Between 1972 and 1978 there were 275 chemical or oil spills in the Sarnia area, and 58 per cent of them put material directly into the river. More than 1 355 tonnes of oil, acid, paint, phenols, styrene, sodium hydroxide, vinyl chloride, xylene and benzene went into the water. Many of the chemicals are toxic to humans, plants and animals and some of them have been detected in low levels in drinking water downstream. Compounding the problem, there are about 2 500 tonnes of agricultural pesticides a year used on the farmland draining into the St. Clair and Detroit rivers. About 70 per cent of these chemicals are potential environmental hazards. In 1984 Alachlor, a widely used herbicide sold under the name Lasso, was found in southwestern Ontario well water. Alachlor causes cancer in test animals and Ottawa has said the chemical will be phased out of use.

But it is the fear of what the toxic blob might represent that sends a chill up one's spine. Environment Canada scientists say it may be the first sign of chemicals oozing up through cracks in the ground and onto the river bottom. The possible source is some 8 billion litres of chemical waste pumped into the ground near the river between 1958 and 1976. Underground injection is a technique used in a number of areas, principally the U.S. gulf coast and western Canada, to get rid of troublesome chemical wastes. At least 16 wells were used by Sarnia industry to pump their wastes into porous rock called the Detroit Formation, 150–250 metres underground. Some material was also injected into a deeper salt formation.

Signs of trouble from underground disposal were visible as far back as 1967, when abandoned wells in Port Huron, Michigan, across the river from Sarnia, started to flow with water contaminated with phenols and hydrogen sulphide. In 1972 an abandoned well behind Sarnia's Capitol Theatre began to flow with a greenish liquid containing high levels of the same two chemicals, plus chloride and organic carbon. The same year two wells on the property of Imperial Oil Limited began to discharge similar liquids. In 1976 the Ontario environment ministry banned the injection of chemical wastes in wells beside the river and said that only limited waste disposal could take place 8 kilometres or more back from the river, and the wastes could only be poured into the ground, not injected under pressure. The fear is that injection might have forced the chemicals back up to the surface through natural cracks in the rock and the pressure of injection itself might have fractured the rock, opening up new pathways. The Detroit Formation is already perforated with hundreds of abandoned and often forgotten oil and gas wells, the legacy of Canada's first oil rush, a century ago.

We know that water from underground sources is bubbling up through the bottom of the St. Clair River but so far no one is certain whether it is carrying chemicals from the 8 million tonnes buried around Sarnia. If the chemicals are coming through the bottom of the river, some people in Environment Canada fear that this could be North America's biggest hazardous waste problem yet. One official estimated that the clean-up cost could top $100 million. A Dow spokesman was quoted as saying that he is not sure the technology even exists to extract the chemicals put far underground. Environment Minister Thomas McMillan said shortly after the discoveries that the problem appears awesome. If large amounts of wastes are coming up through the river bottom, dealing with the situation will tax the resources of "not only my department but of the country...."

From Sarnia south to Lake Erie there are 350 000 Canadians and 3.7 million U.S. citizens drinking the water which flows through the Sarnia chemical complex. By late 1985 government analysts had found 120 compounds, including two forms of dioxin, in the water as far downstream as Amherstburg, near the mouth of the Detroit River. The town of Wallaceburg, 45 kilometres below Sarnia, has lived for decades in the shadow of Chemical Valley. But the discovery of The Blob at Sarnia and 41 chemicals in their own tap water proved too much for the patience of people in this town of 11 223. A number of the chemicals in their drinking water, including benzene, hexachlorobenzene and carbon tetrachloride, are human carcinogens when encountered at high levels. In November, 1985, a group of townspeople asked Ontario Environment Minister James Bradley to pipe water to them from Lake Huron (the same water that Sarnia residents drink), upstream from Chemical Valley. That pipeline would cost $8-9 million. The initial government response to Wallaceburg was that the chemicals in their water fell within guidelines, in the cases where guidelines existed. Mr. Bradley said he would consider carbon filtration of drinking water, if necessary, for Wallaceburg, Windsor and Amherstburg. Close by Wallaceburg is the Walpole Island Indian Reserve, a community of 2 100 Indians who also draw their drinking water from the river and who worry about what chemicals are in that water. People there reported beads of some unknown substance floating on their water and pots blackened after boiling water. Some residents reported more cases of illness than usual. Shortly after Dow's big perchloroethylene spill, the community started trucking water in from Sombra, which gets its water from a pipeline to Lake

Huron. Wallaceburg store owners were doing a land-office business selling bottled water.

The jury is still out on the fate of the Great Lakes. In the case of a number of well-known contaminants, such as PCBs, dioxin and DDT, the pollution levels in the lakes generally have fallen since the 1970s, though they are rising in some specific areas, especially in Lake Ontario. Even if the pollution was stopped tomorrow, the lakes contain such an enormous quantity of toxic chemicals that they cannot flush themselves clean for many decades, possibly even a couple of centuries. Once the chemicals are unleashed into a big lake there is little we can do about them, except wait for nature's slow healing processes. These include the breakdown of some chemicals in sunlight—although they do not always break down into harmless forms—the slow burial of toxins by the age-old process of sedimentation and the flushing of chemicals down the St. Lawrence to the Atlantic. In addition volatile chemicals will evaporate from the lakes' surface and will fall elsewhere as toxic rain.

The chemical history of the Great Lakes is still being written. According to Donald Williams, head of the federal surveillance program on the Great Lakes, the phosphorus clean-up of the past decade "represents the greatest effort ever made anywhere to reverse a serious case of environmental degradation. In one sense the two countries are engaged in a very costly experiment. The world is watching the successes and failures of this cooperative venture."

CHAPTER FIVE

TOXIC RAIN: DEATH FROM THE SKY

IN OUR ORGY OF pollution we have even managed to spoil the rain, a key part of the water cycle and of life on Earth. By filling the air with smoke and gases from factories, mills, power plants, incinerators, cars, trucks and a host of chimneys we have created invisible rivers of air pollution downwind of big cities and industries. In the atmosphere they merge to form a thin but perceptible film extending around the globe. Even in the Arctic a haze of pollutants from southern industries periodically clouds the skies. We have turned the rain into a chemical bath, full of acids, pesticides, industrial chemicals and partially understood byproducts of burning. Kenneth Hare, the renowned Canadian climatologist, writes that the atmosphere which we breathe "becomes heavily charged with sour-smelling, dirty-looking and very alien constituents. Visibility goes down, the sky whitens, the washing line darkens and atmospheric quality obviously deteriorates." The vast tonnages of sulphur dioxide spewed into the air, particularly in the midwest and northeast of North America, produce sulphate particles which create a gauze-like effect, turning blue skies white. "In Toronto, humid, southwest winds in summer invariably bring white skies, a drab haze and a lack of sparkle. A whole generation of young Canadians have grown up to believe that this is the hallmark of summer," writes the University of Toronto professor. "Their earliest ancestors saw the blue skies typical of Texas or Oklahoma."

The relationship between polluted air and water is as simple and direct as the aphorism that what goes up must come down. Many millions of tonnes of pollution fall from the sky every year in what has become a toxic rain. Over the past few decades industries in developed nations have eliminated much of the black smoke which was once considered an emblem of progress. What is left is sometimes called invisible smoke, a clear, chemical soup which we cannot see and sometimes cannot even smell, but which is affecting the air we breathe, the food we eat and the water we drink. It is the reason that fish, seals, penguins, polar bears and humans in remote corners of the world now have significant levels of exotic industrial chemicals in their body fat. It is the reason that there is no place left on the planet where we can hide from pollution.

A succession of environment ministers has called that part of air pollution known as acid rain the greatest environmental crisis facing Canada. And this country is just one of many under bombardment by industrial fallout which sterilizes lakes and rivers, creating an aquatic version of Silent Spring. Large parts of the United States and Europe are being eaten away. Acid rain and its family of related pollutants kill fish—thereby starving wildlife which feeds on them—destroy some crops, threaten forests, dissolve buildings and are corroding our very health by attacking our respiratory tracts and poisoning our waterways. In the past two or three decades thousands of lakes and rivers have died across eastern North America and Scandinavia, killing off the rare Aurora trout in northern Ontario and devastating the forests of central Europe.

Acid rain is relatively complicated in scientific terms but in its essence it is easy to understand. Put simply, it refers to forms of air pollution which shoot out of smokestacks and exhaust pipes, mix with water in the air and turn that water into acids. It does not take much imagination to grasp its effects, as the anti-acid rain posters and political cartoons attest, with their images of fish reduced to skeletons and umbrellas dissolving. In some cases, rain 400 times more acidic than normal, as strong as vinegar, falls to Earth. The more accurate title is acid deposition, which includes corrosive fallout in many forms: rain, snow, sleet, hail, fog, dew and even dry gases and dusts, which can turn into acid on contact with water. In cities local pollution usually lands on buildings in dry form to destroy such structures as the Parliament Buildings, the Parthenon in Athens and the limestone façades of Christchurch, New Zealand. Acid rain which kills wilderness lakes with pollution from sources hundreds, even thousands, of kilometres away is part of a problem called long-range transport of acidic precipitation, or LRTAP in the scientific jargon.

The acids are sulphuric, nitric and sometimes hydrochloric. Most of the research in North America has centred around the problem of sulphur acids coming from sulphur dioxide, a heavy, pungent, color-less gas. It is a byproduct of the burning of fuels, such as coal and oil, which contain sulphur and of the smelting of ores, particularly nickel and copper ores, which contain more sulphur than metal. The pollu-tion also comes from pulp mills, refineries and any furnace that burns coal or fuel oil. Sulphur dioxide is a health hazard in its own right and causes respiratory health problems, particularly for asthmatics. It also directly attacks buildings, metal structures and statuary, accelerating their natural weathering dramatically. In the atmosphere sulphur dioxide gas is changed chemically into sulphates, fine particles smaller than a pin head and themselves a health problem. But it is the conversion of sulphur dioxide and sulphates into sulphuric acid while they blow through the sky that creates sulphuric acid rain. Nitric acid comes from nitrogen oxides, a byproduct of high temperature com-bustion, and the largest sources are coal-burning power plants and motor vehicle engines. The oxides can form acid or can interact with other chemicals in the combustion process to form ozone and other oxidants, which can attack the respiratory tract and destroy vegeta-tion. Nitrogen oxides are responsible for about one-third of the acidity in Canadian acid rain and are a serious part of the acid shock to aquatic life during the spring melt. Hydrochloric acid is the least studied of the three acids in acid rain but is formed from the burning of coal rich in chlorine.

Air pollution and acid rain have a long and dishonorable history, much of which was ignored until severe damage took place. Serious air pollution began with the industrial revolution and the building of large metal smelters and coal-burning factories. In the mid- to late 1600s English researchers noted the harmful effects of the fallout and in 1727, S. Hales of London observed that dew and rain "contain salt, sulphur, etc. For the air is full of acid and sulphureous [sic] particles." Transboundary air pollution reared its head when French farmers found that clouds containing sulphur fumes, floating over from England, were ruining their vines in flower. The term acid rain was probably coined in 1852 by researcher Robert Angus Smith, who lived in the industrial city of Manchester.

In 1942 the *Industrial Waters of Canada* report noted that: "Above large manufacturing areas the air is often laden with dust of all kinds, soot, silica, silicates, sulphates and carbonates, sulphuric and sul-phurous acid. . . . These are all adsorbed in the falling rain or snow, resulting in a very inferior water. . . .even in places where there is no factory pollution of the air. . .the rain water shows appreciable amounts of dissolved and adsorbed matter." During the late 1950s and early 1960s Canadian-born ecologist Eville Gorham, now with the University of Minnesota, warned of the dangers of acid rain but was largely ignored. During the same period Svante Oden, a Swedish scientist, took up the cry because by then Sweden was finding that wilderness lakes, far from industry, were becoming acid and the fish were dying. The Swedes found high levels of acid in the rain borne from the industrial heartland of Europe and Great Britain by southerly winds and they gave acid rain international attention at the 1972 Conference on the Human Environment in Stockholm. The same year Harold Harvey, a University of Toronto professor, was among the first Canadians to successfully publicize the acid rain connection. Along with R. J. Beamish and other graduate students studying Killarney Provincial Park near Sudbury, Professor Harvey found that a number of lakes were becoming acidic and fishless.

One of the great ironies of the acid rain story is the tall smokestacks chapter. By the early postwar period industry was expanding at such a fever pitch that the air in many cities was downright unsafe to breathe. In an effort to improve the air quality of cities, governments in a number of countries ordered factories and power plants to build tall smokestacks to disperse their pollution over a large expanse of the countryside—usually somebody else's countryside. Since 1970 the United States has built more than 175 smokestacks over 160 metres high (the height of a 50-storey building) and 35 of those are over 250 metres. Canada beat them all with the 381-metre-tall superstack built in 1972 by Inco Limited at its giant copper and nickel smelter in Sudbury. The tall stacks are just another version of "the solution to pollution is dilution" trick used to disguise the dumping of poisons. While the tall stacks improved the local air quality they created another problem—the long-range transport of air pollution. Like giant cannons they inject gases high into the atmosphere where they are picked up by the winds and carried far away. The pollution also stays in the air long enough to be transformed into acids. Because the fallout often lands in another province, state or country from that of its origin, many governments have tried to wash their hands of the issue, saying it is not their problem.

No one knows exactly how much air pollution there is, but the world produces an estimated 75 to 100 million tonnes a year of sulphur dioxide alone. In 1980, the year Canada and the United States signed an agreement to fight acid rain, the two countries produced 50 million tonnes of sulphur and nitrogen acidic air pollution, with 87 per cent of that in the United States. In Canada the acid rain damage has been worst in the eastern half of the country and has been linked most strongly to sulphur, so the battle has been focussed on sulphur dioxide, especially from polluters in the area from Manitoba east to Nova Scotia. In 1980 sources in eastern Canada were allowed to produce 4.5 million tonnes a year of sulphur dioxide, although because of a number of factors, including strikes and the recession, they only produced 3.8 million tonnes. The biggest polluters are six copper and nickel smelters and as many power plants. In the same year 2.5 million tonnes of nitrogen oxides came from chimneys and exhaust pipes.

An area of 5 to 10 million square kilometres across North America and Europe is already affected by acid rain and other parts of the globe have not yet been accurately studied. In North America the acid rain is worst east of a line drawn roughly up the Mississippi Valley from Texas and carried north into northern Ontario. The most polluted areas are over the Ohio Valley and southern Great Lakes, both heavy industrial centres, but pollution is serious enough even in rural Ontario, Quebec and the Maritimes to destroy the fish in lakes and streams. The part of Canada believed to be at greatest risk runs east from Manitoba to the Atlantic Ocean and south of the 52nd parallel, a line through mid-northern Ontario and through the centre of Quebec. The local effects of pollution can be seen around smelters such as those in Sudbury and the iron sintering plant at Wawa, Ontario, where sulphur gases have burned away surrounding vegetation.

Not all areas are equally affected by acid rain. It is most destructive to fish life in the Precambrian Shield, which stretches across the Canadian north, and in similar hardrock areas in the eastern and northeastern United States and the western mountains of the continent. These are areas where the rock and thin soils lack the limestone chemistry to neutralize acids. For example, a number of lakes in Killarney Park, including those named in honor of artists in the Group of Seven, are acid. In the Adirondack Mountains of upstate New York, remote fishing lakes, cherished in such a heavily populated state, have died. In Nova Scotia a dozen rivers have lost their salmon. Within the past two or three decades Canada has seen an estimated 14 000 lakes and an unknown number of rivers become acidified and another

300 000 are believed at risk. In the Rocky Mountains acid rain is attacking the high lakes, including those in famous U.S. national parks. Sweden has 2 500 acid lakes and 17 500 more are becoming acidic. The country also has 90 000 kilometres of streams, twice the circumference of Earth, which are dead or dying. Norway studied 5 000 lakes and found 1 750 fishless and 900 seriously affected.

The effects of acid rain are many and varied but it is the fate of the fish which has been most graphic. Acid rain can kill young fish, especially during the spring melt when a winter's accumulation of acid snow suddenly runs into the streams where delicate fish eggs are hatching. And fish are suffocated because acid dissolves aluminum, a common element, from the ground and the substance coats their gills. Other elements, such as iron, mercury, manganese, copper, nickel, cadmium and lead, are found in high concentrations in fish from acidic lakes, affecting the health of the fish and making them dangerous for humans to eat. Fish in some acid lakes are actually deformed and scientists like Dr. Harvey theorize that the effects of acidity cause their spines to weaken, allowing their muscles literally to pull the bodies into contorted shapes. Not only fish disappear but so do phytoplankton and zooplankton, the basic plant and animal life in the water, and frogs, salamanders and other parts of the food chain. A 1985 study by Robert Alvo of Trent University said that young loons have much less chance of surviving if they are raised on lakes affected by acid rain. The young birds die of starvation because the acidic water has killed the fish on which they depend for food. Losing any part of the wilderness hurts us all but if we could no longer hear the haunting cry of the loon across a northern lake, we would suffer a great loss. In acidified lakes in northern Europe the osprey, also known as the fish hawk, is disappearing in a similar fashion.

In the final stages of acidification lakes become crystal clear but later they can be invaded by a foul-smelling filamentous algae, symbolizing the death of the lake.

Acid rain and its co-pollutants are attacking human health. We breathe in the oxidants which attack our respiratory system and there is one estimate that these forms of air pollution kill more than 50 000 people a year in Canada and the United States. Tap water from acidified lakes has high levels of heavy metals, which are dissolved out of the plumbing system by the acid water and possibly dissolved from the lakes' bedrock. Up to twice the recommended maximum level of mercury for eating has been found in fish from acid lakes. In Sweden the leaching of heavy metals has contaminated some water supplies to the point that it has caused outbreaks of illness and was blamed for killing three people on dialysis machines in hospital by aluminum poisoning. Moose livers were banned for consumption because the animals had accumulated high levels of metals which acid rain had leached from the rocks and passed to the plants they ate.

Acid rain and its related pollutants can kill plants and they are implicated in the widespread death of forests in central Europe and the increasing death of trees in parts of eastern North America. There is a major tragedy unfolding in Germany's Black Forest, where, in large areas, up to half the trees have started dying in the last few years. It is more than sentiment, or even the loss of the ancient forest industry, which is causing a rising panic in some quarters. On mountain slopes the trees are all that stop the snow from constantly rolling down into the valleys in what would be an endless series of devastating avalanches. In North America there are signs of forest deterioration in eastern regions of Ontario, southern Quebec and into the Maritimes, with an increase in the death of maples. Pockets of dying trees are found along the Appalachian Mountains and into New England. There are fears that acid rain seeping into the soil will destroy microorganisms which are basic to the life processes in soil and which support growth of plants. In Sweden soil has been acidified to a depth of 50 centimetres in some areas studied.

During the mid- to late 1970s there was growing awareness of the acid rain threat in Canada, particularly in Ontario, mainly because of studies of the Killarney lakes and other acidified lakes near Sudbury. Pressure grew for more controls on the big smelters, particularly Inco's Sudbury operation, which has long been the largest single source of sulphur dioxide in North America and possibly the world. In 1977 federal Environment Minister Roméo Leblanc called acid rain "an environmental time bomb." During the same period the United States complained about plans for new coal-burning power plants in Ontario and Saskatchewan, saying they would send acid rain south across the border. This, coupled with growing Canadian concerns about U.S. pollution, led to bilateral talks and a 1979 report showing that large parts of the continent were sensitive to acid fallout. Also in 1979 the United Nations Economic Commission for Europe drafted a convention to control the long-range transport of air pollution across national boundaries. By 1984 there were 20 countries, from both eastern and western Europe and including Canada but not Britain or

Tall smokestacks such as the one in Sudbury were built in recent decades to reduce local pollution. They simply spread chemicals further, sending acid rain to kill life in wilderness lakes and rivers.

(ONTARIO MINISTRY OF THE ENVIRONMENT)

the United States, which had pledged to reduce their sulphur dioxide pollution by at least 30 per cent by 1993. A number of countries are doing much more than that. Sweden has cut sulphur pollution by 60 per cent and will have reduced it by 80 per cent by 1995, while Canada has promised a 50-per-cent cut.

On August 5, 1980, Canada and the United States signed what was then seen as a historic Memorandum of Intent to control transboundary air pollution. The document pledged the two nations to enforce existing clean air laws equally stringently and to negotiate a clean air agreement, along the model of the Great Lakes Water Quality Agreements of 1972 and 1978. However, the November, 1980, U.S. elections brought winds of change in more ways than one. They swept away President Jimmy Carter and his officials, who were pushing for stronger anti-pollution legislation, and replaced them with President Ronald Reagan, whose administration is plainly unsympathetic to further acid rain controls. The Reagan administration clearly stated that it saw such controls as an impediment to business. That change in Washington has turned acid rain into one of the most contentious issues in years between Canada and the United States. By 1981, when it was obvious that President Reagan had no intention of seeking more acid rain reductions, External Affairs Minister Mark MacGuigan told a conference in Buffalo that U.S. acid rain "is killing our rivers and lakes" and he talked about the "depredations" of U.S. pollution. Keith Norton, Ontario's environment minister at the time, said the problem was threatening good relations between the two nations. In February, 1982, a Canada-U.S. research team established under the 1980 agreement reported on the serious nature of acid rain and Environment Minister John Roberts called for joint 50-per-cent reductions in sulphur pollution in the eastern half of both countries. At first there was no response from the U.S. side; then in June the U.S. negotiators said that it was too early to act against acid rain and more research was needed—the consistent position of the Reagan administration. That did not change until early 1986, when President Reagan endorsed a plan to seek money for projects demonstrating acid-rain control technologies, still short of a full-scale clean-up plan.

The U.S. stalling on acid rain controls helped delay action in Canada by several years. At first Canadians called for a 50-per-cent reduction in sulphur dioxide by 1990, a decade after the signing of the Memorandum of Intent. In a fruitless attempt to draw the United States into negotiations, Canada offered a unilateral 25-per-cent reduction in sulphur pollution and a further 25-per-cent cut if the United States would make a 50-per-cent cut. But the lever was too small to have any effect. Canada is only responsible for about 10–15 per cent of the acid fallout on the United States, while that country creates half the fallout on Canada, and 75 per cent of that in central Ontario, thanks to prevailing northerly winds and the huge power plants of the Ohio Valley. After years of rebuffs from the United States the Canadian federal and provincial environment ministers finally decided this country had to move, with or without a bilateral agreement, and in March, 1984, Canada promised unilateral 50-per-cent cuts in sulphur dioxide emissions by 1994. This will take the maximum permissible sulphur dioxide emissions down to 2.3 million tonnes per year. Pollution control is mainly a provincial responsibility, although the federal government gets involved in negotiations between provinces and countries and is offering up to $150 million to help modernize and clean up the metal smelting industry. The provinces are responsible for cleaning up coal-burning power plants. The attention in North America has been focussed on the east, where the pollution and the damage is worst. But there are significant polluters in western Canada, such as the oil sands plant at Fort McMurray, Alberta, and the southwestern Alberta sour-gas wells which produce sulphur as a byproduct. There are also signs that damage may be more widespread and could hit the southeastern and northern United States.

What pushed Canada's politicians into action was a series of signals from environment groups and from the public. Groups, particularly the Canadian Coalition on Acid Rain, played a major role in goading, encouraging and aiding federal and provincial governments to commit themselves to spend and to order companies to spend what will probably total billions of dollars on the clean-up. A series of public opinion polls commissioned by the acid rain coalition showed that a large majority of people were willing to pay higher taxes and prices in return for a cleaner environment, and this was particularly influential in showing politicians that the public was serious about a clean-up. The coalition, which represents 52 business, environmental, tourism and public interest groups with total memberships of over 1.5 million people, keeps up a steady stream of information about the effects of acid rain. For example, it says, millions of people would be put out of work if acid rain destroys fishing and related tourism industry and attacks the forests. More recently the economics arguments have been picked up by governments. In late 1985 the Ontario government announced a major increase in the pollution cuts to be imposed on the provinces' big polluters, including three smelters and Ontario Hydro. Premier David Peterson said that if left unabated, acid rain would destroy the economic base of the province, so it was worthwhile for governments and industry to spend several hundred million dollars to reduce the pollution.

In fact there have been reductions in the pollution that causes acid rain, though many of these have been related to making local air more breathable or have come as a result of the economic slump of recent years. Between 1970 and 1980 the pollution from Sudbury dropped sharply as Inco cut its emissions by 60 per cent and nearby Falconbridge Nickel Mines Limited chopped 64 per cent. In the early 1970s, Inco had been releasing more than 6 000 tonnes of sulphur dioxide into the atmosphere every working day of the year but by 1984 it was down to 1 871 tonnes per day. This is a big improvement from the previous 2.2 million tonnes a year but is still a huge amount of nearly 683 000 tonnes per annum. In April, 1985, Inco announced it was voluntarily cutting current emissions in half in nine years but in December, Ontario Environment Minister James Bradley said that Inco must chop at least 63 per cent and possibly more by 1994. During the same period Mr. Bradley has also ordered a further 35-per-cent cut from Falconbridge and a 56-per-cent reduction by Algoma Steel Limited at its iron sintering plant in Wawa on the northeastern shores of Lake Superior.

In 1981 the province told Ontario Hydro, its Crown corporation, to reduce its sulphur and nitrogen oxides pollution starting January 1, 1986, and again in 1990. Mr. Bradley imposed a third cut for 1994, which would roll Hydro's sulphur dioxide pollution back to 480 tonnes a day, a 61-per-cent cut from 1982, Hydro's dirtiest year recently. Automobile pollution has long been a sore point in Canada, with our cars allowed to crank out three times as much nitrogen oxides as U.S. vehicles are permitted. It was not until 1985 that the federal government announced that, starting in 1988, Canadian cars would have to be as clean as those sold in the United States. It was hardly a major move, since virtually all cars sold in North America are designed for U.S. standards and the anti-pollution equipment was simply left off most of those vehicles sold in Canada.

The costs of reducing acid rain in Canada vary depending on the source of the estimate, but Environment Canada's acid rain team has calculated that it will cost about $500 million a year for 20 years to cut the sulphur pollution in eastern Canada by 50 per cent. About half that cost will come from the smelting industry and most of the rest from the power plants. In the case of many of the smelters there will be attempts to rebuild them in ways that make them both cleaner and more efficient, thus providing some economic payback. For the power plants there are several options. These include installing "scrubbers"—huge devices which spray a wet limestone mixture into the furnace gases to remove the sulphur dioxide—using low-sulphur coal from western Canada, installing cleaner-burning boilers or using alternate power. Ontario Hydro, for example, is trying to rely more on nuclear power but has the option of importing additional hydro-electricity from Quebec and Manitoba.

It is worth noting that the pollution cutbacks now being ordered will be phased in over nearly a decade, and in the interim the lakes and rivers will continue to die bit by bit. And even when the Canadian program takes full effect, a broad stretch of the country will still be receiving dangerous levels of fallout unless the United States reduces its pollution. It is also worth pointing out the fine print in the Canadian strategy, which says the pollution control levels chosen will protect "moderately sensitive ecosystems." What that means is that a significant number of lakes and rivers now close to the borderline of acidification, or with little natural buffering capacity, will likely be lost. The 50-per-cent controls are aimed at reducing the fallout of wet sulphate to no more than 20 kilograms per hectare per year, which translates into 2 grams per square metre or 2 tonnes per square kilometre. Orrie Loucks, director of the Holcombe Research Institute in Indianapolis, Indiana, and a prominent U.S. acid rain researcher, stated in 1985 that the 20-kilogram level was too high. Mr. Loucks said that research into nearly 650 lakes in the three midwestern states has found damage when fallout levels were as low as 15 kilograms.

There is no realistic way to patch up the damage of acid rain. Liming, the dumping of crushed limestone into acidified lakes to neutralize the acid, can stop lakes from becoming acidic. It can also revive dead acid lakes but the ecosystem will be abnormal, containing such unwanted byproducts as fish full of toxic metals. Liming is also costly—$4 000 to $40 000 a lake—and it must be repeated. This is only practical to save a few very valuable fishing lakes until the time when pollution controls reduce the fallout.

The death of fish in North American and Scandinavian lakes alerted the world to acid rain. The methyl isocyanate leak from the Union

Carbide Corporation pesticide plant, which killed more than 2 000 people in Bhopal, India, on December 3, 1984, drove home the point that there are other toxic chemicals in the air. In fact that spill was an anomaly; there are fortunately very few such serious incidents. But it drew attention to the fact that there are a lot of toxic chemicals getting into the air all the time, albeit in more dilute form. Although they do not cause massive kills they are damaging the environment and harming human health. Following Bhopal, the U.S. House of Representatives ordered an investigation of domestic toxic air pollution. The study found thousands of tonnes of cancer-causing agents and other very hazardous materials being released every year from hundreds of factories. Researchers also found indications of higher than normal cancer rates around some big chemical factories.

While much attention has been focussed on a narrow range of air pollutants, there is growing awareness of the wide range of hazards in the sky. For example most of the government information on acid rain focusses on sulphur dioxide, but the burning of coal releases PAHs, radioactivity and other materials, such as mercury. The smelters which release sulphur dioxide also eject tonnes of heavy metals in their smoke. And there is increasing concern about the long-range transport of a host of pollutants besides those which form acids. In recent years there has been evidence of toxic chemical fallout even in remote areas. A few years ago scientists were sampling fish in tiny lakes on Isle Royale, a U.S. national park on a cluster of wilderness islands in western Lake Superior. To their amazement they found substantial levels of PCBs and Toxaphene in those fish. Tests of other fish in the nearby waters of Lake Superior also revealed chemical levels high enough to cause concern about their edibility. In the case of Lake Superior as much as 90 per cent of the pollution is from airborne fallout. This became obvious when it was found that most of the Toxaphene used in North America was sprayed in the southern and southeastern United States. William Strachan, of the Canada Centre for Inland Waters in Burlington, tested rainfall around the Great Lakes for seven chemicals and found that the fallout on the lakes was in the range of over 20 tonnes per year. Another study calculated 137 tonnes of 8 pesticides plus 29 tonnes of PCBs. Other researchers have estimated that between 130 and 480 tonnes a year of PAHs are falling on the lakes and still other studies have found over 1 800 tonnes of just four metals—cadmium, copper, zinc and lead— falling from the sky onto the lakes every year.

The distances involved in long-range transport of air pollution are startling until one begins to understand just how efficient a mixing machine Earth's atmosphere really is. For example, DDT and PCBs have been found in the fat of penguins and polar bears and the bears also contain the pesticide Chlordane, along with the metals mercury and cadmium. Toxic chemicals are found in remote rivers on Ellesmere Island in Canada's high Arctic, 3 500 kilometres north of the country's industrial heartland, and in headwaters of Rocky Mountain streams. Ice cores drilled from the glaciers on Ellesmere have proven one of the great recording machines of our pollution, as each year's fallout is preserved and covered with another layer of snow, which hardens into ice with time. The ice cores register air pollution arriving around the turn of the century, as smokestacks grew taller and more polluting, and show that the fallout increased 75 per cent between 1950 and 1970.

All this should not come as any surprise. We were introduced to hazardous fallout in the early 1950s, when scientists started measuring Strontium 90 and other radioisotopes spreading across the northern hemisphere as a result of atom and hydrogen bomb tests. Years later researchers studying DDT said that once the chemical was in the oceans the breaking action of the waves would inject it back into the air and DDT would keep migrating long distances.

In fact airborne pollution comes from thousands of sources scattered all over the continent and across the world. Pesticides sprayed on crops and forests do not all make it to the ground and if they do, they do not always stay down. Some of the spray is captured by the winds and carried far away, while another part falls to earth but evaporates back into the sky with the sun's heat, just as water evaporates from a puddle. Eventually the chemical will fall back to the earth, sometimes mixed with rain. Up to 60 per cent of Toxaphene sprayed can be swept away by the wind, and 52 per cent of the amount which reaches the ground has been known to vaporize within two months.

Incinerators built to get rid of our waste are turning into giant pollution machines as they combine plastics, metals and chemical garbage and then spew out vast amounts of partially burned residues into the sky. And chemical factories, refineries and a host of other industries vent gases through chimneys directly into the sky above their plants. There are unexpected sources, like chemical settling ponds, where hazardous substances are supposed to be filtered out of the water or neutralized before the remaining waste water is discharged into our lakes and rivers; some bright scientists are calculating that large amounts of dangerous chemicals instead are evaporating off the surface of these treatment ponds and later falling into the lakes and rivers. Even the tops of dumps, which are supposed to keep chemicals locked in the earth, are sources of air pollution. Some chemicals percolate up through loose fill covering the dumps and others simply waft out of the vent pipes which are installed in the dumps to allow dangerous methane gas to escape before it builds up to explosive levels

All this gaseous soup goes into the earth's atmosphere, which is like a giant refinery. The sun's heat boils chemicals off the surface of polluted lakes and rivers into the air and later they condense in rain, and especially in cold snow. In fact Canada may get more fallout because of its cold climate. Chemicals can probably travel immense distances in one fell swoop before falling as toxic rain, but in some cases they land on lakes and rivers during storms, then are re-evaporated back into the air when the sun comes out. In this manner they hopscotch from lake to lake right across the continent and probably across the oceans of the world, which helps to explain how they travel so far and why fish in pristine wilderness lakes are polluted.

Great Lakes studies have linked this fallout to toxic chemicals in people. For example DDT, PCBs and other chemicals have been found not only in the milk of mothers who live beside the Great Lakes and eat contaminated fish but in that of women who live inland, away from the lakes, and who eat little or no fish. Researchers like Douglas Hallett, a former senior Environment Canada science advisor, believe that chemical fallout is to blame. Dr. Hallett explains that chemicals blow inland where they can be breathed in or can fall into drinking water or onto the land. On land they are taken up by fruits and vegetables and farm animals whose flesh we eat and whose milk we drink. He says that this means it is not enough to stop drinking the lake water or eating the fish. We have to stop the pollution.

CHAPTER SIX

CANCERS
IN THE
FISH

MOST OF THE CONCERN about pollution has been directed towards the people, birds and animals whose health is at risk when they eat fish laden with toxic contaminants. Now the microscopes are focussing on the fish themselves. There have always been some deformed individuals in virtually any species, be it human, fish, fowl, reptile or any other creature. But there is a disturbing cancer increase in North American fish which in some areas is reaching epidemic proportions. The link between pollution and cancers seems clearest among fish such as carp, suckers and bullheads, which root for food in the highly contaminated river and harbor bottom sediments around chemical, dye-making and steel-making industries. In particular polycyclic aromatic hydrocarbons have been associated with the development of cancers in several kinds of bottom fish from both fresh and saltwater areas. It should not be too surprising to find cancers in the wild fish because laboratory tests have shown that certain chemicals cause a wide range of illnesses in test animals, including reproductive failure, stillbirths, low birth weight, reduction of the immune system and retardation.

Abnormal rates of fish cancer have been identified in a number of areas across North America, all of them polluted with industrial wastes. Michael Dickman of Brock University in St. Catharines reported in 1982 that 48 per cent of the hybrid carp-goldfish caught in the Welland River downstream from Welland's industrial and municipal sewer outlets contained large tumors in their reproductive systems. The tumors can grow big enough to render the fish sterile. Only 10 per cent of the fish captured upstream of the city had the cancers.

Carp, goldfish and the carp-goldfish hybrid from Lakes Michigan,

Huron, Erie and Ontario also show tumorous growths on their reproductive organs. Museum specimens of the same species taken from some of the same areas 30 years ago show no tumors. Also in the Great Lakes, a study of white suckers has shown a startling correlation between pollution and the development of skin tumors called papillomas. For example, in the relatively clean upper lakes the papilloma rate is nearly zero but in heavily industrialized areas such as Hamilton Harbor 41 per cent of the fish studied had the affliction. Almost all of the tumors were on the upper lip and mouth area and some were large enough to make it difficult for the fish to eat. Suckers are bottom feeders, raising the likelihood that they came in contact with pollutants which have settled to the lake and harbor bottoms.

There are other close associations between pollution and fish cancers around the Great Lakes. For example the Buffalo River, at the head of the Niagara River, is itself contaminated with a number of chemicals, notably PAHs, which are found downstream from an old steel plant. The river is also laced with chemicals bulldozed into the river bank for cheap disposal by dye industries. These waters are home to cancer-ridden fish, particularly the brown bullhead. The work of John Black of Buffalo's Roswell Park Memorial Institute has been particularly important in linking fish cancers to pollution. Dr. Black took contaminated sediments from the Buffalo river's bottom, extracted the pollutants, fed them to one group of fish and painted them on the skins of another group. The fish fed the pollution developed liver cancer and those painted with the chemicals developed skin papillomas, in both cases diseases like the ones found in fish from the river.

A similar link was drawn between contaminated sediments and cancerous bullheads from the Black River, which empties into Lake Erie at Lorain, east of Cleveland. Three- and four-year-old fish from a section of the river downstream from a steel and coking plant have externally visible cancers. Detailed examination of fish livers shows that nearly 80 per cent of those over two years old have cancer or precancerous lesions. Normally bullheads live seven or eight years but researcher Paul Baumann of the U.S. Fish and Wildlife Service says that in the Black River only a few fish make it to five years. The river bottom is heavy with coal tar, creosote and other chemicals identified with health problems. In Torch Lake, Michigan, on the south shore of Lake Superior, saugers, a close relative of the pickerel, have the dubious distinction of the highest liver cancer rate of all the fish

Tumor of unknown origin on a Lake Erie coho salmon. These large tumors have drawn public attention to the issue of fish cancers but scientists are even more concerned about the liver tumors in many fish, an illness that is hard to spot.
(DR. JOHN BLACK AND THE INTERNATIONAL JOINT COMMISSION)

studied—100 per cent. This small lake has long been a dumping ground for tailings from a former copper mine and the pollution includes nickel, cadmium and arsenic.

In other areas it may be one of the great ironies of pollution clean-ups that we have made some waters clean enough that fish can once again survive but we have left them dirty enough that the fish become ill. For many years the Hudson River was too filthy to support tomcod but in recent years the gross pollution was reduced to the point that the fish could once again swim in from the ocean and survive. John Harshbarger of the Smithsonian Institution in Washington says that virtually all the two-year-olds caught from the river from New York upstream to Poughkeepsie were sick. Dr. Harshbarger said these tomcod had "the biggest and worst-looking liver cancers of fish" from five major locations of fish cancer across the United States. Only 5 per cent of the tomcod caught were two years old, rather than the normal 25 per cent. This and the Black River example suggest that the fish are being killed off by the toxins before they can grow old.

The cancer reports are not unique to the east. A mid-1970s study of cancer in Pacific coast fish found that 58 per cent of young English sole in Vancouver harbor had skin cancer. The study by the British Columbia Cancer Research Centre found this disease rate was proportional to the proximity of fish to pollution. Not far to the south, U.S. researchers studying sole in Puget Sound and its tributaries, near Seattle and Tacoma, found that more than 70 per cent of the bottom-dwelling English sole and some of the flounder suffered serious liver diseases, and 12 per cent had liver cancer. One mud sample from the area turned up more than 500 aromatic hydrocarbons, a family of chemicals known to include cancer-causing agents.

Dr. Harshbarger has been among the most outspoken U.S. scientists linking pollutants and cancers, particularly liver cancers. In 1983 Dr. Harshbarger, director of the registry of tumors in lower animals at the Smithsonian's National Museum of Natural History, explained the link to U.S. politicians. He told the House of Representatives Subcommittee on Fisheries and Wildlife Conservation and the Environment that fish, like mammals, use the liver to eliminate a wide variety of chemical pollutants. Unfortunately the metabolic action of the liver appears to enable the chemicals to cause cancer.

In addition to cancer the chemicals seem to be killing off aquatic life in other ways. The death of beluga whales in the St. Lawrence River has led to suspicions that these marine mammals are dying because of toxic chemicals like PCBs, DDT and Mirex in their bodies. Most of this species of white whales is found in the Arctic but there used to be a colony of several thousand in the open reaches of the St. Lawrence. That colony has dwindled to around 350. Many of the deaths in the past were from hunting, which has now been stopped, but the whales are still dying and washing up on the shores. By 1985 bodies were being found at the rate of one a month.

Autopsies by the federal Department of Fisheries and Oceans has found PCB levels of 575 parts per million in the whale blubber and up to 1 725 ppm in the breast milk of one dead animal. That milk virtually would be poison to young belugas and if these levels are common it means the species could be killed off. By comparison the same department considers fish with 2 ppm too contaminated for commercial sale to humans. Federal researchers say they are almost certain chemicals like PCBs, which are known to cause cancer and other health problems in laboratory test animals, are poisoning the belugas. The scientists believe that the PCBs are at least reducing the effectiveness of the belugas' immune systems, making the sea beasts vulnerable to such ailments as bladder cancer, pneumonia, heart problems and stomach ulcers. Pierre Beland, head of the Fisheries and Oceans research centre in Rimouski, says the belugas, by eating tonnes of contaminated fish, are, in effect, cleaning up the St. Lawrence at the cost of their own lives.

Lake trout can no longer reproduce successfully in Lake Michigan and studies point the finger at high levels of PCBs in their eggs. When the eggs hatch into fry the PCBs are mobilized and the levels are high enough to kill the young fish. This is similar to the case with DDT, which was linked to the reproductive failure of fish decades ago. Ronald Sonstegard of McMaster University has found a high level of goitres in Great Lakes coho salmon, approaching 100 per cent in Lake Erie. The Lake Erie salmon also lack secondary sex characteristics, have impaired lipid metabolism, and are unusually small, and since up to 75 per cent of their embryos die, they cannot maintain their population and must be repeatedly re-stocked. Fish surveys indicate that in the polluted rivers the fish which survive are the so-called coarse or trash species like bullheads rather than the trout and salmon.

The deadly effects of toxic chemicals on our environment were first widely revealed more than 20 years ago by Rachel Carson in *Silent Spring*, the Bible of the environment movement. Miss Carson wrote with passion and precision about how chemicals sprayed to control weeds or insects were also attacking the rest of the web of life. Since then there have been many more cases of birds, fish and animals dying off or their young being stillborn or born deformed. Peregrine falcons and bald eagles virtually disappeared from most of eastern North America. Herring gulls and other fish-eating birds in parts of the lower Great Lakes were born with such ailments as crossed beaks, malformed eyes and extra limbs, or the young died of chick edema, an accumulation of body fluids which suffocated them. This disease was later blamed on dioxin particularly, the deadliest synthetic chemical yet discovered. During the pollution peak of the mid- to late 1970s, herring gulls and double-crested cormorants in Lake Ontario stopped reproducing and the species started dying off.

Many substances which appear safely dilute in the industrial sewers are accumulated in the food chain, first by basic levels of life such as plankton, then by a series of progressively larger fish and finally by the predators which eat fish, including gulls and other fish-eating birds. More than 1 000 substances have been found in the Great Lakes ecosystem and 200 have been analyzed in gull tissues. Some of those pollutants have been found in gull eggs at levels up to 100 000 times those in the nearby water, showing the power of living things to accumulate poisons. Around 1970, fish-eating birds from parts of the Great Lakes had pesticide and chemical levels in their flesh as high as those in any birds in the world. Over the past decade the levels of some of the worst chemicals have declined and the birds are once again reproducing in most areas. However, the status of some species is still not clear and scientists are trying to find out if the birds are suffering less noticeable effects, such as changes in their body chemistry. Part of that research was eliminated in 1984 during federal environment department budget cuts.

Land mammals, too, are suffering food chain effects. In 1971, mink ranchers feeding their animals with Lake Michigan fish such as coho salmon found that the mink were suffering reproductive problems. In 1984 a New York State wildlife researcher said that his department had asked trappers to turn in the bodies of mink from the Lake Ontario shoreline for research but the department had not received any. He speculated that the wild mink have been poisoned off by chemicals in the fish which are a large part of their diet. In the book *Mammals of the Canadian Wild*, author Adrian Forsyth said that wild mink are being killed or stopped from reproducing by PCBs and mercury and this threatens the species in polluted areas. Dr. Sonstegard fed contaminated coho salmon from Lakes Ontario, Erie and Michigan to laboratory rats and within two months all the rats developed thyroid abnormalities and some also showed liver and immune system changes.

As a result of these studies it appears obvious that toxic chemicals in our waterways are causing cancer, birth defects and a series of other ailments in fish, birds and mammals. Drawing a link between wildlife and human health is scientifically difficult until long and expensive tests have been undertaken but Dr. Harshbarger notes that human cancer mortality rates are high in the five U.S. locations where fish cancers were also elevated. "This probably means that humans in those areas are exposed to many of the same carcinogens that fish are exposed to," though the contaminants may or may not be picked up directly from the fish. Dr. A. S. Macpherson, Toronto's medical officer of health, said of fish cancers that it is difficult to estimate the implications for human health, but "Disease in fish may be an 'early warning system' for humans." Dr. Black draws a clear analogy when he says the fish "are like caged canaries used by early coal miners to warn of the unseen hazards of methane gas. The fish are warning us about the hazards of their environment."

CHAPTER SEVEN

IS IT SAFE TO DRINK?

Water, water, everywhere,
Nor any drop to drink
—RIME OF THE ANCIENT MARINER

IS THE WATER DOWNSTREAM from chemical dumps like Love Canal, or from industrial lakes and rivers across North America and around the world, safe to drink—or is it a time bomb in our bodies? The short and sad answer is that no one knows. As a long line of scientists have pointed out, we are accidentally part of an experiment in human toxicology that no ethical person would deliberately conduct. Every day anyone who lives in an industrial city like Toronto, Montreal, New York or New Orleans, or who even drinks chlorinated tap water in a suburban or rural town, is exposed to a shopping list of synthetic chemicals whose safety is, at best, questionable. Health officials agree that there is no evidence that the low levels of chemicals in the tap water in most of North America pose a short-term health risk, but no one can tell what the cumulative effects are over a lifetime. As one Environment Canada official put it, "the risk becomes greater as you extend the time." Douglas Costle, a former head of the U.S. Environmental Protection Agency, said of his advisors: "Scientists will say we cannot tell you that the water is unsafe to drink. By the same token, we cannot tell you it is safe to drink, either."

This is very unsettling news because the water we drink every day is what holds us together. When we exit the womb we are 97 per cent water—close to being jellyfish in human form. With age our bodies accumulate more solid matter but we still remain 65-70 per cent liquid by weight and about 90 per cent by volume, even as adults. As adults we must take in an average of 2 to 5 litres of water per day to keep our personal water balance. On average Canadians of all ages drink 1.34 litres of tap water and tap-water-based beverages, such as soup or coffee, per day. This is the equivalent of four tall glasses of water or six cups of coffee or tea. The intake varies from .61 litres for an infant to 1.57 litres for a person over 55. Women drink slightly more water than men. Although the quantity increases with age the amount in relation to our body weight actually declines, because we put on weight faster than we increase our water intake.

The amount of water in all forms drunk by an average Canadian is actually 2 litres per day when one counts non-tap-water beverages like milk, soft drinks and alcohol. And the liquid intake is even higher because we get another 1 to 2 litres from food, such as potatoes, which are 80 per cent water, and tomatoes, which are 95 per cent liquid. Our bodies, each a tiny ecosystem, release an equal amount of water through perspiration, excretion and in our breath, as you can see when you exhale against a cold windowpane.

Even to discuss the possibility that chemicals in that water could be slowly poisoning us is to ride the edge of public panic and rouse the dark vision of cancer. This explains why most politicians and senior public officials either have taken the easy way out and endorsed tap water as perfectly safe or have cloaked their reservations in a verbal cotton wool of qualifications. Such approaches result in such patently absurd situations as environment ministers announcing that their laboratories have found hundreds of chemicals in the water but that the public should not worry because the water, wherever it happens to be, is the finest on the continent. They usually fall back on statements that the water meets government guidelines without explaining, and in some cases without themselves knowing, how imprecise and incomplete these guidelines really are. For example, there are only 43 Canadian guidelines for health hazards in drinking water, yet more than 1 000 suspect substances have been found in the Great Lakes. And each guideline is calculated for that substance alone and not for the chemical soup we ingest every day.

A growing number of experts are uncomfortable with the old, easy assurances that tiny amounts of chemicals in our glass are harmless. They add up the quantities that we take in over a lifetime and come up with a new equation. It says that some people risk sickness and even death from cancer, birth defects and other illnesses which may not

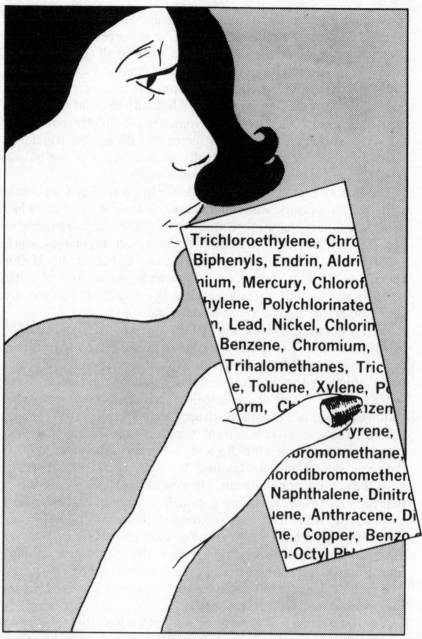

Trichloroethylene, Chro
Biphenyls, Endrin, Aldri
nium, Mercury, Chlorof
hylene, Polychlorinated
n, Lead, Nickel, Chlorin
Benzene, Chromium,
Trihalomethanes, Tric
e, Toluene, Xylene, P
orm, Ch   nzen
                Pyrene,
           romomethane,
        orodibromomether
         Naphthalene, Dinitr
       uene, Anthracene, Di
       ne, Copper, Benzo
       n-Octyl Ph

This graphic representation shows just a few of the hazardous substances which have been found in drinking water from around North America. Unfortunately no one has been able to estimate the risk from this chemical cocktail in our daily ration of water.
(BERNARD BENNELL)

even seem related to drinking water contamination. Many government officials are quietly dropping the word "safe" from their vocabulary when they talk about drinking water. A number of health experts are now suggesting that we prepare to install a new type of treatment system on our waterworks, both to eliminate industrial chemicals and to avoid creating new hazards during the disinfection process.

To understand the debate one has to understand a little history. "As a reservoir and transmission medium of human disease, water has been the leading problem in environmental health throughout history," states the American Academy of Family Physicians. Cholera outbreaks claimed the lives of 50 000 people in Canada between 1832 and 1854. A century ago 180 of every 100 000 people in Canada died each year from typhoid, cholera or similar illnesses contracted from polluted drinking water. There was no sewage treatment then and people were just beginning to understand the warnings of the French chemist Louis Pasteur, who said that microscopic bacteria, often in the water, were causing illness. By the first part of this century people were starting to disinfect drinking water, particularly by adding chlorine. In many areas chlorination is now supplemented with a variety of filtration and chemical treatment systems that remove many of the solid particles from lake and river water, including bits of dirt which can carry bacteria or toxic chemicals. For over half a century people drinking properly chlorinated water have been virtually free of diseases which were the scourge of our grandparents.

But chlorine, the same chemical used by householders to bleach clothes and to disinfect many swimming pools, is a potent substance. About a decade ago researchers found that chlorine added to drinking water reacts with natural organic matter in the water, such as decaying plants, to form a nasty set of chemicals called trihalomethanes (THMs). At least one of these THMs, chloroform, causes cancer in laboratory animals and probably in humans. It is not surprising that chlorine is causing these problems because it is the same chemical used in the production of some of our worst pollutants, including PCBs and a number of dangerous pesticides. A 1977–82 study of drinking water from 138 Ontario communities showed that almost all had THMs but they were almost always below the maximum acceptable level set by the federal and provincial governments for long-term consumption. However, the acceptable Canadian level for THMs is more than three times as high as the U.S. maximum and 350 higher than West Germany's.

While Canadians argue about parts per billion of THMs, much of the world has even more serious drinking water problems. After years of global research the World Health Organization (W.H.O.) issued guidelines for chemical contamination in drinking water, often suggesting maximum levels in the parts per million or billion range for a number of poisons. However, even the W.H.O. says these standards for the long-term protection of health cannot be enforced too literally in many countries because "the adoption of stringent drinking water standards could limit the availability of water supplies—a significant consideration in regions of water shortage." The W.H.O. was referring to the fact that people in some regions, particularly in rural Africa, spend up to half their day seeking water that two out of three times is unsafe to drink, often because of disease-causing organisms. In fact half the world's people, more than 2 billion, cannot get enough clean water and fewer than one-third of the planet's 4.8 billion people have adequate sanitation. The W.H.O. estimates that this combination results in 80 per cent of all the world's illness. People drink contaminated water, they lack adequate water for washing and they lack sanitary disposal for human wastes. In many areas, lakes, rivers and swamps harbor disease-transmitting creatures, including insects, worms and snails.

Residents of developed countries regard diarrhea as a thoroughly unpleasant disease but not one that is likely to kill them. Many tourists often get the illness during visits to areas where the water is inadequately treated. They almost always kill the bugs, however, with potent medicines. People in many poor countries, especially infants, who have not developed their immune systems, also get sick, but the bugs often win. The toll is staggering. The United Nations estimates that waterborne diseases kill 25 million people every year, 15 million of them children. It is as if seven fully loaded jumbo jets crashed every hour and there were no survivors. By the time you finish reading this sentence at least three people will have died because of waterborne diseases. This year 400 million people will suffer from gastro-enteritis, 500 million from trachoma (which can blind), 200 million from schistosomiasis (snail fever) and 30 million from onchocerciasis (river blindness). To that list you can add a host of diseases including typhoid, cholera, dysentery and hepatitis, which are spread by contaminated water, and scabies, yaws, leprosy and conjunctivitis, which are aggravated by insufficient water for washing.

The United Nations estimated that the provision of potable water could cut the world's infant mortality rate in half and in 1980 the world organization announced the decade of clean water and sanitation. But the goal of clean water for all by 1990 failed to grab the headlines the way starvation in Africa has and there has been little support for the waterworks. The poor nations which need water pumps, treatment plants and even latrines, let alone sewage treatment plants, are usually paying off staggering debts, providing other public services and often buying arms.

In most of North America the question of drinking water safety was buried decades ago with the advent of chlorination and did not resurface until the mid- to late 1970s. At first the concerns were usually over well water located within short distances of leaking chemical dumps. But the issue of drinking water safety started to mushroom in areas like southern Ontario after it was revealed that vast amounts of pollution were going directly into the Niagara River and Lake Ontario. Suddenly this involved 7 million Canadian and one million U.S. residents as far downstream as Quebec City.

The incident which galvanized public attention, particularly in Ontario, was the report of dioxin in Lake Ontario in 1980. The next year the Toronto group Pollution Probe caused furor when it issued a report, *Toxics on Tap*, which said there were 16 suspect chemicals in Metro's drinking water and they were likely a health hazard. It was a major challenge to the safety of the 1.25 billion litres of water pumped every day to about 3 million people in and around Metropolitan Toronto and to a large number of industries, including food and beverage plants. In March, 1983, Pollution Probe followed up with a second report, called *Drinking Water: Make It Safe*, which created a new controversy by predicting that between 72 and 156 Toronto residents would get cancer in their lifetimes thanks to pollution in their drinking water. This statement pushed for stronger water quality laws and advanced drinking-water treatment systems. The provincial environment ministry and the Metropolitan Toronto government mounted a combined attack on the report, led by Metro Chairman Paul Godfrey, who called the environment group "alarmist [and] unfair to the public."

The two Pollution Probe reports provoked a hard official look at what was in Toronto's water and led to two studies of bottled drinking water which was being purchased by a growing number of people dissatisfied with the tap brand. The bottled water tests were an attempt to defend tap water by discrediting bottled water but they only succeeded in muddying the issue further by reporting that some bottled waters contained low levels of chemicals or dissolved solids, including natural salts. There was speculation that some of the chemicals in bottled water might have come from machinery used to pump the water out of the ground and bottle it.

Far better was a year-long study by the City of Toronto's health department of all the research it could find on the state of the city's tap water. The report, prepared by Katherine Davies and assisted by researcher Joan Campbell, is a landmark study of chemicals in the drinking water of a Canadian city and is far more sweeping than anything produced by federal or provincial officials. Ironically it listed even more pollutants than Pollution Probe had, in its tabulation of what governments had found in tap water in recent years. The health department study said 83 compounds had been found at least once in Toronto drinking water during the past decade, including seven that are human carcinogens. Only 28 of the substances are subject to government safety guidelines. "There is a widening gap between our ability to detect the presence of contaminants in drinking water and our ability to interpret these data for human health," the report stated. "We simply do not know what the health effects are likely to be from low level exposure or even if there are likely to be any." It did say that the pollution levels detected, particularly of THMs, might cause a slight increase in cancer and infant deaths but this was based on estimates rather than hard evidence. At best the report gave only a qualified endorsement to tap water, saying: "Residents of Toronto can drink tap water with reasonable assurance it is not likely to cause harm or injury," and they need not turn to bottled water or home filters. At the same time it endorsed two of the Pollution Probe recommendations. It said the public should be involved in discussions of what risks exist and what should be done about them. And it said that contamination in Toronto's drinking water is serious enough that governments should test advanced water treatment systems as alternatives to the chlorination method used now.

Dr. A. S. Macpherson, Toronto's medical officer of health, elaborated on the touchy word "safe" by saying, "statements asserting that our drinking water is 'safe' do not reassure the public. Although Toronto's drinking water meets the Health and Welfare Canada guidelines this can no longer be construed as absolutely 'safe'. Clearly water containing carcinogens, or even potential carcinogens such as trihalomethanes, is not free from risk. I therefore suggest that the word 'safe' be eliminated from the discussions on drinking water."

Toronto is only one city concerned about its drinking water. The Science Advisory Board of the Canada-U.S. International Joint Commission on boundary waters reported in 1985 that acute toxicants were present in Toronto and Hamilton harbors, the Rochester area and the Welland Canal area. In addition mutations of test bacteria were caused by the waters from Toronto and Hamilton harbors, the Niagara River mouth, the Bay of Quinte, near Kingston, and the Buffalo River. Such mutations had been found earlier in the St. Clair River and concern flared again in 1985 when toxic chemicals, including a tarry blob of toxins, were found on the bottom of that polluted river. Low levels of chemicals have been found as far downstream as Windsor. A number of contaminants have been found in western Canadian rivers and in Tobin Lake in northeastern Saskatchewan there are both pollutants and high numbers of deformed insect larvae. In fact concerns about drinking water have been reported from all provinces.

Complaints about drinking water are more common in the United States than in Canada. In 1984 the *American Family Physician* magazine warned that: "The quality of our water supplies is deteriorating at an alarming rate." This journal for nearly 57 000 doctors said that the nation was about 20 years behind in its maintenance of water supply systems and these vital systems were being allowed to deteriorate further as governments sought to save money.

In the United States the greatest fears are over the safety of underground water. More than half the population relies on well water and people draw more than 340 billion litres of it a day. Pollution from leaking chemical dumps and other sources is viewed as a time bomb for water quality because it is out of sight and it keeps spreading slowly, even after new pollution is stopped. U.S. Senator David Durenberger, chairman of the Senate Subcommittee on Toxic Substances and Environmental Oversight, said in 1984 that ground water contamination will be the "principal environmental concern for the rest of this decade."

Drinking water quality has become an international issue facing virtually all industrialized nations. The United Nations Environment Program, choosing just two notorious examples, said parts of the Mississippi and the Rhine rivers are "so polluted by organo-chlorine and other compounds that it is doubtful whether they are suitable sources of drinking water. Studies have suggested that their contamination could be linked to the fact that people who have to use these waters suffer slightly higher cancer rates than expected."

It is a commentary on the weakness of our environmental systems that there is no Canadian, let alone global, inventory of the damage done so far to drinking water. Certainly the people who drink the water downstream from Niagara Falls are at some risk, as are those downstream of Sarnia's Chemical Valley. Well waters around dumps in Stouffville and Perkinsfield in Ontario and Mercier in Quebec have been polluted from leaking chemical dumps. The contamination of wells by stray farm pesticides and fertilizers presents a further threat that is poorly understood. For example a substantial number of Prince Edward Islanders risk exposure to the pesticide Aldicarb, which has turned up widely in well water. Alachlor, a weed killer sold under the name Lasso, and used by 45 000 Ontario farmers, was found to cause cancer in laboratory animals. It was discovered in farm wells and in Dresden town water in southwestern Ontario in 1984, and a year later it was ordered phased out of use.

The problems found so far in the United States are far greater. Researchers have identified 700 synthetic chemicals, heavy metals and other substances in drinking water. In 1982 there were reports from two studies about U.S. rural well water. One said that 63 per cent of rural wells tested contained contamination from sources including leaking septic tanks and agricultural chemicals. A second, done by the Environmental Protection Agency, said that nearly 29 per cent of rural households, some 39 million people, had enough bacteria in their drinking water to present potential health hazards. In addition 14–24 per cent of homes had high levels of mercury, lead, cadmium and selenium, heavy metals which can cause health problems. A 1984 study by the U.S. Congressional Office of Technology Assessment said that serious contamination had been found in 35 states and more than 2 800 drinking water wells had been closed.

In some cases the water is not even fit to touch. Most if not all beaches around large cities like Toronto and Montreal have been regularly posted as unsafe for swimming and Ontario Environment Minister James Bradley notes that none of the beaches in his home city of St. Catharines are clean enough for swimming. Even sailboarding over polluted water is dangerous, according to two Quebec doctors, who studied competitors on the St. Lawrence River near Quebec City. They found that 57 per cent of the board sailors became ill after falling into the water and the more often they fell the sicker they got. The ailments included diarrhea, cramps, nausea, vomiting, and skin, ear and eye infections.

One of the problems with polluted water is that you often cannot tell there is anything wrong without complex and expensive tests. Chemical pollution, unless it is at gross levels, is usually colorless, odorless and tasteless. Some chemicals are liberated in steam and can be inhaled in a shower. Others can even penetrate through your skin. Many of the most hazardous chemicals are lipophilic, or fat soluble, which means they prefer to move from water into body fat. In this manner they pass up the food chain and accumulate to levels hundreds, thousands or even a million times their concentration in the environment. They settle in fat areas like the liver and are so slow to be excreted that we may never get rid of them completely. "The adipose tissue of all Canadians has become a rich repository of fat-soluble environmental contaminants, including large numbers of pesticides, flame retardants and industrial transformers fluids," says a report by two noted Canadian environment researchers, Ross Hume Hall and Donald Chant. It is true in Canada and it is true everywhere in the world, even in remote villages. John Laseter of Dallas, who specializes in testing pollution in people, says that each of us now carries a sort of pollution fingerprint in our bodies that enables him to tell where we came from just by the type and level of chemicals in our tissues.

We know from the previous chapter that toxic substances in the water have caused considerable harm to wildlife, which lives constantly with those chemicals or feeds on creatures heavily laden with toxins. But what does that tell us about the risk to humans? One study that seems to show a link between toxins in the Great Lakes and human health is a report in which some U.S. psychologists found that children of fish-eaters in the Grand Rapids and Muskegon areas of Michigan had neural problems such as reduced head circumference and low attention span. During pregnancy the mothers of these children had regularly eaten Lake Michigan salmon which contained high levels of PCBs, Toxaphene and other chemicals. A number of studies have made the point that infants may be exposed to chemicals in utero via placental transfer and, after birth, through their mothers' breast milk, which is high in fat. In many parts of the world chemical levels in mothers' milk are high enough so that the benefits in nutrition, increased immunity to diseases and parental bonding must be weighed against the risks of damage from the toxins.

Speaking in general about the emerging chemical problem several years ago then U.S. Surgeon General Julius Richmond told Congress: "We believe that toxic chemicals are adding to the disease burden of the United States in a significant although as yet not precisely defined way. The magnitude of the public health risk associated with toxic chemicals currently is increasing and will continue to do so until we are successful in identifying chemicals which are highly toxic and controlling the introduction of these chemicals into our environment." Mr. Laseter estimated in 1985 that, based on psychological tests of people who had undergone treatment to reduce their toxic chemical load, North Americans suffer, on average, a 5-per-cent decrease in intelligence from chronic chemical poisoning.

Although cancer is the most frequently mentioned effect of toxic chemicals, it is by no means the only thing they can do to us. They can cause loss of fertility, birth defects, blood disorders, mutations of cells, genetic damage; they disturb the central nervous system, attack a large number of the organs and have psychological effects. Pesticide poisoning can cause depression, emotional sensitivity and failure to understand one's own behavior, which is not surprising since many pesticides are neurotoxins. Even more insidious is the one-two punch of chemical combinations. One substance may not be a strong carcinogen itself but may promote the formation of tumors by another chemical. Chemicals can also suppress or overload the body's immune system, rendering us vulnerable to diseases not normally related to chemical poisoning. There is also a concern that chemicals may be changing the shape of future generations literally, by getting inside our cells and scrambling the coded messages in our genetic material. Ross Hume Hall of McMaster University put it very simply: Adding foreign chemicals to our bodies is like dropping nuts and bolts into a moving engine.

Experience shows that there will be a variety of individual reactions to any substance, depending on exposure levels and the individual's sensitivity. Most people are not allergic to pollen but some of us get hayfever and suffer runny noses during the summer. Most of us survive the daily assault of pollution on our bodies without obvious harm while others suffer what is called environmental illness or the Twentieth-Century Disease. In this state people's immune systems partially break down and they are so sickened by exposure to chemicals that they must live in specially protected homes and eat chemical-free food or they will die. Robert Sugarman, a former U.S. co-chairman of the International Joint Commission, pointed out that even the experts know very little about how much any chemical it takes to produce harm. "We don't know how much you have to eat to get hurt and we don't know how little won't hurt you," he said.

If any groups within our numbers are at higher risk they are probably the young and those of us with immune deficiencies. The fetus is at risk in the sense that it is the victim of any toxins in the mother's diet, a situation which continues for an infant nursing. Young children are also at higher risk than adults because the young eat and drink more than adults in relation to their body size, and their immune systems are less well developed.

Standing between the chemicals and us is a thin line of defence, which consists of advice about maximum acceptable amounts of pollution. There are Canadian guidelines for only 43 toxic substances in drinking water, including bacteria, pesticides, industrial chemicals, heavy metals and uranium, although more than 1 000 substances have been found in the Great Lakes alone. Even with national guidelines there is inconsistency in standards of water quality applied by the different provinces. Each province monitors for a different number of substances in the water, ranging from 16 in British Columbia to 31 in Saskatchewan. In the United States only 17 chemicals are regulated under the federal Safe Drinking Water Act and a number of public officials have called for the inclusion of dozens more which have been found in public water supply systems. The 1978 booklet *Guidelines for Canadian Drinking Water Quality* is sadly out of date and an expanded version is several years overdue. A federal health department official said that the department just does not have enough money in its budget to produce a new list of guidelines to cover more of the substances being found in drinking water, and to deal with other health issues such as indoor air quality. Several years ago the department ran out of money for a service that advised Canadian industries on the safety of chemicals in plumbing materials, such as plastic pipes and the solvents used to fuse them together.

Although the federal health department is the main source of advice on drinking water safety, the provinces are usually responsible for governing the quality of drinking water and on a local level the job is usually delegated to regional health officers. The advice on acceptable limits of a given chemical in our food, air and water is based on a complex but little-known procedure called risk assessment. In a few tragic cases, notably that of mercury, we have direct knowledge about how much it takes of a certain substance to poison people. But most we have to rely on the results of tests on laboratory animals, which are then extrapolated to predict the effect on humans. Batches of animals, usually rats, but often mice and guinea pigs, are fed varying doses of a suspect poison in search of two pieces of information. The first, called the LD50, or lethal dose which will kill half the animals within a short time, gives a relative degree of immediate danger from the substance. The second is the level at which there are no observed adverse effects over a test of several weeks' or several months' duration. This gives the NOEL, or "no observed effects" level.

But the guardians of our health are still left with two difficult questions. How accurately do the tests on animals translate to humans, who have a different metabolism and may be more or less sensitive to a given chemical? And how do you deal with the fact that effects too subtle to show up in laboratory tests could produce cancers 10, 20 or 30 years down the road? The experts try to predict a virtually safe dosage based on the decreasing effects of the chemical on test animals at ever-lower dosages. They may also take the NOEL dosage and divide that by a large number, such as 500 or 1 000, to come up with what they think will be an acceptably small dosage for the public. This does not mean that that amount of the substance is totally inert. But it is a dosage that they estimate is not likely to cause more than possibly one more cancer case among all the people in a city of one million who were drinking that level of a chemical in their water over their lifetimes.

In the booklet *Health Implications of Contaminants in Fish,* Ontario's environment ministry has a section called "Rationale for Consumption Guidelines for Organic Pollutants." After noting that such chemicals as PCBs and Mirex are suspected of causing cancer it adds that, "in the case of carcinogens no absolutely safe level exists," and "any guideline selected is necessarily arbitrary. The guideline therefore does not represent an absolutely safe level. Instead it is derived, taking into account a variety of considerations leading to determination of a risk considered acceptable to society." That paragraph refers to a rarely discussed factor applied to risk assessment called the ALARA principle, meaning As Low As Reasonably Acceptable, when social and economic costs are considered. In other words, the final decision is often taken out of the hands of health officials and given to politicians and economists who then start fiddling with the numbers to meet some economic goal. For example a few years ago the Canadian government discovered that the fungicide Captan had been

A proud fisherman holds a Lake Ontario salmon which is probably hazardous to eat. In a number of areas fish are so contaminated with chemicals that governments recommend limited or no consumption. (ONTARIO MINISTRY OF NATURAL RESOURCES)

registered for use based on falsified safety tests and that it actually caused a cancer in test mice. Rather than remove this presumed carcinogen from the market, Agriculture Canada simply lowered the amount of Captan that could appear on food by the time it got to market, thus leaving the popular chemical in use.

In addition to drinking water, people worry, often with good reason, about eating fish from polluted lakes. It was the discovery of mercury in some Ontario fish in 1970 which gave us the euphemistic slogan "Fish for Fun." That was a polite way of saying the fish were unsafe to eat. Since then fishing bans or warnings have become tragically commonplace around the Great Lakes and in other parts of the world and they have taken a lot of the fun out of fishing. First it was mercury and DDT, then PCBs, and a long list of chemicals including Mirex, Chlordane, Dieldrin, Aldrin, Endrin, heptachlor epoxide, Lindane, Kepone, Toxaphene and now, dioxin, the super-toxic. Fish are particularly vulnerable because they not only swim in polluted water but eat food that has been soaking up the chemicals contained in the water as well. Some environment experts say that eating one big salmon or trout from Lake Ontario will give you the same chemical dose as drinking the lake water for many years. A growing number of people refuse to eat any fish from the lower Great Lakes. Others seem oblivious to government warnings to avoid or limit consumption of suspect fish. You can watch fishermen casting into the Niagara River, right beside leakage from Hyde Park, one of the most dangerous dumps in the area. Native communities and commercial and sport fishermen and their families, groups which all rely heavily on fish for food, are among those who can have high exposures to contaminants. There have been suggestions that some natives who continue to eat fish from mercury-contaminated rivers are showing signs of mercury poisoning.

Health authorities in Canada and the United States warn children and women of child-bearing age to be careful about eating any large salmon or trout from Lakes Michigan and Ontario. In fact New York State recommends no one eat any eels, channel catfish, big trout or salmon from Niagara Falls downstream into the St. Lawrence River. In the 1970s the trout of the Bow River, downstream from Calgary, were all but inedible because they tasted more like diesel fuel or oil than fish. Since Calgary built a modern sewage treatment plant, the taste of fish has improved but one fishermen, when asked if he would eat his catch, replied: "Would you eat fish that had been marinated in a toilet bowl?" There are fish consumption warnings on sections of the South Saskatchewan River and mercury pollution is a problem in fish from parts of Manitoba, Ontario and Quebec.

Federal laws restrict the commercial sale of contaminated fish, which means fish in stores are supposed to meet certain safety standards. When it comes to sport fishing you have to do your own research. Probably the most comprehensive guide anywhere is published annually by the Ontario environment ministry and is called *Guide to Eating Sport Fish in Ontario*. It has health evaluation of fish from over 1 300 locations in the province and provides general tips on how to prepare and eat fish in order to reduce the levels of chemicals and metals.

There are some general rules on how to reduce the risk of catching hazardous fish. Avoid fishing waters around and particularly downstream from industries, including mines and pulp mills, even in wilderness regions. Fish from fast-flowing streams are usually, though not always, cleaner than those from big, slow rivers or from lakes, where the contaminants have more time to settle out and collect in the life. Smaller members of a species are virtually always cleaner than the big, old fish, which have had a longer time to soak up fat-soluble chemicals. Also, fish lower on the food chain generally tend to have lower levels of chemicals than predators, which accumulate the toxic loads of fish they eat. Bottom-feeding fish such as bullheads, catfish and suckers are likely to have higher contaminant levels, particularly when they live in polluted areas. Many toxic chemicals accumulate in the fatty portion of fish, so the cleanest portion is generally a boneless, skinless fillet without the belly fat. Grilling fish allows the fat to drip away from the meat.

It is the drinking water and fish which have received the worst press as sources of toxic chemicals but they are not the only sources and they may not even be the worst ones. A major report on the Great Lakes by the Royal Society of Canada and the U.S. National Research Council created a furor in late 1985 when it stated that the food grown inland from the Great Lakes contains a number of contaminants normally associated with water pollution. The report said that PCB levels are much higher in beef from the Great Lakes-St. Lawrence provinces of Ontario and Quebec than in that from the Atlantic or western provinces. A survey of Canadian mothers' milk found that the highest PCB levels were in Ontario.

Douglas Hallett, then an Environment Canada science advisor, added to the controversy when he elaborated on the issue. After reviewing studies dating back to the 1970s, Dr. Hallett found reports of PCBs in such dietary staples as fruits, vegetables, grains, dairy products and meats. Although they have PCB levels much lower than the ones found in fish, these other foods make up a much higher percentage of the average diet. Dr. Hallett estimated that, based on a typical diet, the average southern Ontario adult's daily intake of PCBs is quite high. This means that children, who eat almost as much as adults but who have less body mass to dilute the chemicals, may be at an even greater risk than currently assumed by most people.

In a 1986 study Katherine Davies of the Toronto Department of Public Health tested a number of foods, grown in southern Ontario and sold in Toronto, for a batch of persistent toxic chemicals. Then she compared the amount of the chemicals in a typical diet of those foods with the amount of the same chemicals one would get from drinking Toronto tap water (which comes from Lake Ontario) and with the amount of those chemicals in the air Torontonians breathe. Ms. Davies estimated that city dwellers would get 86 per cent of their intake of these chemicals, including PCBs and a number of pesticides, from food grown in the region. By comparison only about 9 per cent would come from drinking water, and the rest from the air.

What these dramatic new findings mean is that while much public attention in recent years has focussed on the risk from drinking water, people eating food grown in or near an industrialized region may also face a considerable risk. This does not mean that chemicals in the water do not pose a risk, just that water is only one of several pathways to our body. No one has yet done a detailed analysis of all the chemicals in the food, air and water and compared the relative risk from each one.

The researchers also strongly make the point that even if further research proves that drinking water is not the greatest source of the toxins studied, water in general is a key link in delivering them to our bodies. In fact water turns out once more to be a medium of transmission of hazards back to us through our food chain. At first it was disease-bearing organisms from our human sewage, and now it is our chemical sewage.

Where are these chemicals coming from? Many volatile organic chemicals from industrial smokestacks or from the spray guns aimed at farm fields are carried far and wide to land on crops and pasture. In addition many chemicals fall into lakes, then evaporate back into the sky to fall on foodlands as another part of our toxic rain.

Another pathway for hazards is the use of sewage sludge as a fertilizer. Though it makes good plant food, the residues from sewage treatment plants collect heavy metals and organic chemicals dumped into sewers. Now many sewage plants which offer their sludge fertilizer suggest that it not be used for growing food.

Mixed in with all the bad news, there is some good news about food. The amount of PCBs in Ontario milk dropped by two-thirds between 1973 and 1983 and a provincial official said there has been a similar decline in PCBs in meat samples collected from Ontario slaughterhouses in the past 15 years. The decline follows controls on the uses of PCBs, particularly on the amount allowed in waste oil sprayed on roads to keep down the dust. The food research simply raises one more set of questions about yet another source of pollution, to be added to those of drinking water and the air. To date we do not have very good information on the levels of even the key chemicals, let alone the total chemical burden for any one of these potential sources.

In the vacuum created by the paucity of official advice, many people have been making their own risk assessments of drinking water and turning away from tap water. Several years ago Statistics Canada recorded that Canadians spend more than $20 million a year on bottled water and that figure has likely risen. A former senior federal health official noted a phenomenal increase in the sale of home water filters, with one estimate that sales reached 40 000 a year, worth more than $4 million. A survey of metropolitan homes found that 3 per cent had some kind of private water treatment.

There have also been repeated suggestions that drinking water be piped to southern Ontario from the relatively clean northern waters. In late 1985 senior Toronto alderman June Rowlands likened the pollution in the Great Lakes drinking water to a smoking volcano. She said Metro Toronto should study the idea of a 180-kilometre pipeline from Georgian Bay, near Wiarton, to Metro Toronto and possibly to the rest of southern Ontario. Joseph Curtin, a Toronto planning consultant, estimated the cost of such a pipeline at about $220 million but there are estimates that it would cost far more.

For several years after the discovery of leaking dumps along the Niagara River, an increasing number of citizens of Niagara-on-the-Lake, the picturesque home of the Shaw Festival, refused to drink

Niagara River water. Driven by fears of chemical poisoning, the town made the provincial and local governments pipe in an alternate water supply from St. Catharines, which draws Lake Erie water running through an offshoot of the Welland Canal. Before they got the pipeline the residents "were becoming positively unhinged about the water," said Margherita Howe, head of Operation Clean-Niagara, an important environment group. Since the discovery of the toxic blob on the bottom of the St. Clair River, residents of Wallaceburg and Walpole Island, downstream from the Sarnia chemical complex, have pushed the province for a pipeline to bring them cleaner Lake Huron water. For years Sault Ste. Marie, a city of 83 000, has been drinking water tainted with phenols from the big Algoma Steel Limited mill, sitting just upstream from the public drinking water intake. Although Algoma Steel is under orders to reduce its discharges, Sault Ste. Marie installed a new water intake about 15 kilometres north of the city and the 13 million litres a day of drinking water come from Lake Superior, upstream of the industry.

The worries about current water treatment methods have provoked interest in new types of water treatment, such as disinfection with ozone instead of chlorine, and chemical filtration with granular-activated carbon (GAC). Carbon, in the form of charcoal, has a long history of removing impurities from water and for millennia has been put in water storage vessels to clear the scum, slime and algae which gave stored water a foul taste and musty odor. GAC is a form of carbon, with an incredible number of tiny pores which trap the molecules of many toxic chemicals. It can be up to 90 per cent effective in removing organic chemicals from the water. Ozone is an unstable form of oxygen, with three molecules instead of the normal two, and is formed by passing an electric arc through the air. It is a powerful oxidizing agent, capable of destroying bacteria, and is used for purifying water in a number of regions including France and Quebec. However, the byproducts it creates in water, called epoxides, are still a matter for health research. In addition ozonation, unlike chlorination, leaves no germicidal residue in the water to kill stray bacteria and many health officials say some chemical, probably a form of chlorine, wou'' ve to be added to ozonated water to keep it pure in the pipes.
tage of post-chlorination, as this process is called, is that
e is needed by this stage of treatment and most of the
er is out of the water so there is less chance of forming

One 1983 estimate reckoned that it would cost up to $235 million to give advanced water treatment to Metro Toronto drinking water. Operating such filters is also more costly than normal treatment, since the carbon must be replaced or cleaned of chemicals at high heat lest it overload with toxins and start releasing chemicals back into the water. Ontario has been slowly getting a $1-million test of GAC set up in Niagara Falls. In the United States GAC has already won some acceptance. Douglas Costle, a senior U.S. environment official in the late 1970s, said that he authorized tests because "as a policy maker I had to decide, what does a reasonably prudent man do in the face of scientific uncertainty?" He considered GAC "a reasonably prudent insurance policy against our own ignorance on health effects." Tests were done at a federal water laboratory in Cincinnati, a city which draws its drinking water, contaminated with at least 225 chemicals, from the Ohio River. In early 1983 the city was so impressed with the study results that it voted to spend $38.5 million on building a full-scale GAC plant to purify water for its one million customers. That was despite the fact that all the contaminants in city water fell within U.S. Safe Drinking Water Act limits, where such limits existed. GAC is also used in Jefferson Parish, a suburb upstream of New Orleans on the highly polluted Mississippi River. Carbon filtration is used in at least 100 European plants, in such countries as Switzerland, France, West Germany and the Netherlands.

While boiling water for five minutes is still an accepted way to kill most bacteria in drinking water, there is no agreement on home remedies for chemical pollution. Water experts say, for example, that home water distillers vaporize, then condense, water into a clean container but that volatile chemicals will vaporize and condense with the water. Small household filters using activated carbon can improve the taste of water by removing at least some of the chlorine but federal tests suggested they were too unsophisticated to remove much industrial pollution. The federal health department nearly banned home carbon filters several years ago because it feared that bacteria would collect and multiply in them, presenting an unexpected health hazard. The department backed away from that position under pressure from the industry, which said there was no proof that this would happen in chlorinated tap water. The government does warn against using the filters on untreated water, such as that found in many rural areas. Bottled water is a popular option, both because it lacks the chlorine taste and THMs, and because it is widely felt to be free of industrial pollution. As the tests in Toronto showed, that assumption is not always correct. Bottled water comes under even fewer restrictions than tap water because in the days when those regulations were set, federal health officials assumed people drank little bottled water.

Another way of tackling the problem of drinking water contamination is through stronger laws to protect our water. Current environmental laws are not strong enough and in many cases fines for polluting are so small, they are simply a licence fee to keep dumping. There are signs that the penalties will be increased and when polluters are caught the fines will really hurt them, but this discipline is still the exception. Secondly, there are calls from a number of environment groups for national safe-drinking-water laws to make the supplying of polluted water an offence. Only Quebec has so far enacted such a law. During a January, 1984, speech the federal deputy health minister said Ottawa was considering a safe drinking water act but since then Ottawa has been silent on its plans. In 1985 the federal inquiry on water policy recommended that Ottawa pass a safe drinking water law that would at least apply to federal lands such as Indian reserves, military bases, federal airports and the northern territories. This would set a national standard which would be difficult for the provinces to ignore.

The permanent solution to our drinking water problems is not advanced filtering, just as liming lakes is no solution to acid rain. In both cases the answer is to eliminate much more of the pollution at its source, and this is the philosophy that environment departments are finally starting to endorse. But the clean-ups will be slow and for the next few years at least, we will have to muddle through with partial advice on the hazards in our drinking water. We must seriously look at ways to avoid creating hazardous chemicals during disinfection and we may even have to consider advanced filtration as a stopgap buffer against our pollution excesses.

CHAPTER EIGHT

DRYING UP THE WEST

A LARGE PIECE OF central and western North America is naturally desert or semi-desert, something obvious to anyone who has watched the dry and dusty setting of many a cowboy movie. Over the past century persistent settlers have defied that harsh climate, which can wipe out fortunes with a sudden drought and a spate of windstorms. In large areas farmers have partly insulated themselves from the climate by irrigating the dry but fertile ground. Farmers in parts of the U.S. southwest have literally made the desert bloom into rich farmland by flooding it with water pumped from underground or diverted from distant rivers.

The heartland of this arid region is the North American grasslands, a vast area stretching from the centre of our Prairie provinces, down almost to the Gulf of Mexico and from the Rocky Mountains east toward the Mississippi River. It has long been a land of periodic severe droughts, including one between 1200 and 1500 that transformed forests into grasslands, replaced deer with bison and wiped out the Mill Creek Indian farming culture in what is now Iowa. When white explorers rode across the dry prairies in the nineteenth century they warned that it was an inhospitable land for settlement and they called it The Great American Desert. In 1857 Captain John Palliser, a British explorer and big-game hunter, crossed what is now the Canadian Prairies. He later declared that a large, pie-shaped area, reaching north from the U.S. border and stretching from Manitoba to Alberta and including most of what would become southern Saskatchewan, was unfit for settlement. This zone of low rainfall and hot, dry and windy summers has been called the Palliser Triangle. To the south, geologist-explorer John Wesley Powell surveyed the semi-arid land in the United States and issued a similar warning to prospective settlers.

But land speculators and railway agents renamed the region The Great Plains and waves of immigrants seeking homesteads of their own broke the prairie sod to carve out farms where the buffalo once roamed. Western farmers have faced five great droughts from the 1880s to the 1970s, including the dustbowl conditions of the Dirty Thirties, when drought and winds combined with the economic Great Depression to drive thousands from the land in both Canada and the United States. But each time farmers stuck it out or came back, living for the good years when a decent rainfall would create great fields of rich crops. While most of the Canadian Prairies still rely on dryland farming and natural rainfall, an important number of farms in Canada and many more in the United States now depend on irrigation water. As a result of using that water to the limit and beyond, the farmers are facing current or future shortages in sections of three of the world's great breadbaskets: the Canadian Prairies and the U.S. High Plains just to the south, and the Central Valley of California.

There are 145 000 Canadian Prairie farmers, one-half of all the farmers in Canada and 98 per cent of our wheat farmers. The region holds 246 000 of the country's 310 000 square kilometres of farmland. To understand water in the Canadian Prairies you have to understand the rivers, and the key word is variability. Almost 90 per cent of Prairie water flows off the eastern slopes of the Rocky Mountains, mainly during the spring melt. It dashes eastward towards Hudson Bay, then it is gone. In midsummer when the need is greatest, the rivers run slow, low and muddy. On top of that there is a tremendous fluctuation of river levels from year to year, depending on how much snow fell, how quickly it melted and what rains fell during the summer. Even the South Saskatchewan, the biggest river on the prairies, has only one-seventh the annual flow of a major eastern Canadian river such as the Ottawa.

In the Prairies, the disparity between population and water resources is the greatest in Canada with most people living in the southerly band of farms, not far from the U.S. border, and most of the water in the north. Alberta watches 87 per cent of its water flow to the Arctic Ocean while most of the demand for it is in the south, and that demand is growing. In a ratio guaranteed to cause problems, the Prairies and parts of southern British Columbia already produce half the nation's crops with only four per cent of Canada's water. Farming in the dry west has always been a risky business and crop losses due to drought have been estimated at $50 million a year. In the drought years of 1984 and 1985 they were estimated in the $1 billion range. Because of the great variability of the climate many farmers used to plan on getting by with one good crop in three, but this is no longer practical for many in a day of high interest rates and constant bank payments.

As a result more and more farmers and western government planners see irrigation as the answer. It is expensive but virtually guarantees a crop that is four to six times as abundant as a dryland crop watered only by sparse and intermittent rains. Irrigation also allows the planting of such thirsty crops as soft wheat, sugar beets, alfalfa hay and vegetables in areas where they would not normally survive. Western Canada has irrigated 5 400 square kilometres of farmland, with almost 90 per cent of that in Alberta and most of that

The centre pivot irrigation system has opened up vast areas of dry land for farming but it has also drained large amounts of underground water faster than it can be replenished by nature.   (MICHAEL KEATING)

centred around the southern city of Lethbridge. Irrigation dates back to the late 1880s, when land companies and railways put in their own water supply canals to attract settlers. A century of expansion has laced that part of Alberta with 10 000 kilometres of canals, some of which rival local rivers in size. To the east, in Saskatchewan, irrigation is only starting to reach serious proportions, thanks to the Gardiner Dam on the South Saskatchewan River, which created Lake Diefenbaker, smack in the middle of the dry prairies. This provided a stable reservoir of water from which farmers can draw during the dry summers.

Such reservoirs are necessary because irrigation farming is responsible for 60 per cent of the water consumption in Canada and most of that is in the Prairies. Consumption refers to water that is taken from lakes and rivers and not returned after it is used. Irrigation draws vast quantities of water and spreads it on fields. Some of the water evaporates into the sky to fall far away as rain, some transpires from plant leaves and is evaporated, some becomes part of the crop, which is shipped elsewhere as food, and some seeps into the ground. It is often a very inefficient process, with estimates that on average 40 per cent of the water does not reach the plants. Irrigation could expand dramatically on the Prairies if there were more water in the rivers, with some officials estimating that 10 times as much land could be irrigated if the water could be found. But the water is not there and even now there are years when some rivers run nearly dry and farmers cannot get the water supplies they need.

Farmers are not the only ones bidding for the scarce western water resources. Western provinces, seeking to diversify their economies to be less reliant on the vagaries of droughts and agricultural markets, are trying to attract more industrial development. Many of their growth plans call for industries that consume vast amounts of water. These include huge plants to extract more oil from the ground, potash mines, coal-burning power plants that need large amounts of cooling water and food-processing factories that need lots of pure water. Alberta's oil sands contain more petroleum than the entire proven conventional oil reserves of the Persian Gulf and already the oil sands account for 10 per cent of Canada's oil production. That so-called heavy oil can only be recovered with the aid of large amounts of water. The oil industry also needs water to flood old, conventional wells, and float some of the remaining oil to the surface. These processes both consume and pollute water with oily residues, making it unfit for other uses.

Burning coal to generate electricity also puts a heavy load on local supplies because water is needed for cooling purposes. For example in the 1970s Saskatchewan built the Poplar River power plant along the river of that name, to take advantage of large coal deposits just north of the Montana border. But so far the province has only built two of four planned generating units because there is so little water in the river and Montana does not want any more of the flow reduced. Now Saskatchewan is looking west to the Estevan area where lignite coal fields could be used and the Souris River might be dammed, creating a narrow, 130-kilometre-long lake to provide a basin of cooling water.

More and more, the small water reserves will impose limits to growth on the Prairie economies. For example water in the west, or the lack of it, will play a pivotal role in the success or failure of the federal agriculture strategy, which calls for Canada to double its food production between 1980 and 2000. In fact water is already rationed on more than a dozen southern Prairie rivers, forcing planners to consider building more dams to trap the spring runoff. As more water is withdrawn from the rivers for agriculture and industry, less remains to supply drinking water, dilute sewage, provide for recreation and create a home for fish and other wildlife. Parts of four river basins are already reaching their limits. In dry years there is not enough water for all the demands now on the Milk and St. Mary rivers, which run along the Alberta-Montana border, on parts of the North and South Saskatchewan rivers, the major watercourses which sweep across the Prairies, and on the Red-Assiniboine river system in Manitoba. The Okanagan Valley of the southern British Columbia interior is really an extension of the semi-arid lands to the south and several years ago it appeared the region might have to divert water in from the north. So far it is making do with water from Okanagan Lake. One federal water expert said that at the current rate of irrigation expansion, Alberta has a 10-year supply and Saskatchewan a 20-year one. After that there are two options. One is to stop development. The other—political and economic dynamite—is to divert north-flowing rivers to the south.

One of the issues which will grow in importance in the west is water pollution. Shallow Prairie rivers have little water to dilute wastes and pollution from Edmonton has been tracked as far away as eastern Saskatchewan. Small Prairie lakes and ponds are prone to turn soupy with green algae anyway but a heavy runoff of farm fertilizers is accelerating this process of eutrophication, creating a thousand miniature Lake Eries, each becoming clogged with vegetation as a result of overfertilization. Algal pollution has long been a sore point with Regina and Moose Jaw residents, who complained of having the foulest-tasting, smelliest water in Canada. They draw their water from a shallow lake called Buffalo Pound, which becomes a giant algal bowl in the summer sun. Many residents pushed for a $130-million pipeline to bring "real water" directly from Lake Diefenbaker, more than 100 kilometres northwest of Regina. This was too pricey for governments which, in 1985, put a $142-million granular activated carbon filtration system in the water treatment plant to remove most of the objectionable taste and odor from Buffalo Pound water.

Prairie wildlife is also suffering from the competition for water. Western wetlands were once among the richest in the world but they are disappearing at a terrific pace. Prairie potholes, the breeding grounds of 70 per cent of the continent's ducks, covered 750 000 square kilometres before the start of agriculture a century ago. Studies by the Canadian Wildlife Service show that Manitoba, Saskatchewan and Alberta have lost from 27 to 61 per cent of their wetlands and the remaining marshes and swamps are being drained and turned into farmland at the rate of 11 to 21 per cent a year. In addition as much as three-quarters of the crucial wetland margins, where ducks nest and hide from predators, are being ploughed under in the human quest for ever more farmland. The combination of recent droughts, the disappearance of wetlands and heavy hunting in the United States sent the 1985 fall duck migration plunging to the lowest levels in this century. We know even less about the effects of changes in the natural water regime on fish and can only roughly estimate how much water aquatic life needs to exist, even as we lower river levels. We do know that dams block fish migration routes and reduce the flushing action of spring floods. This flushing normally removes pollution and provides a gush of water for spawning fish, water laden with nutrients from upstream.

In western Canada, irrigation has generally been restricted to areas where rivers flow and this water must be transported through expensive canal systems. By comparison large U.S. areas have generous underground water reserves which can be tapped with relative ease. As one envious Canadian irrigation expert said, many a U.S. farmer can get up in the morning and simply decide to sink a well to irrigate the farm. However, that advantage is proving short-lived in many areas. While Canadian rivers will keep flowing indefinitely, a growing number of U.S. farmers are pumping up their underground water faster than it is being replenished, a situation called mining or overdrafting. In other parts of the U.S. west, the rivers have been over-allocated and customers are having their water rationed in dry years.

Across the western United States more and more people are competing for less and less water. That water is dammed, pumped and canalized until Texas cattle can feed on corn grown on the semi-desert High Plains and on alfalfa grown on what were true deserts in southern California. The High Plains, an area from Nebraska south into Texas, are made arable with water pumped from the ground, while California's deserts bloom with water diverted across sand dunes from the Colorado River or from northern rivers or pumped from wells. It is ironic that New Jersey, with a generous rainfall, boasts on its licence plates that it is the Garden State but California and Texas, two of the driest states, have become first- and second-ranked agricultural producers because of overdrafting their ground water. At the same time New Jersey has become one of the most polluted states, thanks to industry which has dumped large amounts of hazardous chemicals that threaten water supplies.

It is the rapid expansion of cities and industries which often have the image of straining the water resources of the west and southwest but it is farming which uses most of the water. This strip of warm-weather states, from Florida to California, which has been growing rapidly as so-called snowbirds migrate from the northern states and Canada, has been dubbed the Sun Belt. Over the last few decades millions of new settlers have been lured south from the cold but wet northeast, bringing with them water-hungry industries, farms and the demand for swimming pools, golf courses and green lawns. This has changed the face of some states such as Texas, which long had the image of being cowboy country but is in transition, becoming an urban society fuelled by oil, gas and microelectronics industries such as Texas Instruments.

Perhaps the best known of the Sun Belt states is California, which has the population of Canada on one-twentieth the surface. California is two diverse environments tied together by politics: the north has two-thirds of the water and the dry south two-thirds of the population. It is more than Disneyland that makes California a fantasy. The real wonderland is in the vast, irrigated farms sitting on former deserts, and the huge cities built with water carried hundreds of kilometres and pumped over mountain ranges. Just north of the Mexican border lies the Imperial Valley, an example of what the world's greatest plumbing system has done. At the southeast corner are sand dunes where Hollywood often films its African desert sequences. Spanish army captain Juan Bautista de Anza crossed this desert two centuries ago in what he called the "journey of death." Now, slashing through that desert like a mirage, is the All American Canal, a thin blue artery tying the dry but fertile Imperial Valley to the Colorado River. What was once a valley of death is now sprouting with life. The Imperial Irrigation District, 2 000 square kilometres of irrigated land, is the largest single irrigation district in the Western Hemisphere. It drinks through a 1 500-kilometre-long network of canals and excretes through 50 000 kilometres of drainage tiles. Lettuce planted here in October will be on Canadian tables in the dead of winter. Just to the north, the Coachella Valley blooms with groves of date palms, orange, grapefruit and tangerine trees and grapevines. And on its northern fringe sits Palm Springs, home of golf tournaments and a symbol of human determination in its efforts to transplant a game conceived in the wet foggy Highlands of Scotland to what was once just a water hole in the California desert. It is a city where sprinklers hold the desert at bay and where there are more swimming pools per capita than in any other U.S. city.

To the west, across the San Jacinto Mountains, lies the dry, coastal plain of smoggy Los Angeles, an agglomeration of communities that outgrew their local rivers and wells by the turn of the century and now import two-thirds of their water. Three great canal systems are lifelines keeping the area from reverting to its natural desert state. The Colorado River Aqueduct reaches out 400 kilometres to that overtaxed river and the Los Angeles Aqueduct stretches 500 kilometres northeast over the Sierra Nevada Mountains to the Owens Valley and Mono Lake. The California Aqueduct carries water more than 700 kilometres south along the Pacific coast, starting in the San Joaquin-Sacramento Delta, just east of San Francisco. Along the way that water must be pumped 600 metres up over the Tehachapi Mountains, 10 times the height of Niagara Falls and the greatest lift of its kind in the world.

California's other huge farming district is the Central Valley— running between San Francisco in the north and Los Angeles in the south. Though rainfall averages only one-quarter of that in New

Jersey, the land is lush. With the intensive overuse of underground sources and massive water diversions from northern California, farmers irrigate 32 000 square kilometres of land, an area nearly six times the size of Prince Edward Island. In total California has 40 000 square kilometres of irrigated farmland, some of which produces three or four crops a year. To the east, Texas is the number-two farm state, again largely because of irrigation and excessive use of underground water reserves which are vanishing much faster than nature replaces them.

Even Arizona, drier than California, is a major farm state, in total defiance of its desert climate and its original Indian name, Arizonac, meaning "little spring." In a land suited to a few cows eating wild grasses, farmers irrigate 5 000 square kilometres of crops such as cotton, alfalfa hay and pecans with ever-scarcer water pumped from underground. In fact 90 per cent of the water used in the state is drawn from diminishing underground sources for farm irrigation. Over the past couple of decades Arizona has changed its ecology to such a degree that it is losing its prized status of a haven for allergy sufferers. There used to be so few allergy-producing plants that hay fever victims moved to Arizona for the clean air, but so many immigrants planted pollen-producing lawns, gardens and trees that the air is no longer allergen free in many parts of the state.

Over the past 15 years Arizona's population has grown 50 per cent to the current three million, including many who yearn for watery symbols in the desert. Now Phoenix, the state capital, boasts that it has the world's tallest fountain, spouting 170 metres into the sky, the height of a 50-storey skyscraper. And in another burst of hubris the city claims the world's first authentic inland surfing centre: Big Surf. It says the mechanically driven waves in "Arizona's ocean on the desert" are more reliable than those on the real ocean, far to the west.

Now Arizona is running short of water and joining the raid on the Colorado River. For centuries that river has wound its way south on a 2 500-kilometre journey from the high mountains of Colorado to the bay that is called the Gulf of California or the Sea of Cortez, depending on whether you are in the United States or Mexico. For most of its life the river was totally unimpeded by humans as it cascaded down the mountains, carved through the Grand Canyon and sprawled across the desert towards the salt sea. But over the last century this river has become one of the most over-used in the world and it now supplies water and hydro-electric power for 20 million people, more than half the population served by the infinitely larger Great Lakes. Now the

Colorado's profile looks like a giant snake that swallowed a bunch of watermelons. It starts as a small creek then grows into a large river, but 10 big dams along the way create huge bulges which have become the largest lakes in the southwest. At the same time it is drained by hundreds of diversion pipes and canals to irrigate nearly 14 000 square kilometres of farmland. By the time it reaches Mexico the snake has slimmed down to as little as 10 per cent of its historic flow, the minimum amount of water guaranteed to Mexico by treaty. Once Mexican farmers have taken water for their own irrigation, the mouth of the river is often just a dry strip of land, dampened only when rainstorms upstream send down more water than can be captured by the dams.

The second major water source in the west lies underground in the form of reserves called aquifers, the equivalent of hidden lakes. The largest of them all, in fact the largest in the world, is the Ogallala Aquifer, a vast resource underlying 460 000 square kilometres of the Great Plains region. The aquifer is a layer of sand, gravel and silt averaging 60 metres in thickness, with the spaces between stones filled with water. In profile it looks like a shallow dish of stones and water tilted on its side. To the north, in Nebraska, the water-saturated layer is thick but to the south, in Texas, it is very shallow and parts already have been virtually drained. The aquifer lay underground, untouched since the retreating glaciers sent meltwaters surging across the continent 12 000 years ago. Every year since then, sparse rains add a bit more water to this storehouse.

Before 1930 the aquifer was virtually untapped, as most of this land was used only for cattle grazing and dryland farming. But the great drought of 1930–39 wiped out many of the farmers and after that they started drilling into the Ogallala for irrigation water, pumping up this priceless reserve the way they pumped oil. The aquifer underlies eight states and now is an important factor in the economies of six: Texas, New Mexico, Oklahoma, Kansas, Colorado and Nebraska. It supports one-fifth of the irrigated cropland in the United States and was watering 65 000 square kilometres of farmland by 1978, the peak year. The Ogallala region is a key part of the U.S. economy. It produces about one-quarter of the U.S. food, including a large share of the fresh fruits and vegetables found in major U.S. cities. For example it produces 40 per cent of the fed beef in the United States, cattle kept in pens and fattened for slaughter. It is the source of 40 per cent of the grain sorghum, 30 per cent of the upland cotton, 20 per cent of the alfalfa hay, 15 per cent of the corn and 10 per cent of the wheat. A study several years ago said that this was worth $15 billion a year.

All this wealth is produced at a huge cost in water. More than 160 000 wells suck 34.5 cubic kilometres of water from the ground every year, twice the annual flow of the Colorado River, and only one-tenth of that is replaced by nature. Already 500 cubic kilometres of water have been taken out and hydrogeologists estimate that the aquifer is one-half depleted under 9 000 square kilometres of Texas, Kansas and New Mexico. Wells are running dry in some areas or the remaining water is just too deep to draw up for irrigation at a reasonable cost. The Ogallala provides 95 per cent of the irrigation water in its region and there is no replacement for that aquifer in this land of ephemeral streams, some of which evaporate before they ever reach a river. A senior Texas political aide said that growing irrigated crops like corn on the High Plains has been a "freak of nature" that may have to be abandoned or at least modified. A 1982 study of the Ogallala warned that falling water levels foretell "a potential reduction in the agricultural production capacity that has contributed substantially to both feeding and clothing" the United States.

The draining of the Ogallala is symptomatic of serious water depletion across the U.S. west, a situation which will force change. Parts of the west are still budgeting for between 70 and 200 per cent more water than will be available in the future. Large farms in Arizona are already being closed as cities outbid them for the scarce water, and in west Texas land is being returned to semi-desert rangeland as water becomes too expensive to keep pumping it for crops. Between 1978 and 1982 irrigation was reduced on 6 700 square kilometres of land in Arizona, Kansas, New Mexico, Oklahoma and Texas. The drop was most severe in Texas, where 20 per cent of irrigated land was affected.

The plight of people who overuse their water resources is not always greeted with offers of more water. Those who live outside Los Angeles tend to look at the three great canals to that city as three great greedy tentacles, reaching out for their water. Since 1913 Los Angeles has been drying up the Owens Valley and more recently extended the pipeline north to Owens Lake, which it has sucked down by 10 metres, threatening to destroy its environment. For example, islands where birds could nest undisturbed are now connected to the mainland and are accessible to predators. Southern California is also losing water from the Colorado River, thanks to a 1963 U.S. Supreme Court decision which awarded some of the water traditionally taken by

California to Arizona instead. Arizona is only starting to take advantage of that decision, since its own canal to the river was not opened until 1985.

Southern California estimates it has enough water to last through the decade at projected rates of demand and population growth but after that "it is getting to crisis engineering," says one senior state official. There are big rivers in northern California and the California Aqueduct could carry twice as much water south from them, but further water diversions have been held up by regional splits and partisan politics.

Arizona is now paying the price of being the state with the greatest over-use of its underground water. North of Phoenix the water table has dropped as much as 100 metres, causing the surface of the land above to sag as much as five metres. In some areas the earth is cracking open, causing fissures in highways, train derailments, cracked buildings and dislocated natural gas pipelines. Faced with a precipitous drop in water, Arizona lobbied for and got a $3.5-billion federal lifeline from the Colorado River. The Central Arizona Project, a 500-kilometre-long canal visible from the space shuttle, reaches first to Phoenix and later will be extended to Tucson. Even that artificial river will only compensate for one-half the overdraft of ground water, so the state must economize radically. In return for the canal the U.S. government exacted a water conservation plan that, although stringent by comparison with most states, still will not bring Arizona into balance with its water resources for 40 years. The key to the plan is eliminating irrigation on more and more farmland and ploughing the water into less-thirsty, higher-paying industrial or housing developments. Once more, tumbleweed rolls across what, briefly, were croplands.

Texas, which faces severe shortages in the west and north, considered a $2-billion plan to divert water from the Mississippi River clear across Arkansas, then across Texas, as far as New Mexico. This so upset Arkansas that it passed a law saying that water could not be removed from that state in amounts larger than a bucketful. In any case Texans decided the project was too big even for them and they have decided to live within their means. In some cases that decision will let irrigated farmland go back to dry ranchland. In others it means trying to irrigate with less water, or planting salt-tolerant crops like cotton so they can use brackish underground water which would kill most other plants. Like Arizona, Texas faces problems from dropping ground levels, caused by the removal of water underneath. Land within a 60-kilometre radius of Houston has sagged almost three metres and the houses of astronauts, along with those of the earth-bound, are slowly sinking.

It is not only the draining of aquifers and rivers that is threatening the water resources. Western water quality is often marginal at best and in a number of places is barely acceptable for long-term human consumption because of high natural levels of trace metals, dissolved solids and salts. An addition of pollution from industry or agriculture does not have to be large to push it over the edge. Pollution is a serious problem, especially when there is much less water to dilute wastes than, say, in the Great Lakes. In California and Arizona orange groves, pesticides suspected of causing cancer and sterility in humans have seeped into the underground water. The same thing is happening around some industries, as chemicals, particularly the metal-cleaning solvents such as trichloroethylene (TCE), percolate down as much as 100 metres through the sandy soils. This type of pollution has been found around Silicon Valley, the home of the computer chip industry near San Francisco. One of the nastier cases to surface is the discovery that about 20 000 Tucson residents have been drinking TCE in their well water for as long as 30 years, apparently the legacy of chemicals dumped at a nearby airport. Large amounts of TCE were sprayed on aircraft to clean them and the chemicals percolated down into the water. TCE has been suggested as a possible cause for an apparent outbreak of illness that has left a number of young people stricken with such afflictions as brain tumors.

Salinization is an unpleasant side effect in a number of irrigation areas. It is a process in which excess irrigation water lying in the soil dissolves natural salts in the upper layer of the earth and floats them to the surface. When the water evaporates, the salt is left behind as a dry, white crust which sterilizes the land, making it unfit for any crops unless it is removed. In a number of areas farmers install drainage tiles to flush the salts away but this extracts another price, particularly when the drainage runoff also includes pesticides and fertilizers. A former senior U.S. wildlife official in California said that polluted irrigation water draining from the farms of the Central Valley had caused "unparalleled destruction" of migratory birds and fish in the region and "turned the San Joaquin River into the lower colon of California—a stinking sewer."

Already the west faces the growing spectre of spreading water shortages. This could be made dramatically worse by two events, one natural and the other caused by an unexpected form of air pollution. The first threat is the prediction of natural climate fluctuation. A 1984 Canadian study paper on world deserts stated that some researchers believe droughts lasting two centuries occur every 550 to 600 years on the western plains. If this is correct the region is due for another drought like the one which wiped out the Mill Creek culture. The second threat is the so-called greenhouse effect, in which air pollutants such as carbon dioxide and other industrial gases collect in the atmosphere, gradually raising Earth's temperature, just like the temperature in a greenhouse. This effect is predicted to start within 15 years and gradually will make western North America even warmer and drier. It could turn large tracts of farmland from semi-deserts into true deserts and the terrible droughts of 1984 and 1985 on parts of the Prairies could become the norm.

Richard Thomas, a senior official of the Canada-U.S. International Joint Commission on boundary waters, said that if the climate change turns out to have severe effects on the U.S. west, the rainfall runoff to some already heavily used western rivers could be reduced by between 40 to 70 per cent and water shortages could be devastating. Mr. Thomas said that at the extreme, this could provoke the "decline or collapse of North American society."

With such predictions, farmers must be asking themselves, is there only dust at the end of the rainbow?

In the face of declining water reserves, they are looking for alternatives. One, which has been debated for years, is the diversion of water from the great northern rivers of the continent. John Carroll, a University of New Hampshire specialist on Canada-U.S. environmental relations, has predicted that Oklahoma, Kansas, Texas and New Mexico "will become panicky" as they use up the Ogallala Aquifer. "They are starting to look north." But the costs of water diversions are stupendous and a number of people are promoting water conservation as the alternative, saying there is enough water for many years if it is used wisely. These issues will be dealt with in future chapters.

CHAPTER NINE

CLIMATE CHANGE: DRYING US UP

WITHIN THE NEXT half-century we are likely to begin the greatest climatic upheaval of the 10 000 years or so over which civilization has evolved. There appears to be scientific consensus that the planet is heading for a warming trend virtually unprecedented since the last ice age, that it will be caused by forms of air pollution and that no one is sure how to stop it. The prediction from national and international climate experts, including the World Meteorological Organization, is that the average temperature of the globe will increase by 1.5 to 4.5 degrees Celsius by as soon as 2030, and the first effects will likely be felt within the next 15 years. This increase may not seem much compared to the fluctuations in temperature even on a typical day but it threatens to be an upheaval in our global weather patterns and the planetary water balance. Scientists calculate that there will be major changes in rain and snowfall patterns and in the amount of water that is evaporated back into the sky from various regions before it runs to the sea. This will wreak drastic changes in agriculture, forestry, navigation, power generation, drinking water quality and the environment in general. The change is predicted to further dry up the great breadbaskets of Canada's Prairies and the U.S. Great Plains, areas which already suffer periodic droughts. Similar disruptions of major food sources are predicted in other parts of the world and this could shift the global balance of power, an issue already being studied by some intelligence services. The African drought and subsequent famine have given us a taste of what can happen when there is no longer enough water to sustain normal life. There are other political implications, such as the reduction in arctic ice—which could open the north to both commercial and military shipping—and the eventual possibility that melting icecaps will raise the oceans and flood coastlines around the planet.

In the long term our climate has been highly variable, even during the past 10 000 years since the last ice age ended. During the mid-Holocene period, about 5 000 to 7 000 years ago, the average global temperature appears to have been about 1.5 to 2 degrees Celsius warmer than at present. Then there was a longer growing season in Alaska, parts of Canada and northern Europe, all of which are now marginal for agriculture. It was also much drier in what are now the major wheat and corn belts of the U.S. midwest and Great Plains and the Soviet Union, and the forests of Minnesota, Illinois and Missouri retreated as the prairies spread northward. There was moderately more precipitation in what are now the Sahara, Arabian and Kalahari deserts and across Australia. Much of Eurasia was also drier and the Caspian Sea was much smaller than today.

This was followed by a cooler and wetter period that corresponds to the Iron Age and that reached its chilliest peak more than 2 000 years ago, allowing great, dark forests to spread southwards in Europe. Again the climate rebounded into a warmer period, which peaked in the early Middle Ages, about 800 to 1 000 years ago. Although summer temperatures averaged only 1 degree warmer than now in North America and Europe, it was possible to grow crops at much higher latitudes. This was the period when Norse explorers sailed across the relatively warmer and ice-free north Atlantic to found farming colonies on Iceland, Greenland and North America, notably at L'Anse aux Meadows on the northern tip of Newfoundland. The warm period came to a brutal end with the onset of the Little Ice Age, which lasted from the 1400s into the early 1800s and was severe enough some winters to freeze the Thames River. During this big chill, the Viking colonies retreated from North America and Greenland as permafrost increased its grip on farmland and ice once more choked the northern sea routes. Again it took only a 1-degree change in the global average temperature but this time it was a drop. Since about 1880 the world has warmed up again and the interval from about 1910 to 1960 has been the mildest half-century of any in the past millennium.

The climate that permits life as we know it on this planet is governed by a number of factors, including the distance from the sun and the state of that thin, clear envelope of air that we call the atmosphere. Less than one per cent of the gases, principally carbon dioxide (CO_2), in that atmosphere play a crucial role in maintaining Earth's heat balance. They regulate the amount of sunlight which reaches the planet's surface, and the amount of heat which can escape back into space. For the first time in history, human activity is capable of upsetting the natural equilibrium to the point where the world appears perched on the edge of another momentous climate shift. There is scientific consensus that certain forms of air pollution are able to block partially the escape of heat from Earth and that the amount of these gases, especially CO_2, is increasing in the atmosphere above us at an unprecedented rate, thanks to air pollution.

Carbon dioxide is what gives fizz to soft drinks, beer and bubbly mineral water. We have been taught in school that CO_2 is an odorless, colorless and virtually harmless gas, but in the atmosphere it behaves like a one-way mirror. It lets much of the sun's ultra-violet light and heat continue to reach Earth, but it traps some of the infrared wavelength heat normally radiated from the planet's surface into space. Without CO_2 and certain other gases in the sky, too much heat would escape from the planet and the temperature would plunge to levels which would freeze all water and life. The action of CO_2 and some other "greenhouse gases" has been compared to that of a glass greenhouse, which traps the sun's heat and allows us to grow tomatoes and delicate flowers in cold, northern climates. Until now the amount of CO_2 in the sky has been governed by natural processes, including volcanoes, which release the gas, and plants, which absorb the gas and convert it to living matter. Since the industrial revolution we have been setting the stage for a major change in the natural balance by burning increasing amounts of fossil fuels like wood, coal, oil and gas, which suddenly release their carbon back into the sky. We now inject five billion tonnes a year of carbon into the atmosphere and an estimated three billion tonnes stay up there while the rest is apparently absorbed by living matter, possibly plankton in the oceans, and land plants.

As carbon dioxide levels build, less and less heat will escape, thus raising global temperatures and changing the weather and the climate as we now know it. The predicted warming has been dubbed the greenhouse effect. At first the effect was linked almost solely to increasing levels of CO_2 but recent calculations indicate that other industrial gases, particularly chlorofluorocarbons (CFCs), have an even greater heat-blocking effect and enough of them are escaping to have as much impact as CO_2 alone. These CFCs are used as aerosol

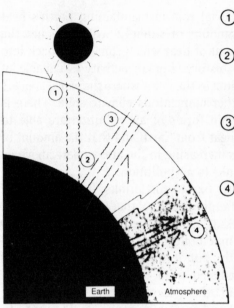

① Solar energy enters the atmosphere (unimpeded by CO_2).

② Light is absorbed by the earth. It is reradiated at longer heat wavelengths, some of which are captured by CO_2; the others escape into space.

③ At the normal atmospheric CO_2 level the quantity of light and heat escaping into space determines the earth's temperature and climate.

④ Higher concentrations of CO_2 trap more reradiated heat. Atmospheric and surface temperatures increase, affecting weather and climate.

Earth   Atmosphere   Space

The "Greenhouse Effect".

(ENVIRONMENT CANADA)

propellants in some spray cans, as refrigerator fluids and in the manufacture of industrial foams. Each time one of those spray cans is used, each time a refrigerator or air conditioner leaks or is scrapped and each time foams are produced in factories, more of these very light gases escape and migrate into the atmosphere.

As the gas levels increase and more of the heat that normally escapes into space is trapped in the lower levels of the atmosphere and radiated back to the ground, global temperatures will slowly rise. The smallest temperature increase will be felt near the equator and the greatest at high latitudes, such as the northern reaches of Canada, Europe and the Soviet Union. In the far north the effects are predicted to be most noticeable in the late fall and winter, which means January in cities like Yellowknife and Whitehorse might be as much as seven degrees warmer than at present. The effects could be dramatic and often welcome. Heating costs would decrease and there would be a longer summer travel period. Ice seasons would be shorter and the ice thinner, possibly resulting in ice-free arctic summers in the Canadian

Archipelago, and a Northwest Passage open to ship traffic for a good part of the year. This will be a boon to oil and gas exploration, promising less damage to oil rigs in the Beaufort Sea and lengthening the time in which supplies can be shipped in and oil taken out by tanker. Easier navigation for normal ships could change military strategies by allowing warships and commercial ships from many nations to penetrate this zone. This would further test Canada's claim to national sovereignty in the Arctic Archipelago.

There would also be a major change in the northern environment, including an estimated 20 to 30 per cent increase in precipitation in what is now a frozen desert. This would put more water in northern rivers and more snow tires on northerners' cars. The absence of sea ice is predicted to increase the severity of storms, and the greater winter snowfall, combined with more summer melting, would increase the production of icebergs in the eastern Arctic. A temperature rise would restart the northern march of the tree line, which was 100 kilometres farther north during the warm period 1 000 years ago.

In the temperate mid-latitudes, which include much of Canada, virtually all of the United States, and much of Europe and the Soviet Union, the climate will probably be warmer and drier. There may be increases in rain in some regions but this could be more than offset by greater evaporation of water back into the sky. Several climate experts have said that southern Canada may experience more winters like that of 1982–83, which was several degrees warmer than usual. That winter was so mild that it was almost snowless in southern Ontario, saving millions of dollars in snow removal but costing many jobs in winter recreation. It was followed by a wet spring, then a hot, dry summer which reduced Ontario's usual $2.5-billion farm crop by 25 per cent. In a few decades Toronto may have weather now typical of St. Louis, Missouri, or Nashville, Tennessee, while northern Ontario and the Prairies could inherit Toronto's slushy but relatively milder winters. In the winter it will take less fuel to heat homes but in the summer there will be greater demand for air conditioning, which will require more electricity. Southern Canada might also experience some of the wilder weather of more southerly latitudes, including hurricanes, tornadoes and flash floods. The Prairies are predicted to get much warmer, so they are likely to experience even more droughts like the disastrous years of 1984 and 1985. British Columbia might become wetter than it is now, increasing the risk of mudslides, avalanches and flooding. In the Ukraine and central Asia hot, dry winds will sweep out of the mountains of Afghanistan to shrivel the crops, forcing agriculture farther north into more marginal soil types.

Tropical latitudes are likely to get more rainfall but higher transpiration by plants and evaporation by the sun means that they could face a net loss in usable water. If so, this means that already marginal lands like the Sahel belt, which stretches across Africa south of the Sahara, will become drier and the desert will spread. On a continent that is now chronically short of food and has a rapidly expanding population, the effects could be catastrophic.

The warming will also have effects on the seas. When the oceans warm up they will gradually swell, as a result of the same heat expansion effect that makes a pot boil over. This rising water level will be augmented by melting glaciers, leading to a sea level rise of 50 to 100 centimetres in the next century. Over a much longer period, possibly 200 to 500 years, there is a risk that the gigantic West Antarctic Icecap will collapse into the seas, causing them to rise five to seven metres. This could flood parts of coastal cities like Vancouver, Victoria, Charlottetown, Halifax, New York, Washington, London, Leningrad, Stockholm, Calcutta and Singapore, leaving them looking like Venice. Prince Edward Island could be split into as many as four islands and most of Florida could vanish beneath the waves, becoming a modern-day Atlantis. One-third of the Netherlands and parts of Louisiana and Bangladesh could be submerged.

While people in coastal areas may start building dykes and seawalls to hold back ever higher tides and storm waves, the continental interiors will face growing water shortages. In some parts of central North America rainfall could be reduced by 40 to 70 per cent, while in others any increase in rainfall may be lost to the warmer air. This means more droughts and less water in the rivers to irrigate crops. Major changes in water levels in the grain belts of Canada and the United States would have a tremendous economic and social impact. They would be felt both in these countries and around a world that now depends on these breadbaskets for a large part of its food. One prediction said that Saskatchewan could have up to a 37-per-cent decrease in spring wheat yield and a significant increase in the already-serious wind erosion, because there will be less moisture to hold the soil in place. This could mean drastic shifts in Prairie agriculture, with some cropland becoming too dry for anything but occasional farming and grazing. The corn belt would shift northwards into Wisconsin, Minnesota and southern Canada, where, because of soil types, yields would be lower. Agricultural productivity in the United States could fall dramatically if, just to pick one example, corn were not available to support the cattle feeder industry which now relies on that crop. If things get too dry much of the U.S. west could resemble the Saharan fringes. The soil would still be rich but the air would be so hot and dry that only a few crops like millet, lentils and sorghum could be grown. Instead of being a major world food exporter, the United States could have a problem just feeding itself. To make matters worse, the dry period would coincide with a major decline in underground water resources such as the Ogallala Aquifer, which is now being over-pumped across a huge part of the western farm belt. Already rivers like the Colorado are stretched to the limit and states are squabbling over future water rights.

Canada's southern Prairies face a very uncertain future but the area does have some room to expand. As the present fringes of farmland warmed up, farmers could push north for some distance but they will be stopped by the rugged Canadian shield, particularly in Manitoba and Saskatchewan. To the east the warmer climate might mean that parts of northern Ontario, including the clay belt of the Hudson Bay lowlands, could be farmed. In the northern territories a longer warm season, combined with the midnight sun of midsummer, could produce some spectacular crops where there is fertile land. It is predicted that growing conditions around Yellowknife, Whitehorse and Fort Simpson will approach those now found around Edmonton and farming will improve in the valleys on the Peace and Liard rivers of Alberta and the Northwest Territories.

The Great Lakes region would face serious changes in a drier climate, because water levels would tumble at the same time that a burgeoning population would increase its demand for water. There are predictions that the outflow of water from the lakes to the St. Lawrence River could drop by as much as 15 to 28 per cent, when one combines the reduction in available water with increases in demand. This could result in a drop of as much as one metre in the level of the lower lakes, which would mean that the new average levels would be nearly down to their historic low points. The effects would be extensive and very expensive. For starters nearly $1 billion in power production alone would be lost every year because of less water to turn the giant turbines at Niagara Falls and the St. Lawrence River. This reduction in hydro-electricity would come at a time where there would also be heavier demand for more air conditioning. The power utilities would have to consider a number of unpalatable alternatives, including damming more northern rivers, building more nuclear power plants—which are expensive and have as yet unresolved waste disposal problems—or burning more coal, which can produce more acid rain and more CO_2 to add to the gaseous greenhouse.

Reduced water levels would dramatically affect shipping. It matters little if the open lake is one metre lower but the drop would have a big effect in the relatively shallow connecting rivers and the harbors the ships must enter to unload. Dredging costs would skyrocket and so would public concern about the many tonnes of pollutants which would be stirred up from the muds of these industrialized regions. This would present one threat to drinking water and another would come from the fact that the lakes would have less volume to dilute the pollution.

Wildlife habitats would be dramatically affected as the shoreline marshes, which are the breeding and feeding grounds for many species of fish, amphibians, birds and animals, gradually dried up. New wetland areas would probably emerge along the changing shorelines but this would be a long and disruptive process. About the only people to benefit from shoreline changes would be cottage owners, who would face less loss of property to erosion and would have wider beaches. This would be somewhat offset by the fact that marinas would be much shallower and many boat docks would be left high and dry. Shipping would likely benefit from a longer season of open water and farmers in the southern Ontario, Quebec and Maritimes regions would have longer growing seasons and could grow more delicate crops, if they could get enough water for irrigation.

What the greenhouse effect portends is a pollution issue surpassing even that of acid rain in its potential effects on our water resources and our society. Although scientists are still running complex computer models in an effort to be more precise about its details, there appears to be solid agreement that the change is coming. The only questions are exactly how fast and precisely what will happen in various corners of Earth. Most of the major predictions are based on a time when the levels of CO_2 in the atmosphere are estimated to reach double the 1900 level. A few years ago that was calculated to be between 2050 and 2070 but new calculations based on the effect of other gases, like the CFCs, has moved the target date ahead to around 2030. Since the effects will start gradually, this means that people should start noticing changes in the long-term weather by about the year 2000.

Already there is enough information about what is coming for people to start thinking and developing plans for major economic and social changes. The first and obvious one is, can we stop the greenhouse effect? When the issue became front-page news in 1983, initial reactions were that CO_2 comes from too many sources to stop it, the burning of fossil fuels is an underpinning of our modern economy and there is no technology to capture the gases. Now some planners are talking of at least delaying the effect. They say, for example, that if we decrease coal and oil use to save energy and reduce acid rain, we will also cut the amount of carbon dioxide. CFCs are not only a greenhouse gas, but they can attack ozone high in the stratosphere. High-altitude ozone is important in filtering out some of the sun's ultraviolet radiation. By cutting the escape of CFCs we can both slow the greenhouse effect and save ourselves from excessive ultra-violet radiation, which can cause skin cancer.

Assuming that the greenhouse effect is going to arrive later if not sooner, we have to plan such water-related works as canals, dams, reservoirs, bridges, harbors and hydro-electric developments like the second part of the James Bay project. These are structures planned to last for 50 to 100 years but current designs are based on historical climate and water data, which will likely not give an accurate prediction for the future. If we build based on historical data, our structures may be too big or too small for future water volumes. We may also have to plan on a whole new type of water project, such as dykes, to protect coastal cities. Farming all over the world, but especially on the Prairies, appears headed for major changes, which may start to be felt by this generation and will almost certainly have a major effect on the next one. The west will probably face a social upheaval that will make even that of the dustbowl years pale by comparison. The country will have to decide whether to subsidize farmers to stay in areas which become very dry, or pay them to move north and start again.

Forestry is a major issue, for several reasons. First, if the tree line marches north, so will the transitional zone of mixed hardwoods and conifers, and a forest industry geared to cutting and processing one type of tree could find itself facing another. On a much greater scale the already serious global deforestation will become an even bigger issue, since the cutting and burning of trees release vast quantities of CO_2 into the atmosphere while reducing the number of trees which naturally convert CO_2 into oxygen. They have another linkage to the world water balance as well: tree roots are vital in holding water in the soil and trickling it gradually into the rivers, while tree leaves release water into the air to help form rain clouds. Finally, a serious drying up of the west could increase the pressures for massive water diversion projects to bring water from the northern rivers south, both into the Canadian Prairies and the U.S. west, to provide for irrigation. The issue of water diversions will be discussed in the next two chapters.

CHAPTER TEN

DIVERSIONS: EXPORTING OUR ENVIRONMENT?

For MORE THAN A century North Americans have been defying the dry western climate and settling in areas where the rains are sparse and the rivers small and irregular. In some areas, notably the High Plains of the central United States and parts of Arizona and California, people have found water underground but they have tapped these sources so fiercely that the wells are starting to go dry. By now large farming regions are being forced to reduce irrigation and either stop planting completely or make do with the less bountiful crops which the rain will support. The bottoms of the wells and the limits of the rivers became visible two decades ago and since then people have been dreaming of grand schemes to stave off the inevitable droughts. They have talked of towing icebergs to the California coast, desalting the sea or moving water right across the continent.

It is the concept of water transfers from the wet to the dry areas of North America which has attracted the most attention and the greatest fear. Engineers have always been fascinated with the fact that drops of water falling only a few centimetres apart will run down different sides of a hill and end up in different oceans. On a continental scale they see too many rivers flowing the "wrong" way to the Arctic Ocean while millions of people who settled in warm but dry regions such as the Canadian Prairies and the U.S. southwest need more water. The engineering solution proposed involves nothing less than changing the face of the continent in a way it has not been changed since the glaciers melted, releasing cascades of water which carved many of our rivers and filled our lakes. When engineers look for water, their eyes fix on such sources as the Great Lakes, which hold 80 per cent of all

153

the lake water in North America, and on the wide and deep rivers which flow through the Canadian north. In the past two decades there have been at least a dozen major proposals to divert northern water to the drylands of western Canada and the United States through huge canal and reservoir systems, with the water lifted over mountains by immense pumps. Some of the schemes call for international projects that would take water from Canadian rivers and move it south to the United States. Others suggest that the United States simply take water from its side of the Great Lakes, leaving it unclear what, if any, compensation would be given to Canada for water taken from the lake system.

While the idea of diversions has been around for decades, the signal for their appearance on a major scale was a 1963 U.S. Supreme Court decision that southern California would have to give up some of the water it was taking from the Colorado River and let Arizona have it instead. The fear of water shortages was fuelled in the early 1960s by a major one in the U.S. northeast. It was a period when New York forbade restaurants to serve water unless patrons asked for it, swimming pools and fountains were shut, car washing and lawn watering were banned and air conditioning was limited. In some areas there was not even enough water to flush away sewage.

In 1964 Los Angeles engineer Ralph Parsons proposed solving the problems of dry areas from California to Mexico to New York by taking water from the northwest corner of the continent and diverting it across North America. This scheme, called the North American Water and Power Alliance—NAWAPA—was for years the focal point of discussions about possible water diversions, and a number of similar proposals were modelled on it. Parsons suggested a series of gigantic dams in the northern river valleys of Alaska and the Yukon. First he would reverse the flows of the Tanana and Yukon rivers in Alaska. To augment that water he would then build the world's largest dam on the headwaters of the Copper River in southern Alaska. That dam, 540 metres high, would be just a bit shorter than the CN Tower in Toronto. Behind it, the waters of the Copper would be backed up, then diverted by tunnel through a mountain to join those of the Yukon and Tanana in a reservoir three-quarters the size of Lake Michigan. From there the water would be pumped uphill into the Peace River basin in British Columbia, then would cascade south to flood the Rocky Mountain Trench, creating another lake 800 kilometres long, or nearly one-half the distance from the Yukon to the Montana border. At that point it would also pick up the waters of the Columbia, Fraser and Kootenay river systems.

Mr. Parsons outlined a continent-wide water distribution network which incorporated 240 reservoirs, 112 irrigation systems and 17 navigation canals handling 136 cubic kilometres of water a year. While some of the water was to be pumped east across the Prairies as far as the Great Lakes, most of it was to go south via the Columbia and Snake rivers to the Colorado River. Water would be spread far and wide to irrigate about 220 000 square kilometres of dry farmland in the United States and Mexico and even provide water for New York City.

NAWAPA was hardly designed to please Canadians. From 70 to 80 per cent of the water would come from Canada but 61 per cent would go to the United States, Mexico would get 19 per cent and Canada would keep only 20 per cent. The artificial lakes would inundate some of British Columbia's richest farmland and block Canada's major transportation routes, effectively turning the westernmost province into an island. Major western rivers would trickle rather than flow to the sea, changing whole biological regimes and destroying large salmon fisheries. There were even fears that the pressure of the water on the earth's crust might be so great that earthquakes could be triggered along this fault zone. They could burst the giant dams, unleashing floods of biblical proportions. To top off the problems, the project was estimated to cost $200 billion in 1977 prices.

But it was a Canadian proposal from the other side of the continent which was first off the mark and which is back in the news. In 1960, even before the water shortages became apparent in the U.S. West, mining engineer Thomas Kierans suggested to the Canadian government that water from rivers flowing into James Bay could be captured and pumped to the Great Lakes. From there he outlined virtually the mirror image of Parsons' distribution system, this time sending eastern water as far as California and Mexico. Mr. Kierans was a bit ahead of his time and over the years his idea became simply another in the pack created by NAWAPA and imitators of both schemes. Now his James Bay proposal has come back into public debate. The Kierans plan, called the Great Recycling and Northern Development Canal, or Grand Canal for short, is on the same scale as NAWAPA. It calls for a 160-kilometre-long system of dykes and causeways across the mouth of James Bay. This would allow fresh water from north-flowing rivers in Ontario and Quebec to gradually flush out the salt water into

Hudson Bay. Over time that river flow of 13.6 million litres per second, twice that of the St. Lawrence River, would turn James Bay into a 70 000-square-kilometre reservoir of fresh water. Then batteries of gigantic pumps would start lifting as much as one-fifth of that flow back, 292 metres up and over the Canadian Shield. Mr. Kierans says he has not picked a final route but the water could be pumped up the Harricana river valley in Quebec, just east of the Ontario border, to Amos and be transferred by canal into the headwaters of the Ottawa River near Noranda and Rouyn. Part of this flow would go down the Ottawa River to the St. Lawrence, while part would be pumped west, up the Mattawa River to Lake Nipissing where it would flow down the French River to Georgian Bay and the Great Lakes. Moving an estimated 347 cubic kilometres of water each year along the 640 kilometres from James Bay to Georgian Bay would require about 10 000 megawatts of electrical power, eating up the entire output of the James Bay power project. One proposal has been to build nuclear power stations to provide at least some of the power and Atomic Energy of Canada Limited is looking at the idea.

What is the aim of adding as much as 30 per cent of the flow of the Great Lakes? For starters, Mr. Kierans says that this extra influx of water would stabilize lake levels in the face of increasing consumption by cities and industries. But a large amount of water would be moved by canal and pump, west to the dry farmlands and thirsty cities. Mr. Kierans' maps show that water would be transferred via an existing canal at Chicago on the south end of Lake Michigan and from a canal to be built from Green Bay, further up Lake Michigan. These canals would link up with the Missouri and Mississippi rivers and from them water would be picked up downstream and distributed west and south via a network of canals. A separate northern canal would be built to the Prairies from the west end of Lake Superior, again pumping uphill all the way. Mr. Kierans says his continental system would bring water to about 100 million people in the three countries. He estimates the cost at about $100 billion, with half needed to get the water to the Great Lakes and the other half to move the water west. This is 10 times the cost of the Apollo project to put humans on the moon.

Mr. Kierans says he became interested in western water shortages when he saw Prairie dustbowl conditions during the 1930s at the age of 19. He got the idea of enclosing James Bay after he read that the Netherlands was finishing a 32-kilometre-long dyke in 1932 to close off much of what had been the Zuider Zee, an arm of the ocean, and

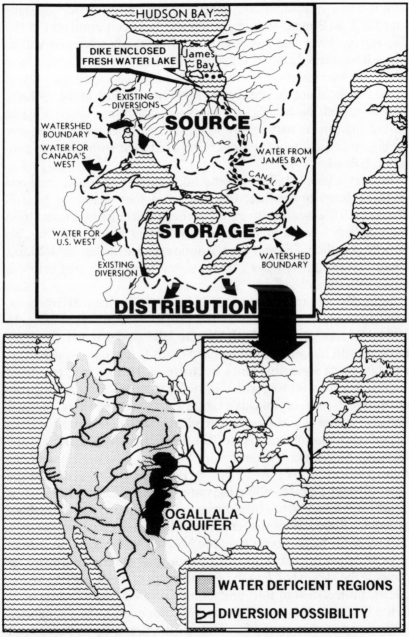

This proposal called the Grand Canal, would dike James Bay and pump some of the fresh water flowing into it from tributary rivers uphill then south and west to the Great Lakes. From there water would be pumped and sent by canal to the Prairies and to the dry western U.S., according to engineer Thomas Kierans. (BERNARD BENNELL)

turn it into a freshwater lake called the IJsselmeer. About the same time the U.S. Bureau of Reclamation was busy collecting part of the Sacramento River and pumping it south to the San Joaquin Valley, where it has turned a desert into one of the world's richest agricultural areas. Mr. Kierans also likes to compare his project to China's Grand Canal, built about 2,500 years ago. Now living in St. John's, Newfoundland, he has picked up experience in big water projects during his career, particularly when he was chief mining engineer during construction of the Upper Churchill Falls hydro-electric project in Labrador.

Whenever people talk of moving huge amounts of water from one drainage basin to another, the first word that comes to mind is diversions. However, Mr. Kierans has tried to distance his project from the criticism levelled at diversions by finding a new word for his project: recycling. To carry the semantic exercise further he also talks about "creating new water" by capturing fresh water just before it mixes with the salt seas.

So far Mr. Kierans has convinced a handful of influential engineers, politicians and economists that the project is worth examining. In 1984 Mr. Kierans created GRANDCo., the Grand Canal Company Limited, with himself as president and Louis Desmarais, former chairman of Canada Steamship Lines, as chairman. He then entered into an engineering joint venture with four major companies: the SNC Group in Montreal, one of Canada's largest engineering firms; Bechtel Canada Limited of Toronto, the Canadian branch of one of the world's largest engineering companies; the UMA Group of Calgary; and Rosseau, Sauvé and Warren Inc. of Montreal. The project also has some political support. As an MP in 1983 Mr. Desmarais raised the issue of water exports, calling the water "white gold." In 1985, when he was still leader of the then opposition Liberal party in the Quebec assembly, Robert Bourassa endorsed the Grand Canal project in a chapter of his book, *Power from the North*. That book was written to draw attention to his bid to return to power as premier of Quebec, to promote the idea of building the second phase of the James Bay hydro-electric project, and to start promoting the sale of more hydro power to the United States. In an interview Mr. Bourassa said he supported engineering studies on the feasibility of the Grand Canal because "it could create spectacular wealth for Canada...that could change the political equilibrium in North America."

The most controversial backer of the project is Simon Reisman, former deputy finance minister, former deputy minister of industry and former secretary to the Treasury Board. Mr. Reisman was also the senior negotiator of the 1965 Canada-U.S. Automotive Products Agreement, known as the Autopact. He has retired from public service to become a consultant to business and government and was a key advisor to Liberal leader John Turner during the 1984 federal election campaign. He has also been an advisor to the Grand Canal Company and an outspoken supporter of the proposal. In April, 1985, Mr. Reisman told a conference sponsored by the Ontario Economic Council that the United States wants Canadian water badly and that this is the playing card that could give Canada its best opportunity of obtaining secure, long-term access to the U.S. market for Canadian goods. He said Canada could probably negotiate a deal to have the United States pay almost all the cost of water diversion, pay for the water itself and give Canadian goods and services immediate free access to U.S. markets, while giving Canada 10 or 15 years in which to adapt its industries to meet increased competition from U.S. imports. In an interview with newspaper reporters Mr. Reisman said, "The Americans have a desperate need for water...I think they would go crazy for the idea." Mr. Reisman has also called water the "missing link" in trade talks and said of the Grand Canal: "This bargaining lever is so great we can get anything we want so long as it is reasonable."

In November, 1985, Prime Minister Brian Mulroney set off a flurry of speculation about the federal attitude towards water exports when he appointed Mr. Reisman as Canada's ambassador for free trade talks with the United States. Early in 1986 Mr. Reisman commented that while he has strong personal views that water will play a key role in Canada-U.S. relations "in perpetuity," those views are private and not relevant to his role as chief negotiator. Mr. Reisman said that he has no formal links with the Grand Canal concept.

Backers of the Grand Canal project have been seeking federal financial support. GRANDCo. has asked the federal Department of Supply and Services and the National Research Council to put up to $750 000, about half the cost of a feasibility study on the scheme.

Canada already exports water in the form of bottled mineral water and a number of politicians have declared that this is the largest quantity they want to see leave the country. There is another type of export, by tanker, which water experts say is still not a big threat to the environment since the amount of water taken would not likely be more than the volume of a small stream. So far there have been two recent tanker proposals. A Vancouver business man wanted to have one or two small tankers a week pick up water that now falls into Hotham Sound from a stream draining Freil Lake, 90 kilometres northwest of Vancouver. It would be shipped to Southern California or Mexico, bottled and sold as drinking water.

A similar idea was broached on the other side of the country: a proposal to ship water from Sept-Iles, Quebec, on the Gulf of St. Lawrence, to the United Arab Emirates, which must now get part of its fresh water supply by desalting ocean water at great cost. Two companies were formed to negotiate a deal with the Arabs but the estimated cost of $400 million for a fleet of 16 tankers to transport 16 million litres a month apparently stalled the project. Some commentators also pointed out that fresh water was available much closer to the Arabs, from European rivers. Another study suggested that empty oil tankers could carry water back to the Middle East, although they would have to be lined with giant plastic bags or the water would have to be purified at the other end. This would cost about $2 per 1 000 litres, as opposed to $3 if one sent an empty tanker over for water only.

At least one company apparently found the concept worthwhile. In the spring of 1984 it was reported that Exxon Corporation, the world's largest oil company, was quietly taking fresh water from the Hudson River. Oil tankers were transporting the water 3 000 kilometres to the arid Caribbean island of Aruba, where Exxon operates a refinery and needs fresh water for cooling. Starting in 1977 a number of Exxon oil tankers unloaded their cargoes in New Jersey, loaded with sea water for ballast, then steamed more than 100 kilometres upstream to a freshwater section of the river. There they pumped the sea water and filled up with fresh water, a scarce commodity on Aruba. In 1983, when a desalination plant failed on the island, Exxon sent 61 tankers, including some that arrived empty just to pick up fresh water. After environmentalists spotted the sudden flood of tanker traffic and complained to governments about pollution from the tankers emptying their holds, Exxon stopped the shipments. Aruba has since been importing tanker loads of water from other Caribbean countries.

Water exports are a touchy issue in many countries, particularly in Canada, and the Kierans proposal has drawn fierce opposition from a number of politicians and native and environment groups. Mr. Kierans promises jobs for northerners and a freshwater fishery in James Bay. His opponents say the interruption of natural river flows into James Bay would upset whole ecosystems, affecting life that depends on them, including human communities, fish, amphibians, birds and animals. Damming rivers across North America as part of the distribution system would reduce the flushing action of spring floods, which carries away pollution and provides surges of water essential for breeding fish. Changing natural lake levels would either flood or dry up wetlands which are crucial breeding areas for much wildlife. The building of canals and water storage reservoirs across the continent would flood a number of valleys, which are often excellent farmland. The new water links across the continent would also create a migration route for different life forms which have been separated by natural barriers. These include some unwanted fish species, parasites and fish diseases. One past example of what happens when natural barriers are removed is the invasion of sea lamprey which were able to get around Niagara Falls when the Welland Canal was opened. Lampreys had virtually wiped out trout fishing on the upper Great Lakes by the 1950s and are now held at bay by a costly and complex poisoning program which must be repeated indefinitely. The transfer of foreign biota was one of the main Canadian complaints about the Garrison Dam irrigation project in North Dakota. If built to full scale, Garrison's pumps and canals would have transferred water and foreign life forms from the Mississippi drainage basin over the height of land into the Red River and Lake Winnipeg systems, threatening Canadian fisheries. After years of complaints from Canada, the United States has apparently agreed to reduce the scale of the Garrison project and keep the Mississippi water south of the continental divide.

Mr. Kierans' ideas about reclaiming "wasted" water from James Bay have been challenged by people like James Bruce, until recently a federal assistant deputy environment minister. Dr. Bruce said that the mix of fresh and salt waters has important impacts on ocean currents, salinity and fish production. The fresh water becomes part of an aquatic life cycle which has effects far away from the shores where the water enters. Some commentators have said that the freshwater flow from James Bay affects fish as far away as Newfoundland's Grand Banks. The James Bay diversion would also upset the tourism community. It would turn historic waterways like the Mattawa and French rivers, once key links in the fur trade route and now popular recreational canoe route and fishing areas, into industrial canals. The Mattawa is a provincial park and the French is an historic waterway, so any plans to turn them into canals would require changes in the designation by the Ontario government and this would meet with stiff opposition. Even the water sales idea is under fire, by people who believe it would irrevocably commit Canada to water exports, even if the water was needed at home in the future.

The strength of opposition to water exports, which has marked Canadian reaction since the days of NAWAPA, is interesting because we have long exported non-renewable resources such as minerals, oil and gas and renewable resources such as wood products and wheat. The reluctance to part with water obviously goes beyond economic reasons and touches a chord deep in the Canadian psyche. Frank Quinn, a senior federal water planner, seemed to capture the prevailing mood when, during a 1983 interview, he said that major diversions "would be a tragedy...exporting our environment." Perhaps, too, one can look at an 1849 statement by Nova Scotia scientist Abraham Gesner that has become a Canadian cliché on the resource industries. In a critique on the disadvantages of free trade with the colonies of Upper and Lower Canada he wrote: "The suppliers of raw materials at last become hewers of wood and drawers of water to the manufacturers."

Whatever the reasons, the Canadian reaction to water export proposals has been hostile. In 1967, during the NAWAPA debate, General A. G. L. McNaughton, a former Canadian co-chairman of the International Joint Commission, called water exports "a monstrous concept, a diabolical thesis." Northern Affairs Minister Arthur Laing said, "there is no continental water in Canada. There is only Canadian water." There was a long lull in which the diversions issue faded away but it has been revived with the Grand Canal proposal and so has political opposition. "Large-scale diversions would play havoc with the ecological and economic balance of the Great Lakes basin," said Environment Minister Charles Caccia in 1984. The federal water inquiry which Mr. Caccia appointed reported that 9 out of 10 Canadians asked about the issue opposed major water exports.

In 1985 Prime Minister Brian Mulroney was dragged into the debate when a U.S. magazine quoted him as replying "Why not?" to the idea of water exports to the United States. Mr. Mulroney's press assistant said that the Prime Minister was only endorsing the much smaller concept of water export by tanker to the Middle East. In late 1984 Mr. Mulroney wrote a letter endorsing one of the plans to export water from Sept-Iles, in his riding, to Arab states. In late 1985 the new federal environment minister, Thomas McMillan, was the first Conservative cabinet minister to publicly attack diversions, when he referred to the Grand Canal scheme as "an elusive dream" and an attempt to turn water into "white oil." Mr. McMillan criticized the plan as not well thought out, declaring the huge cost and environmental damage made it "doubtful at best and potentially disastrous at worst." He said it would reduce the amount of fresh water reaching Hudson Strait and this would affect fishing and the livelihood of native peoples.

The provinces have generally opposed water exports and Ontario has become the most outspoken critic. For example in 1983 Natural Resources Minister Alan Pope attacked the idea of one diversion studied in the United States, a $27-billion, 980-kilometre canal from the west end of Lake Superior to the Missouri River in South Dakota. Mr. Pope said it would take 280 cubic metres of water per second from Lake Superior and that would drop Lakes Huron, Michigan and Erie, creating an "almost catastrophic effect." The same year he rebuffed the proposal of two Illinois and Wisconsin businessmen who wanted Ontario's permission to divert Great Lakes water, either by tanker or by expanding an existing canal from Lake Michigan to the Mississippi river system. "They called us the OPEC of water," said Mr. Pope (a reference to the world's major oil cartel). His position was that "We do not have any water to give away," and the Great Lakes are "a reservoir that cannot be touched without serious, wide-ranging impacts on our economy and way of life." Any drop in their levels would reduce the amount of water to dilute pollution in drinking water; lower hydro-electric generation; reduce boat access to harbors and rivers; damage spawning grounds for fish; and harm tourism. Since then, studies on growing industrial consumption around the lakes and the drying up that is predicted to come with the greenhouse effect predict that the Great Lakes levels could drop by as much as one metre over the next few decades.

Among the provinces only British Columbia seemed to be interested in water exports. In 1981 B.C. Premier William Bennett told some California businessmen that his province's water was not for sale. But he added: "Come and see me in 20 years." In 1984 B.C. Environment Minister Anthony Brummett predicted that in about 15 years a global water shortage would create an opportunity to export some of the province's "superabundance" of fresh water, particularly from streams flowing to the sea.

Not all the opposition to water exports comes from Canadians. There has also been strong opposition to water diversion from some

U.S. quarters. Part of this stems from the fact that a number of schemes called for either drawing water from rivers in the humid U.S. northwest, or transporting water through that area by flooding valleys. In either case politicians in the regions that would be affected did not like what they heard and mounted such effective opposition in the U.S. Congress that in 1968 they won a 10-year moratorium on even studies of major water transfers between different U.S. river basins. This ban was renewed in 1978 for another decade. In fact the ban is not completely watertight because it did not apply to all U.S. agencies and in 1976 approval was given to the U.S. Army Corps of Engineers to study the Ogallala Aquifer and determine how to get more water to it. Some of the U.S. opposition is based on purely economic grounds, particularly now that the U.S. deficit is around $200 billion. U.S. studies have also concluded that even if water were shipped to the dry west, the farmers could not afford it. The U.S. Army Corps of Engineers studied the idea of transferring water from the Missouri or Arkansas rivers west to the Ogallala region, but found it would cost from $500 to $1 000 per thousand cubic metres. Canada's federal water inquiry estimated that it would cost more than $1 300 per thousand cubic metres to deliver Canadian water to the U.S. southwest. Both studies concluded that these prices were too high unless the price of irrigated crops were to skyrocket. For example, the Canadian study estimated that U.S. farmers could not afford to pay more than $130 per thousand cubic metres and in fact they only pay one-tenth of that price now to pump water from the ground or to get it from subsidized water projects. One U.S. expert dismissed water exports as unlikely by saying that the only crop which could pay for them was truffles. But just because they are outrageously expensive does not mean that diversions will not happen. Senator David Duren-berger of Minnesota told a 1984 water conference in Toronto, "The first principle of water policy, in my country, at least, is that rational thinking does not apply."

The first serious attempt to block water diversions in the east has come from a coalition of all the provincial and state governments bordering on the Great Lakes-St. Lawrence system. In early 1985, Ontario, Quebec and the eight states, Minnesota, Michigan, Wisconsin, Illinois, Ohio, New York, Pennsylvania and Indiana, signed an anti-diversions agreement called the Great Lakes Charter. Since the provinces and states cannot sign international treaties the charter has been described as "a good faith agreement," based firmly on self-interest. It pledges the signatories not to permit any significant increase in water consumption or diversion without consulting with the other parties. The agreement also calls on them to share information on current water consumption and to develop a regional water-use strategy.

The 10 governments are bound together by a complex series of factors that make the Great Lakes ecosystem an economic as well as a biological entity. Even Quebeckers living along the heavily populated St. Lawrence Valley have concerns about increasing water withdrawals from the Great Lakes. Any diversion which reduced the downstream flow would hurt them. Ontario would be affected even more than Quebec and has expressed concerns not only about the possibility of unilateral U.S. water diversions from the lakes but about the increasing demand for the shared waters by the much bigger U.S. population and industry along the lakeshore.

The Great Lakes states have their own reasons to sign the pact, because any major drop in the lake levels caused by one state would affect all of them. This charter has made it clear that the states would have more to gain from holding on to their water than from diverting it to their western cousins. For years the Great Lakes states have watched the Sun Belt states lure industry away with the promise of a warm climate and water projects paid for with federal money, including taxes from the east. Now the Great Lakes states, dubbed the Rust Belt because of their industrial decline, are calling themselves the Water Belt and claiming that this is the lure which will being industry back when the wells run dry in the south. "The American breadbasket, feeding the country, is using up its water reserves," said William Hoyt, a New York State assemblyman, and "all the criteria are there for a crisis growing in those parts of the country." When their water is gone, Mr. Hoyt predicted, "the pressure is going to be extraordinary" to divert water from areas like the Great Lakes. But New York and the other states plan to hold onto the water and tell industry to move north. Michigan governor James Blanchard said the charter "is a signal to the Sun Belt that we stand together internationally to protect our water resources." In 1985 Ohio governor Richard Celeste told a conference that "companies are finding it is delightful to bask in the sun but sooner or later you get thirsty."

In fact this attitude on the part of the Great Lakes states is likely the strongest protection that Canada has against water diversions. At present Canada has no formalized policy on water diversions, only a

Part of the Central Arizona Project canal snakes its way across the desert, bearing precious Colorado River water toward Phoenix, about eighty kilometres away, and eventually to Tucson.   (U.S. BUREAU OF RECLAMATION)

collection of statements by various cabinet ministers, past and present. In 1985 the federal water inquiry, headed by Vancouver resource economist Peter Pearse, reported on the state of Canada's waters. The final report did note that Canada now exports small amounts of water to the United States on a local scale. For example Coutts, Alberta, pipes water just across the border to Sweetgrass, Montana, while Gretna, Manitoba, sends water to Neche, North Dakota. St. Stephen, New Brunswick, sends water across the St. Croix River to Calais, Maine, and some of this water returns to an industrial plant in New Brunswick. This minor sort of water export poses no threat, the report said. When it came to the idea of massive canal schemes the inquiry did not take a clear stand but suggested that if the government ever even considered water exports, it should first set up a regulatory system to review each proposal. The system it proposed is so stringent that, if followed to the letter, it would probably make exports unlikely. For example, the recommendation advised that before approving any water diversions, the government should consider their impacts on fisheries, navigation, boundary waters, northern residents, tourism, fishermen and the environment in general. It said that the government should also consider the possible need for increasing water supplies in Canada in the future to cope with the drying effect of climate changes. Finally, the inquiry pointed out that any water export would bind Canada even more closely to the United States.

What are the alternatives to major water diversions to the U.S. west? Water conservation is the most attractive alternative right now because it will stretch out existing water supplies, though no one is sure for how much longer. The main target of conservation is agriculture, which takes 80 per cent of the water consumed in the United States and which wastes up to half that with inefficient irrigation techniques. Critics also say that a lot of water is wasted because many irrigated crops have relatively low value or are surplus commodities. They maintain that this is the result of turn-of-the-century U.S. water policies which have not been updated to deal with water shortages. In 1902 the United States passed the Reclamation Act and created the Bureau of Reclamation to provide water for homesteaders in dry western areas, as part of the settling of the west. Since then more than 48 500 square kilometres of land, an area nearly the size of Nova Scotia, have been irrigated under that act. In recent years questions have arisen about the real value of much of the irrigation. A 1981 federal study of six federal irrigation projects found that the water rates farmers were paying covered less than 10 per cent of the cost of the dams, reservoirs and canals needed to supply that water. It even found that the value of the crops grown was less than the actual cost of the water delivered to the fields.

The question is, will governments continue with the old philosophy on a grand scale and subsidize water transfers to the dry west in order to support local economies? Dr. Derrick Sewell, an international water expert at the University of Victoria, believes that large-scale water exports from Canada will only take place if there is a real crisis in western U.S. farm areas, and a deal is struck on the costs and environmental damage which would result from diversions. Dr. Sewell suspects that this kind of deal could only be worked out if there is a shift away from current environmental priorities. Former Ontario premier William Davis once stated: "The pressure for access to Great Lakes water will no doubt intensify in the future as drought-stricken southern states contemplate gigantic engineered diversion projects as the solution to their difficulties." However, a number of U.S. water experts say that, given the tremendous costs of such a project, water transfers do not appear to be affordable at this time.

CHAPTER ELEVEN

INTERNAL DIVERSIONS: WINNERS AND LOSERS

ALMOST AS SOON AS the first Europeans arrived in Canada, they started trying to change the way nature had laid down the waterworks. People were not satisfied with rapids in the rivers so they made small canals and locks to move heavy freight canoes past obstructions and avoid portaging. Now Canada diverts more water than any country in the world but very few of us realize it. Our tiny boat canals grew into the Rideau, the Welland and finally the St. Lawrence Seaway. These waterways let the world's freighters cruise 3 700 kilometres from the ocean to the head of the Great Lakes, rising 143 metres along the way. We are world experts at building huge power dams to reshape rivers like the Churchill and La Grande. In the west there are networks of dams, reservoirs and canals to hold part of the spring runoff and meter it out for irrigation across semi-arid plains in southern Alberta and Saskatchewan. In populated areas we are starting to move water around for another reason. About 700 000 Canadians are or soon will be drinking diverted water because they have built cities too big for the local supplies or they have polluted their normal sources of drinking water.

Canada already diverts about 4 400 000 litres of water per second—more than the United States and the Soviet Union combined—but most of that happens in the far north, out of sight of most people. If Canada's 54 diversions could be combined into a single giant waterway they would create the third-largest river in the country, after the St. Lawrence and Mackenzie rivers. Most diversions are over very short distances and are for hydro-electric megaprojects like James Bay, Churchill Falls and the Churchill-Nelson River diversion in Manitoba. This country ranks third in the world for water storage,

169

with 518 cubic kilometres held behind its dams. We have 97 big dams, storing at least 100 million cubic metres (100 billion litres) of water. Over 80 per cent of these are for hydro-electric power production, while only 7 per cent are for irrigation, and the rest are for flood control or water supply.

By now the world has tens of thousands of dams with a capacity of about 2 000 cubic kilometres of water. This has the effect of capturing about 17 per cent of the stable runoff of the world's rivers and holding it for use when needed to produce hydro-electricity or to irrigate crops. Most of the big dams have been built since the Second World War. Now the planet is running out of narrow valleys to dam up. These projects are also getting more costly and are running into growing opposition from conservationists and from farmers, who want to save the remaining rich valley bottom lands.

This leaves another option: moving water in from other river basins. "Large-scale transfers are appearing more attractive to a number of nations which have already used up their local river flows and want to expand farming and industry," writes Mostafa Tolba, executive director of the United Nations Environment Program. His comment appears in a recent book, *Large Scale Water Transfers: Emerging Environmental and Social Experiences*, outlining a number of existing and proposed water diversions around the world. The amounts of water involved are staggering. Most of the figures are given in cubic kilometres of water per year, which is the equivalent of 1 billion cubic metres or 1 trillion litres.

In North America, more domestic water diversions within Canada and the United States are likely before Canada considers exporting water southward. For example, northern California has more water which could be shipped south and the Pacific northwest has many large rivers which, at least in theory, could be diverted to dry western areas. The Missouri and Mississippi river systems have long been viewed as possible sources of water to replenish the Ogallala Aquifer on the High Plains. There have been studies in taking water from the U.S. side of the Great Lakes and diverting it westward. The question is not whether such plans are technically possible, but if they will succeed politically and financially. For the present, water transfers are opposed by the potential source regions and in any case appear too expensive to be paid for by the major consumer, agriculture, given current food prices. In Canada, hydro-electric power projects will continue to dam up free-flowing rivers. And there will continue to be relatively small water diversions in the east to supply cities which outstrip their rivers by growth or pollute them out of use. But the major question lies in the west, where expanding agricultural demand, coupled with new industrial projects, has sparked demands to divert water over long distances to the dry southern Prairies.

Water diversions are nothing new in history. For thousands of years people in North Africa and Asia have made short-distance water transfers to irrigate fields and allow agriculture in dry areas. By hand-drawn bucket or by water wheel, humans and animals lifted water from nearby rivers and poured it into irrigation canals, which then branched into furrows between the rows of crops. Since early times a number of cities have had to import some of their water supplies. The Romans raised water diversions to an art form, with superb aqueducts which delivered millions of litres of water per day over many kilometres to some of their major cities.

Water diversions to dry areas are not new. Pont du Gard, built about 19 B.C. in southern France, was part of a supply system carrying water forty kilometres to Nîmes.
(MICHAEL KEATING)

The manipulation of rivers has obvious benefits but it can be very expensive and cause considerable ecological and even social impact. The Bennett Dam on the Peace River in British Columbia has, since 1968, changed the water flow far downstream in the Peace-Athabasca delta in northeastern Alberta. By storing the spring freshet behind the dam and adjusting the release of water to suit power demands, the dam reduced the natural rush of water and created problems for wildlife and people by upsetting seasonal water levels downstream. Some dams have also caused unexpected mercury pollution problems. After Manitoba Hydro plugged the outlet of Southern Indian Lake at Missy Falls, part of the Churchill River spilled southward to augment the flow of the Nelson as it sped through a major powerhouse. But the artificial lake on the Churchill spread water into soils naturally high in mercury and natural organisms converted the metal to the dangerous methylmercury form. In the slow currents the methylmercury accumulated to unsafe levels in the fish, meaning native people could no longer sell them commercially and were at some risk if they ate this traditional food. The same problem has taken place behind the giant dams in the James Bay power project in Quebec. One researcher reported that mercury levels in the fish behind these dams were as bad as any in the world.

There are many more controversial power projects for northern rivers but they have stayed on the drawing board because hydro exports to the United States had been limited in the past and the increase in the demand for power tapered off during the recession of the early 1980s. A change in federal policies towards hydro-electric exports in recent years has created a new type of market and a new concern. Now that long-term power exports are being allowed, more and more provinces, notably Quebec, British Columbia and Manitoba, are rushing to build more huge hydro dams. As they drown one northern valley after another and dry up river deltas downstream, there is a growing outcry that in effect Canada is exporting its water and its environment via high-voltage transmission lines.

Hydro reservoirs and river diversions have already changed the face of Quebec more than any other province. The land is dotted with a series of new lakes as a result of hydro-electric reservoirs: the Cabonga and Gouin to the south; the Pipmuacan and Manicouagan to the southeast; and, to the north, as part of the James Bay project, the Caniapiscau, the largest body of water in the province. Just across the border in Labrador the biggest lake is the Smallwood Reservoir, the water storehouse for the Churchill Falls power project.

Quebec's James Bay hydro-electric project, sprawling across the sub-arctic wilderness about 1 000 kilometres north of Montreal, was launched by Premier Robert Bourassa in 1971 as "the project of the century." The plan to turn part of northwestern Quebec into North America's biggest power plant is centred around La Grande Rivière, already a huge watercourse. It has been swollen even more by the diversions of most of the waters of the Eastmain and Opinaca into its channel. Even some of the waters of the Caniapiscau, which flows north into Ungava Bay, have been diverted over the height of land to flow west through La Grande. The project has created five giant reservoirs covering 11 900 square kilometres of Quebec. The waters are controlled by eight dams, up to 40 storeys high, and 198 dykes, which, if placed end to end, would stretch for 125 kilometres. The $15-billion first phase of this project can produce more than 10 000 megawatts of electricity, about 20 per cent of Canada's present hydro-electric capacity. In his 1985 book, *Power from the North*, Mr. Bourassa explained that he wants to built the 8 000-megawatt second phase of James Bay by damming the Great Whale River to the north, and the Nottaway, Broadback and Rupert to the south. He would even augment that power by damming rivers on the north shore of the St. Lawrence to generate another 4 000 megawatts. All this power is far more than Quebec can absorb and already part of it is flowing into the New England states. Mr. Bourassa is promoting the idea of further sales to the United States. The cost of developing the 12 000 megawatts of power is estimated by Mr. Bourassa at $25 billion in 1984 dollars.

British Columbia, like Quebec, regards its huge rivers flowing to the seas as power sources waiting to be tapped and sold to the big U.S. market, this one on the west coast. As he opened the $2-billion Revelstoke Dam in the summer of 1985, B.C. Premier William Bennett announced that he was reversing the policy of not building dams for power exports. After discussions with utilities in California a month later Mr. Bennett said he was ready to start work on the controversial Site C project on the Peace River in northeastern British Columbia. This site has been opposed in the past because it would flood some of the best northern farmland in the valley of the Peace. Site C would be another megaproject, costing $3.2 billion over 9 years and creating 5 000 construction jobs. There is another controversial project on the drawing boards for northern British Columbia. For more than two decades B.C. Hydro engineers have been studying the 600-kilometre-long Stikine River. This wild river flows from the remote Cassiar

Mountains through a series of gorges, including one called the Grand Canyon, before it empties into the Pacific in a wide delta near Wrangell in the Alaskan panhandle. B.C. Hydro would like to generate 2 800 megawatts of power by erecting five major dams, as high as 75 storeys, in the canyon which is now home to hundreds of mountain goats.

Manitoba, which developed the huge Churchill-Nelson power diversion in the early 1970s, is now going ahead with the Limestone generating station to take further advantage of the Nelson's increased flow. This $2.1-billion project on the Nelson River, about 800 kilometres north of Winnipeg, will produce 1 200 megawatts of electricity when it is finished in 1990 and in the meantime will create 6 000 construction jobs. Nearly half the power is slated for export to the United States and Limestone may be just one of a series. If Manitoba Hydro can sell more power to the United States, Ontario and Saskatchewan, it may go ahead with the Conawapa generating station downstream from Limestone and in the future with other developments on the Nelson drainage basin.

Alberta is waiting in the wings for the opportune moment to develop its own hydro megaproject in the north. For years the province has been studying the idea of a major power dam on the Slave River, just south of the border with the Northwest Territories. However, this project could be the most controversial of all, because of its potential for ecological damage. Critics say the dam would flood islands which are nesting sites for the world's northernmost colony of white pelicans, a species listed by Alberta and Ottawa as threatened. These pelicans nest on granite islands near the thundering Mountain Rapids, the only colony in the world known to nest on river islands rather than lake islands. Even more controversial is the fact that the project, including its huge power transmission towers, would encroach on Wood Buffalo National Park, one of the largest parks in the world and home to a wide variety of wildlife including eagles and peregrine falcons. Most important of all, the park is the world's only wild nesting site for the whooping crane. A small colony of birds is being nursed back from the brink of extinction by Canada and by the United States, where the birds winter, and any threat to their survival would be seen in the same light as the killing of the last passenger pigeons. Environmentalists have warned that flooding the rapids in the Slave River might allow Arctic lamprey, which suck the blood of the fish, to migrate south into the upper Slave and Peace and Athabasca systems just as the Welland Canal allowed sea lamprey to invade the Great Lakes.

Far to the south there are water problems of a different kind as one area after another in Prairie Canada outgrows its water resources or bumps up against the limits to growth and is forced to restrict development. Already there are water shortages in the North and South Saskatchewan, Red, Assiniboine, Milk and St. Mary river systems. A number of development interests are calling for major water transfers from the north so that farmland can be irrigated in order to defeat the periodic droughts. The reason is obvious. The earth is as fine and dry as brown talcum powder and as it trickles through your fingers the ever-present hot, dry wind picks it up from the ground and swirls it into dust devils. On one side of a dirt road lies the unbroken Prairie, where short grasses and wild roses half hide the yellow bloom of a cactus. On the other side of the road green crops sprout from a field watered by a giant mechanical sprinkler as long as a dozen railway cars. The machine slowly rotates on its rubber wheels around a central water pipe, literally holding the desert at bay. The water comes from a river many kilometres away via a system of canals and none of it will return. As far as that river is concerned the water is gone—bound up in a food crop which will be exported, evaporated into the air to land far away as rain or simply lost into the soil where it will percolate deep underground. Without this type of irrigation, farming in the dry southlands of the prairies is a risky, often futile business. With it there is a growing drain on the local rivers, which even now do not always have enough water for the farmers in dry years. At such times the last farmers to hook up to the irrigation system are the first to get cut off and must watch their crops wilt in the hot summer sun.

In southern Alberta local rivers are giving their last for irrigation. The provincial government has just promised $200 million to build the Oldman Dam where the Oldman River joins the Castle and Crowsnest rivers in the foothills west of Lethbridge. But when this dam is completed around 1991, it will use up the last major irrigation dam site in southern Alberta. There still will be some valleys where reservoirs can be created to gather some of the spring runoff and hold it for use during the growing season, but their capacity is limited by topography and law. The law is an agreement that Alberta and Saskatchewan must each let half the flow of their prairie rivers continue downstream to the next province until it reaches Manitoba and finally Hudson Bay. Once the southern prairie rivers have been milked of every drop they can safely yield, there are two alternatives. One is to call a halt to further irrigation farming. The other is to seek water in the north.

That idea of diversions from the north has been proposed for decades and was the subject of a major study in the mid-1960s when the Alberta government produced a master plan for the province's waters, called PRIME (Prairie River Improvement, Management and Evaluation). It suggested diverting water from the Peace and Atha-basca rivers, south to the Saskatchewan and Bow river systems. The water would irrigate crops, provide for growing cities and industries and dilute their wastes. This proposal was announced by the Social Credit government and drew immediate public criticism, including the catchy bumper sticker: PRIME is a Crime. When the Progressive Conservative government of Peter Lougheed was elected in 1971 it promised that the plan would be shelved, but several years ago it was revealed that senior people in the government were studying water diversions. In 1982 the Alberta Water Advisory Committee talked about a 22-million-cubic-metre-per-year diversion from the Peace River to irrigate 25 000 square kilometres in southern Alberta. There was an immediate public outcry which Mr. Lougheed tried to defuse by appointing an Alberta Water Commission to examine emerging water supply problems and consider strategies.

But PRIME was not unique. In 1972 the three prairie provinces and the federal government released the Saskatchewan-Nelson Basin water supply study, which looked at potential water diversion in all three prairie provinces. Its list of possible water manipulations includes 54 dams and diversions which would send water from the Peace, Athabasca and Churchill rivers south, turning the prairie rivers into a gigantic plumbing system on the scale of California.

Massive diversions are not popular with a number of people, including farmers whose land would be flooded to create reservoirs and canals, fishermen who see good trout streams being sacrificed and citizens who oppose the destruction of natural areas. In Alberta the anglers are among the most vocal opponents. They are already upset that the Oldman Dam will partially flood two of the province's best trout streams, the Oldman and the Crowsnest. One provincial official said that he suspected the name of the project was changed from the old title of Three Rivers Dam to Oldman Dam "so it would only look like we were messing up one river instead of three." Fishermen are also concerned that Alberta some day may go ahead with a proposed irrigation dam on the world-famous trout river, the Bow, about 20 kilometres south of Calgary. This would flood the river's fast-flowing, shallow stretches, destroying them as trout habitat. (The federal water inquiry found that charges to farmers for federally assisted irrigation projects are only about one-fifth of the cost of getting that water to the farms.)

Drinking-water diversions involve much less volume than irrigation canals or hydro-electric water channels but are controversial because they point out how we are using up or polluting local supplies. Between 1913 and 1919, in Canada's first big drinking-water diversion, Winnipeg built a 150-kilometre-long aqueduct to Shoal Lake, an arm of Lake-of-the-Woods, because the Red River was silty and its flow unreliable. In Ontario a growing number of pipelines bring Great Lakes water to cities like London, St. Thomas and a group of municipalities on the northern fringes of Toronto. Several Ontario communities, such as Niagara-on-the-Lake, Perkinsfield and Whitchurch-Stouffville, have piped water to people whose drinking water was polluted. The growing fears that toxic chemical dumps along the Niagara River will poison Lake Ontario has provoked a number of people, including scientists and politicians, to predict that southern Ontario will look to the relatively pure waters of Georgian Bay, more than 100 kilometres to the north, for a massive drinking water diversion.

In fact Canada and the United States have two "internal" diversions which result in Canada exporting a small amount of water to the United States. The Canadian diversion resulted from a decision more than 40 years ago to redirect 160 cubic metres per second of the Ogoki and Kenogami rivers away from the Albany River, which flows into James Bay. The water was diverted south to Lake Superior in the Nipigon area and from there it continues downstream to provide more hydro-electric power from generating stations. In effect that water transfer, generally referred to as the Ogoki-Long Lac diversion, is partially compensating for water that the United States has long removed from Lake Michigan at Chicago.

The Chicago diversion was originally started in 1848 as a minor ship canal, the Illinois and Michigan. It connected the lake with the south-flowing Illinois river system but in its early years rarely carried much water out of Lake Michigan. In 1900 the waterway was enlarged and renamed the Chicago Sanitary and Ship Canal. The canal was

This map, adapted from those in a study by the federal and Prairie province governments, shows how planners have looked at ways of diverting water from the northern rivers into the dry southern Prairies, where farmers are chronically short of water. However, such

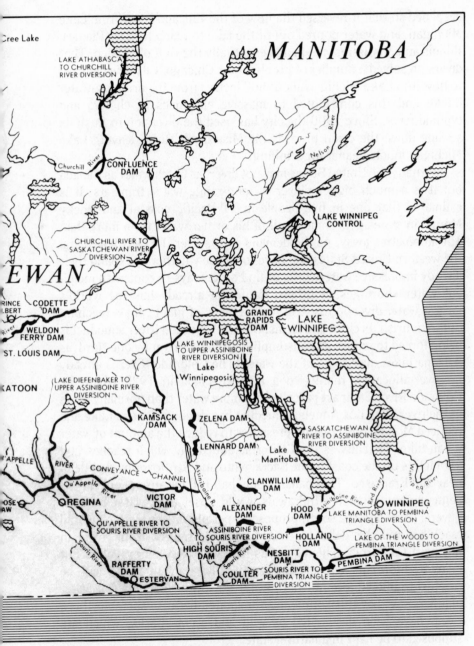

major changes in the Prairie environment would face stiff opposition from people who want the area left in a more natural state. In addition the costs of diversion would be very high.   (BERNARD BENNELL)

deepened so that it reversed the flow of the Chicago River from Lake Michigan, and water poured out of the lake to reach the Des Plaines, Illinois and Mississippi rivers and eventually the Gulf of Mexico. That diversion solved a number of problems for Chicago. City sewage used to flow into Lake Michigan about 600 metres from the drinking-water intake and this contributed to massive epidemics of cholera and typhoid fever. Since 1900 the city has used the diversion to flush its sewage down the canal towards the Mississippi River, leaving Lake Michigan much cleaner for drinking.

Internally the United States may not divert as much water as Canada but it is a much bigger player in long-range water transfers. It is estimated that one in five people in 11 Pacific coastal and Rocky Mountain states gets some or all of his or her water from more than 150 kilometres away. As the demand grows over the next few years, the western United States will have to decide whether to expand their already impressive waterworks or find other ways to cope with incipient water shortages. Southern California already has the world's largest water diversion system, with a maze of giant canals reaching out to nourish its cities and farms. But the Colorado River aqueduct is being forced to reduce its consumption from that river by one-third, as Arizona takes over some of the water. The Colorado River is already far over-allocated, thanks to a mistake made in 1922 when the Colorado River Compact parcelled out more water than normally flows in the river. The Los Angeles aqueduct has dried up Owens Lake and reduced Mono Lake, creating pressures to reduce the amount of water it can take. That leaves the California aqueduct, which reaches 700 kilometres up the coast to the Sacramento and San Joaquin river delta near San Francisco. That canal is only half full because people in the delta say any further withdrawals would upset their water balance. Several years ago the south proposed a peripheral canal which would reach around the delta for water flowing straight from rivers in northern California. This plan was narrowly rejected by voters but many Californians expect that eventually a compromise will be reached to allow more northern water go south. A number of water planners say that this source may be limited because some northern rivers have been designated as wild and scenic parks, which are supposed to be kept in a natural state.

Texas dabbled with the idea of water diversions but seems to have decided they are too costly. In 1968 a state water plan stipulated that Texas should have diversions from rivers outside its boundaries by

1988. It targeted the Mississippi in particular, though it considered getting water from as far away as the Columbia River in Washington or from sources in Canada. In 1969 Texans narrowly defeated a $2-billion bond issue that would have started a $53.5-billion plan to transport water 2 300 kilometres from the lower Mississippi to dry west Texas and New Mexico. Now the state is trying to make do with local sources and gave up irrigating large tracts of dry land when the wells ran dry.

The most contentious area is the High Plains, where underground water reserves in the Ogallala Aquifer are running out. By 2020 two-thirds of the irrigated land may have to go back to dryland farming unless as much as 13 cubic kilometres of water a year can be found somewhere else. For many years water experts have been studying the situation but so far no action has been taken. There are a number of possible water sources, including the Arkansas and Missouri river systems to the east and even the Great Lakes, which hold almost one-fifth of the planet's fresh surface water. One major problem is that water would have to be transported from 550 to 1 800 kilometres, depending on the source, and lifted uphill as much as 1 000 metres to reach the plains. The cost has been estimated at anywhere between $2.6 and $40 billion. And the farming region which needs water is so vast that a massive network of local delivery canals would have to be constructed at a cost equal to the price of the main system. In addition there would be a constant need to power gigantic pumps to keep the water flowing against the natural pull of gravity.

While North America talks about the possibility of very long-range water transfers, the Soviet Union is showing signs of proceeding with one. On both continents most of the great rivers drain north into the Arctic, while farm production in the dry southlands is limited by a lack of water. In the Soviet Union the Southern European, Central Asian and Kazakhstan republics contain 75 per cent of the nation's population and produce almost 80 per cent of the food, but have only 16 per cent of the water. The Soviet Union has chronic food shortages, often because of inadequate rainfall, and as a result imports large amounts of grain from countries such as Canada and the United States. At the same time the Central Asian Republics are undergoing a population explosion, with growth of up to 30 per cent in a decade. Water is needed for the people, for their burgeoning industries and for more farmland irrigation.

Already rivers in the southlands are heavily over-used, reducing the amount of fresh water to reach the Caspian, Azov and Aral seas, which causes them to shrink and threatens their fisheries. Since the Caspian's major tributary, the Volga River, has been tapped for irrigation water, the sea level has dropped as much as three metres. The Caspian produces 90 per cent of the world's sturgeon catch, including the world-famous caviar, and if water levels keep falling that fishery is endangered. Consumption of tributary rivers of the Azov has caused this sea to drop so quickly that instead of draining into the Black Sea, the reverse is happening, making the Azov saltier. To the east the Aral Sea has dropped 9 metres and its surface area has shrunk by 30 per cent since 1960. As a result its fisheries are disappearing, since its tributaries, the Syr-Darya and Amu-Darya, are almost used up by water withdrawals. If irrigation demands keep growing, the sea will vanish completely.

For a century, planners have talked about diverting north-flowing rivers to the dry southern regions. Recent statements concerned channelling as much as 20 cubic kilometres of water a year from northern rivers, such as the Onega, Upper Sukhona and Pechora, which lie northeast of Moscow. The water was to be pumped into the south-flowing Volga and Don rivers to irrigate land and replenish the Azov and Caspian seas. But even this amount of water is only half what is really needed to stabilize their levels and most of that would be directed to the Caspian, with its valuable sturgeon fishery.

The second and much more ambitious project would be to tap the mighty Ob River, its tributary, the Irtish, and possibly the Yenisei, all of which flow north through Siberia. Some of their waters would be diverted as far as 2 500 kilometres southwest, to rescue the Aral Sea, its tributary rivers the Amu-Darya and the Syr-Darya, and the Urals. Recent proposals planned that at first 27 cubic kilometres per year of water would be taken, and this amount might grow to 60. The water would irrigate 45 000 square kilometres of farmland and save the Aral Sea from disappearing. However, the diversions would take as much as 20 per cent of the Ob and lower it as much as 2.5 metres.

Scientists, including some in the Soviet Union, have warned that the massive diversions and their dams will change arctic wildlife by reducing water flows and blocking the migration of fish such as salmon, which stream up the Pechora. The withdrawals from that river are being limited to leave water to dilute pollution and allow some navigation to continue. A number of scientists from countries including Canada have expressed fears that if enough water is diverted away from the Arctic, the circumpolar climate could be affected. Fresh water flowing into the Arctic Ocean naturally reduces the salinity of the seawater. There are concerns that if too much fresh water is diverted south, the Arctic Ocean would become saltier, decreasing the amount of ice which could form each winter. This increase in open water could contribute to an increase in the amount of water vapor in the air and in the snowfall on the land areas around the arctic regions, the scientists say. Two Soviet scientists, G. V. Voropaev and A. L. Velikanov, wrote in 1985 that the amount of water involved in even the major diversions discussed might affect the climate in the immediate vicinity of the river mouths, but the effects would be local, not hemispheric.

While in recent years it appeared that major diversions were in the offing, Soviet statements in early 1986 indicated that plans had been scaled back dramatically. The latest ones called for only a small diversion from the Sukhona river system into the Volga and a Soviet official said that the nation will try to scale back the demand for water in the dry region by conservation and recycling. The same official forecast that the major diversions still may have to come in another decade or two, as the population grows in the southern regions.

China has the Soviet problem in reverse. Most of its water is in the south but it needs more water for agriculture, industry and a growing population in the north near Beijing (Peking). North China has only eight per cent of the nation's surface water and has only moderate rainfall, much of which arrives at the wrong time of the year for farmers. Like the Soviet Union, this country has also been heavily dependent on grain imports and there is pressure to divert water from humid areas to increase domestic food production. In China's case it would be a south-to-north diversion. Since the early 1950s China has studied the idea of diverting water from the Chang Jiang (Yangtze) River, in the south. At 5 800 kilometres this is the longest river in Asia, flowing from the Tibetan highlands to the East China Sea. Three diversion routes have been studied but two are very expensive and the Chinese have, at least for now, opted for the easier eastern route. This would utilize the ancient Beijing-Hangzhou Grand Canal and a chain of lakes, to move water north 1 150 kilometres from Nanjing to Tianjin, southeast of Beijing. The expanded canal will bring between 14 and 30 cubic kilometres of water to the dry North China Plain, increasing the amount of land which can be irrigated, or better irrigated, by close to 5 000 square kilometres. The project will also improve navigation on the ancient canal route, which was started 2 400 years ago for military purposes and was gradually lengthened over the centuries to transport grain to the capital.

India is another big nation with water in one area and dry farmland in another. The three main rivers, the Brahmaputra, Ganges and Indus in the north, have nearly two-thirds of India's river flow. To the south more and more underground sources are being used up by farmers desperate for irrigation water. India has suggested building a grid of east–west and north–south canals to bring water to drought-prone Rajasthan in the west, Madhya Pradesh in the centre and Tamil Nadu at the southern tip of the subcontinent. The backbone would be a 3 200-kilometre-long Ganges-Cauvery river canal running nearly the length of the country. So far the project does not appear to have gotten past the planning stage.

What is obvious is that around the world, important farming and population areas are running up against limits to water supplies and they face difficult decisions, often made harder by local political and business interests. While some countries simply will not have the money to build costly canal and pumping systems, others will have to choose between spending money on diversions, or trying to limit demand and make scarce water resources last longer through conservation. Even these tactics may not be enough if population growth is not checked or if the greenhouse effect suddenly creates permanent droughts in what were once fertile farming areas.

CHAPTER TWELVE

JUST WHOSE WATER IS IT, ANYWAY?

CANADIANS HAVE ALWAYS treated water as a free good, a birthright to which we were entitled in unlimited quantities. We tend to look at our giant lakes and rivers as water there for the taking by the first entrepreneur to grab it. Historically that is just what happened. People dammed up rivers to supply their mills and factories with water and hydro-electric power and treated lakes and rivers as a public garbage dump, often ignoring the complaints of less powerful neighbors who were injured by the pollution. Former Environment Minister Charles Caccia frequently made the point that free enterprise companies pride themselves in not requiring public subsidies. In fact, he said, they are getting a free slice of a major public good, the natural resource of clean water that they consume and pollute in vast quantities. The result has been a cost to the public of many hundreds of millions of dollars, to pay for sewage treatment of industrial wastes, provide alternate water supply systems and maintain environmental protection agencies.

Perhaps the issue of who gets the water is most brutal in the Canadian northland, where time is measured by the strokes of the paddle, not the ticking of a clock, and the calendar is marked by changing seasons. Part of that seasonal change is the natural rising and falling of water levels in the local rivers following the spring melt, summer dryness, fall rains and winter freeze-up. This natural life cycle has supported the growth of a wide variety of plants and animals, including humans. But in one river after another that age-old cycle has been shattered. To pick just one example, the Kamiskotia River near Timmins, in northern Ontario, for many years has been virtually killed by arsenic and acid leaching from a huge pile of mine wastes left by industries. One tributary creek draining from the waste pile is as acidic as vinegar and no fish can live in the waters downstream of the wastes. Industry has walked away from the mess and the province is reluctant to spend the $4–17 million needed to stop the pollution. This story is repeated time after time across the north when mines that are worked out are then abandoned, to poison the surrounding lands and waters indefinitely.

Even more dramatic is the effect of hydro-electric dams. The James Bay hydro-electric project flooded 12 000 square kilometres of north-western Quebec with five huge reservoirs which fluctuate wildly, revealing mud-rimmed, stump-choked waters. Release of an abnormally large amount of water from the biggest of the reservoirs has been blamed for the drowning of about 10 000 caribou that were crossing the Caniapiscau River downstream in September, 1984. Fishing at the mouth of the same river has deteriorated because the inter-tidal zone at Ungava Bay now fluctuates up and down the river for 60 kilometres, depending on how much water is released by Hydro Quebec. On the James Bay side, the Cree who lived at the mouth of the Eastmain River are now living on a saltwater estuary and have lost their traditional source of fresh running water. However, the Cree and the Inuit did get $225 million in compensation in return for damage caused by the hydro project when, in effect, they sold off some of their aboriginal rights to the water. Across the country the native peoples in the Peace-Athabasca Delta in Alberta were not so fortunate. They found out about the Bennett Dam in British Columbia in 1968 after it changed the natural flow of water downstream. And they simply have to live with its effects on the wildlife they hunt and fish and on their own water travel patterns.

Until recently the wildlife that inhabits or depends on waters affected by human actions was not really considered to have any rights. Some anti-pollution laws impose penalties for discharging wastes which kill fish but the aim of most such laws is to protect desirable species of fish for human consumption. Even there the law only deals effectively with cases of gross pollution that knock the fish dead overnight and it fails to prevent the insidious pollution that gives fish cancers or makes them unfit to eat. The laws are virtually silent on the need to protect aquatic life on its own merits, which would help to protect the biosphere of which we are all a part.

In fact our perspective on water issues has long been blinkered and we have failed to give a proper value to the water itself. For example, much of the philosophy of our pollution laws is geared to protecting drinking water or fish in the vicinity of towns and cities. This has allowed pollution to spread in remote areas. In the case of consumption, particularly in the west, water has often been allocated in generous quantities to the first person who asked for it, precluding other future uses. Now that limits to water are coming into sight in more and more parts of the world, environmental planners are saying it is time to stop talking of "free" water. Most people get their water simply for the cost of pumping it to their homes. Resource economists say water is a valuable commodity—an irreplaceable one—which should have a price and possibly be bought and sold like oil. They suggest that this would make people think of conserving it.

One group that has long been aware of the value of water in North America is the people who live in the dry west. Historically farmers and cattle barons, particularly in the United States, have been willing to fight for the waterhole, as anyone who has watched western movies knows. In a speech to a major water conference in Toronto in 1984, Scott Matheson, then Governor of Utah, the second-driest state, drove home the point. "Not only have political fortunes been lost but blood has been shed many, many times in the history of our two countries in the allocation of water...our most precious natural resource." The U.S. Council on Foreign Relations told a Canada-U.S. conference in 1984 that: "Fresh water, long considered inexhaustible and hence a free good, now begins to appear as perhaps the major long-range resource issue on the continent." The council warned that, "if unaddressed, rising demand over the next decades, especially by Americans, can cause problems of unprecedented seriousness since water is clearly the most precious of all continental resources."

This raises the question of just who owns the water on the continent and what laws control its use. Canadian water law is actually a myriad of rules, regulations and customs, some written down and some not. The country has 10 federal departments and agencies administering 20 statutes governing water, but they wield little authority since the provinces have the real control over water and other resources. Within the provinces and territories literally dozens of departments, agencies and boards make decisions affecting water. Jurisdiction is further fragmented by the fact that municipalities also have powers which affect water, ranging from sewage treatment, a prime element, to policies on agricultural, housing and industrial development and whether or not to meter water use. One of the unfortunate results is that those responsible for governing the use of water are often not the same ones who have to pick up the pieces afterwards with, for example, pollution controls. A report released by the federal inquiry on water said: "As water has emerged as a mainstream issue so has the perception that water policy is disorderly, fragmented and weak."

A pillar of water law in a number of countries, including Canada and the United States, is the old English common law which says that someone on the shoreline, a riparian landowner, can use water but cannot diminish its quality or quantity for downstream users. Obviously this riparian law, or riparian right, has been greatly modified in areas, particularly the west, where large amounts of water are withdrawn for irrigation, lowering the downstream flow. Riparian law has been affected by provincial statutes which allow landowners and companies to make major withdrawals or to divert whole rivers for hydro-electric projects. There is even a legal debate as to whether the fact that provinces issue permits for water use abolishes the old riparian right of a downstream victim to sue those people who damage the water quality. A research paper for the federal water inquiry pointed out that a number of people argue that this right to sue should be preserved because it is a method of maintaining water quality. Another problem is that some provinces find themselves in a bind because in the past they assumed there was unlimited water and they allocated water to users without imposing time limits. Now that there are new demands for a limited resource it is hard to abrogate those old agreements. Some provinces have also negotiated pollution control agreements with companies behind closed doors and later had to defend those companies when, for example, a citizen took the company to court for poisoning a river.

We seem to have approached water quality backwards. With our shortsighted attitude towards natural resources we have treated water as something that is virtually inexhaustible and therefore in little need of protection. As a result there is no broadly drafted law that "thou shalt not pollute our common heritage." Instead there is a mishmash of specific laws and guidelines that are usually so vague that companies can pollute at will unless a specific law has been passed to stop them. Instead of insisting that nothing can be discharged into the water without permission, we say that chemicals are considered innocent until proven guilty, so companies are allowed to discharge vast amounts of virtually unknown substances. Even the controls on pollution are based on a thoroughly discredited principle that the solution to pollution is dilution. As a result companies are allowed to dump highly toxic substances into our drinking-water sources, as long as they dilute the stuff so that it usually does not kill everything downstream overnight. Even when citizens try to tackle polluters they are sandbagged by the legal system. In order to sue, you commonly have to mount a case on your own, a highly expensive proposition given the many levels of appeal courts and the wealth of many polluters. And you have to prove that the substance is harming you, something that is extremely difficult to do when you are talking about many polluters putting many substances into common drinking water. With tap water that may contain several dozen substances, how do you prove it was Company A's toxin that got you rather than Company B's?

As water use increases, the various political jurisdictions bump up against one another more and more often. The greatest potential conflict is on the Prairies, where there is little water to begin with and virtually all of that flows east from the slopes of the continental divide in Alberta to Hudson Bay in Manitoba. Several decades ago Alberta, Saskatchewan and Manitoba decided they needed a way to share that water, particularly in the North and South Saskatchewan river systems. In 1948 they and the federal government formed the Prairie Provinces Water Board and in 1969 updated the agreement by signing a master agreement on apportionment of the Prairie waters. The water board, chaired by the senior water official in Environment Canada, is to oversee that sharing arrangement. The key element is an agreement that Alberta will pass half the flow of its eastbound prairie rivers on to Saskatchewan, and that province will do likewise to Manitoba. This further enshrines a 50-50 principle, which says that the state of origin has the right to at least half its waters but must pass half of them on to downstream users.

Water laws in the United States share a link to riparian law but were long ago modified to incorporate a principle called "reasonable use" which gave people the right to alter stream flows. This was further changed in the dry west by the Doctrine of Prior Appropriation, which means the first person to get the water has the legal right to use all of it forever. This instills a "use it or lose it" philosophy which discourages water conservation. It also encourages upstream users to build dams to capture water just in case they want to use it later on. The doctrine is somewhat modified by the "beneficial use" clause, stipulating that the water must be put to some purpose considered "useful," such as irrigating crops. For example, people establish a beneficial use by diverting the water to use on their land. As in Canada there is a plethora of laws, rules and regulations over water in the United States, but much more of the law seems to be hammered out in litigation. For example, it was a long series of court cases involving other Great Lakes states and the U.S. government that finally forced Chicago to reduce its diversion of Lake Michigan water. For years California appropriated water from the Colorado River to divert to its dry southlands but in 1963 Arizona won a court case which gave it some of that water.

When Texas debated a plan to reach eastwards for a piece of the Mississippi, Arkansas passed a law to stop anyone from taking water out of the state in amounts greater than a bucketful. A confrontation was averted when Texas abandoned the water diversion plan as too expensive. But Texas did get a similar law struck down on its western border. El Paso has been steadily outgrowing its local water supply so it negotiated to buy water from landowners in New Mexico. That state tried to stop the export of its scarce and precious water but a U.S. district court overruled a 1953 New Mexico law prohibiting the export of water from underground sources. The court found that El Paso's need for drinking water was greater and so that city has drinking-water wells in New Mexico. In a similar case Nebraska tried to stop the sale of its water but a 1982 U.S. supreme court decision said it could not automatically stop such exports, because water is an article of commerce. This decision sent a chill through water planners across the United States since it appeared that businessmen would be permitted to move water across state lines the way they transport food, oil, gas and other commodities—for private profit. This would run counter to the plans of states that want to hold on to their water resources to attract industry, and the taxes and employment it creates. But a number of state water experts contend that the court decisions are not a carte blanche for water exports. The removal of water from one state could be stopped or at least reduced, they believe, if the source state has implemented water conservation measures to prove that it was not wasting water, and could show that it needed the water at home for the health and welfare of its own citizens and did not have any to spare.

Like Prairie Canada, the southwestern states have had to try to divide up some of their waters, notably the Colorado River. The Colorado basin drains one-twelfth of the U.S. land mass in seven states and is a source of water and hydro-electric power for 20 million people. Back in 1922 the seven states signed the Colorado River

Compact in an effort to carve up its waters. Unfortunately for a lot of people, they goofed and allotted themselves 22.3 cubic kilometres of water per year, based on records from an abnormally wet period, when the actual long-term average flow is less than three-quarters that amount. To make matters worse they left virtually nothing to Mexico, a reflection of an 1894 U.S. policy called the Harmon Doctrine, which tried to pretend that the United States had no obligation to let water from its rivers flow beyond its borders. It took Mexico until 1944 to obtain a treaty allotting it 1.85 cubic kilometres of water a year from the Colorado. For many years the water the state received was so polluted with dissolved salts, as a result of U.S. irrigation practices, that it was sometimes unusable. The treaty guaranteed water of at least usable quality and in order to meet that obligation the United States has opted to build a $225-million desalination plant at Yuma, Arizona, on the Mexican border. By desalting some of the polluted river flow the United States will not have to release more water from upstream to dilute the pollution.

Canada-U.S. relations over boundary waters also have had their tense moments and this current period includes many of them. For several years now Canada has virtually accused the United States of poisoning Lake Ontario with wastes from the Niagara River and destroying much of eastern Canada with acid rain. Numerous Canadian politicians have lashed out at the United States, saying that it uses this country, in addition to its own, as a garbage dump for industrial discharges.

It is not really surprising that Canada and the United States have had some boundary water disputes. After all they share a 9 000-kilometre frontier, with 3 800 kilometres of that running through 300 lakes and rivers. John Carroll of the University of New Hampshire wrote about relations between Canada and the United States in his 1983 book, *Environmental Diplomacy*. Professor Carroll stated: "Bilateral environmental disagreements are becoming more numerous, more serious and less tractable and are beginning to represent greater stakes than ever before. They now constitute a substantial portion of all of the bilateral difficulties between the two nations and are strongly represented on any list of the top five or ten most serious diplomatic differences outstanding at any one time."

Tensions have run high in the past. For example the St. Mary River rises in the Montana mountains before running north across the border to become an important source of irrigation water for Alberta farmers in the Lethbridge area. But there was competition for that water with U.S. farmers, starting late in the last century. A long-running dispute came to a head when the United States announced that it was going to divert the St. Mary River into the more easterly Milk River, which also rises in Montana. The Milk flows into Alberta but then it plunges south and east back into the United States to link up with the Missouri River and later the Mississippi. Canada retaliated by declaring that it would head the water off at the pass and it hired a contractor to start digging a canal to the Milk River. In a game of one-upmanship Canada threatened to take the entire flow of the Milk. At one point it looked as if there was going to be a shootout over the water, which is critical in that dry area. The problem was resolved without either country making a diversion and the time-softened ditch near the Alberta village of Warner has become just a blip in Canadian history.

It was incidents like this that led to a remarkable attempt to find a permanent way of resolving such water issues: the 1909 Boundary Waters Treaty between Canada and the United States. The treaty, which was actually signed for Canada by Great Britain, has few parallels in the world and is so sweeping that many observers maintain that it would be virtually impossible to duplicate today. Dams and waterworks, according to the treaty, on either side affecting boundary water levels would become subject to approval by a special body, the International Joint Commission. It called for free and open navigation on boundary waters and Lake Michigan, which is entirely within the United States. And it contained a farsighted anti-pollution clause that reads, "Boundary waters and waters flowing across the boundary shall not be polluted on either side to the injury of health or property on the other."

Since then eight significant boundary water treaties and agreements have been signed by the two countries, covering everything from shipping and power generation to pollution and flood control. They include:

Lake of the Woods Convention and Protocol of 1925
Rainy Lake Convention of 1940
Niagara River Water Diversion Treaty of 1950
St. Lawrence Project of 1952
Columbia River Treaty of 1961 and Protocol of 1964
Great Lakes Water Quality Agreements of 1972 and 1978
Skagit River Treaty of 1984

In fact there have been dozens of other investigations, discussions and agreements covering boundary air and water issues.

But something even more important than a string of treaties came out of that 1909 agreement—the formation of the International Joint Commission (I.J.C.). Temporary joint commissions with one or more representatives from each country have long been appointed by nations to collect the facts about international disputes and offer recommendations for their solutions. Great Britain and the United States used commissions to settle the original Canadian boundary after the U.S. Revolutionary War.

But the I.J.C. is a permanent commission. Three of its members are appointed by the prime minister and three by the president. They have small secretariats in Ottawa and Washington and a Great Lakes regional office in Windsor. The six-member commission takes an investigative role to study and report on boundary water issues when asked jointly by the two governments. It also can be given a quasi-judicial role to set terms and conditions for the operation of boundary water projects and decide on compensation for affected parties. Since 1912 the I.J.C. has dealt with more than 50 cases involving the apportionment, conservation and development of water, including hydro power along the international boundary. Since 1918 it has been issuing reports on Great Lakes water quality and has been the key agency in preparing for and monitoring the progress of two Great Lakes water quality agreements.

This does not mean that the I.J.C. has no shortcomings. The national governments do not always treat it seriously. Both countries have left long gaps before appointing members and twice in recent years Canada has failed to appoint two of its three commissioners for extended periods. Sometimes the appointments are treated as just another slot to fill, rather than posts which need highly qualified people, so the commission often has been slowed down while new members try to understand the complex issues. The saving grace is that the commissioners usually seem convinced of the seriousness of the issues and often rise to the occasion. In addition the I.J.C. staff is small but highly effective in analyzing the issues and proposing recommendations.

Whatever their weaknesses, the treaty and the commission have given Canada, a much smaller country, bargaining rights with the most powerful nation on earth over a very contentious issue. As far as Canada was concerned, the 1909 treaty revoked the U.S. Harmon

Doctrine, which said an upstream state could do what it wanted with its waters. Canada's first federal water inquiry, chaired by Vancouver resource economist Peter Pearse, wrote in 1985: "If we had not had the Boundary Waters Treaty and the International Joint Commission to articulate our water interests during the past 75 years, we would almost certainly have had fewer cooperative projects, less consideration in unilateral developments and more strained relations with the United States. Its principle of equality is particularly important in view of the relative size and power of the two countries. In this respect it is superior to assurances afforded by international law."

Possibly the greatest fruits of the treaty and the I.J.C. are the Great Lakes Water Quality Agreements of 1972 and 1978. After years of watching rivers turn into soapy, oily sewers, and lakes into soupy ponds, the two countries signed clean-up pacts. In 1972 the goal was to stop the premature eutrophication of the lower Great Lakes by controlling the main villain, phosphorus from sewage and from laundry detergents. The two nations have limited phosphates in detergents everywhere but in Ohio and Pennsylvania and have spend billions of dollars on sewage treatment plants. Lake Erie and Lake Ontario are already much healthier and an ecological crisis of major proportions has been averted. The 1972 agreement called for a five-year progress review, and this led to the 1978 agreement. It, like the 1909 treaty, was more sweeping in its impact than governments probably first realized. While the 1972 agreement focussed almost entirely on phosphorus, the second attacked the full spectrum of industrial pollutants, toxic substances and radioactive wastes. It set specific water-quality objectives for almost 30 chemicals and it called for the countries to recognize the fact that the Great Lakes is an ecosystem. This means that they should accept the reality that all activities on land, water and air affect all living things, including humans, around the Great Lakes. And most importantly it pledged the two countries to "virtually eliminate discharges of persistent toxic substances" and to monitor the lakes for any violations.

That is pretty strong talk and they have not even succeeded in eliminating one chemical, PCBs, from the environment. Since 1978 the I.J.C. has been monitoring the state of the lakes, usually through research done by federal, provincial and state governments. The result has been some fascinating insights into just how polluted the lakes are, but little good news about clean-ups of toxic discharges. One of the reasons for the failure of the agreements to stop toxic chemicals lies in the fact that the documents are simply agreements, lacking treaty powers. Treaties in effect become domestic law, while agreements are only statements of intent and impose no legal requirements on business or lower levels of government. They can only be enforced by the passage of federal laws, where such laws do not conflict with provincial or states' rights. As a result the work done has been carried out unilaterally or under special agreements between the federal and regional levels of government.

The I.J.C. has been successful in resolving a number of contentious disputes over border water, including the monitoring of the shared waters of the Milk and St. Mary rivers. More recently the I.J.C. has dealt with two significant cases, the Garrison Diversion and the Skagit Valley. The Garrison Diversion was supposed to irrigate large tracts of dry land east of Minot, North Dakota. As originally designed, the Garrison would have pumped water from the Missouri-Mississippi river system, which drains to the Gulf of Mexico, over the Continental Divide. The water would then flow into the Red river system, which drains to Lake Winnipeg and thence to James Bay. As work started and the implications became clear, Canada complained bitterly that the U.S. water would be polluted with pesticides and fertilizers. More importantly, Canada was concerned that fish and fish parasites native to the U.S. rivers would be introduced into Lake Winnipeg, possibly damaging or even destroying the valuable fishery. A lot of questions about the value of Garrison were also raised in the United States, with some people maintaining that farmers would lose as much in good farmland flooded by the reservoirs as they would gain in increased crops from irrigation. For a number of years the U.S. federal and state governments appeared to ignore Canadian complaints. But more recently the U.S. government, concerned not only about Canadian reaction but also about the escalating cost of the work, seems to be promising that the project will be scaled down and that the U.S. water will stay south of the Continental Divide.

The Skagit case was another long-running dispute. In 1967 British Columbia rashly sold off the beautiful Skagit Valley by giving Seattle City Light the right to flood it to produce power for Seattle. The Skagit River was dammed in Washington State, 50 kilometres south of the British Columbia border, but the dam only flooded about two square kilometres of B.C. land. Several years ago the power company decided to raise the Ross Dam to impound more water and provide more electricity. This would have backed up the water at least 15 kilometres into Canada, flooding out about 20 square kilometres of one of the last flat-bottomed wilderness valleys in the area and with it a beautiful forest and a wild river with good canoeing, fishing, camping and wildlife habitats. The threat of flooding sparked an angry reaction from a generation which valued the valley as it was. The flooding was averted in 1983 after British Columbia bought its way out of the deal by offering to supply power from alternate sources.

An interesting air pollution case happened not far east of the Skagit many years earlier and it should set a precedent for acid rain controls by both countries. In the Trail smelter case it was Canada that was fouling the U.S. air. Sulphur dioxide fumes from a giant Canadian lead and zinc smelter in Trail, British Columbia, on the Columbia River, were damaging apple orchards and crops across the border in Washington. The I.J.C. started studying the case in 1928, and in 1931 it recommended that compensation be awarded to the farmers. There were a number of delays and the fumes continued so the United States brought pressure to bear by linking the clean-up and compensation to a trade agreement sought by Canada. The countries appointed an ad hoc tribunal which, in 1941, finally awarded damages, many of them paid to the survivors of farmers. In addition the smelter was cleaned up. The tribunal also ruled that: "No state has the right to use or permit the use of its territory in such a manner as to cause injury by fumes in or to the territory of another, or to the persons or property therein, when the case is of serious consequence and the injury is established by clear and convincing evidence."

It is a notable landmark for a more recent air pollution problem that directly affects water quality: acid rain. In fact the acid rain debate between the two countries actually began in the late 1970s when the United States complained to Canada about coal-burning power plants planned for southern Saskatchewan and northern Ontario, on the grounds that they would send acid rain into the United States. Following joint research the countries realized that each of them was producing extensive air pollution harming both themselves and each other. They signed the 1980 Memorandum of Intent to control transboundary air pollution, a document that pledged both countries to do their best to limit air pollution immediately, using existing laws, and to negotiate a clean air agreement, on the model of the Great Lakes water quality agreements but without the involvement of the I.J.C.

After Ronald Reagan became president in early 1981, Canada's attempts to negotiate an air pollution agreement were rebuffed on the grounds that more research was needed. It was not until 1986 that President Reagan agreed to the re-establishment of bilateral discussions on the issue between a full range of government officials from both countries.

Another potentially divisive issue is water consumption from the Great Lakes. This refers to the cumulative effects of hundreds of individually modest water withdrawals around the lakes by many thousands of users ranging from industries to whole cities. The settlement of 37 million people around the lakes and the creation of farms and industries are actually consuming water and not returning it. Water is taken up through thousands of pipes and canals, some of them no bigger than your wrist and others as wide as a small river, and their cumulative effects are starting to be felt. A recent study, quoting 1975 figures, said that every second of every day, Ontario and the eight boundary states withdrew 2 140 cubic metres of water from the lakes. That 2 140 000 litres of water is equal to one-fifth of the flow of Lake Ontario into the St. Lawrence River. Most of the water is pumped out of the lakes through giant intake pipes and returns anywhere from a few minutes to several months later after being used for such purposes as drinking, cooking, washing, flushing, watering, manufacturing and especially for cooling giant coal- and nuclear-fired power plants. However, six per cent of the water withdrawn, 140 cubic metres per second, is removed from the lakes and not returned. This is called water consumption.

Where does the water go? Some of it goes into our food and drink and becomes part of our growing bodies, or it is exported to be eaten and drunk somewhere else, away from the Great Lakes basin. Part of the water used by factories becomes manufactured products, such as chemicals and paper. The portion used to water livestock, irrigate crops, pastures, orchards, golf courses, lawns and parks is bound up in plants and animals. Some of the water simply leaks into the ground from old pipes and some is evaporated off industrial or power-plant cooling towers into the sky, where it becomes clouds and falls as rain somewhere else. As the lake levels drop, it means less water to turn giant hydro-electric turbines at Niagara Falls and the St. Lawrence River, less water to float cargo and pleasure boats in and out of harbors and even less water to dilute pollution. A small drop can cost millions of dollars in lost power production and reductions in the amount of cargo that ships can carry. Shallower lakes will mean present shoreline wetlands will dry up, disrupting wildlife which needs them as breeding areas or as a place to live.

There is a disturbing factor in the amount of water being taken from the lakes. Although Lake Michigan is entirely within the United

States, the four other Great Lakes are, at least in principle, divided more or less down the middle between the two countries. However, the I.J.C. reported that it is not working that way. According to 1975 statistics the United States is consuming more than seven times as much water from the Great Lakes as Canada. It is not spelled out in the report but one can infer that this is costing Canada money.

Several years ago one Canadian negotiator on Great Lakes issues said in an interview that his U.S. counterparts seemed to feel that since there were more U.S. than Canadian residents around the lakes, they had the right to more water. In 1983 Alan Pope, then Ontario's natural resources minister, told an I.J.C. meeting on the consumption issue: "While we are sensitive to U.S. needs and will continue to try to be the best kind of neighbor...we are opposed to any additional direct or indirect diversion of waters from the Great Lakes system."

At present the effects are barely visible but as the Great Lakes population increases to a predicted 80 million in the next 40 years, its thirst will also grow. One study done for the I.J.C. estimated that total consumption could increase as much as seven times between 1975 and 2035. This estimate would mean that 1 000 cubic metres of water per second would be drained from the lakes, causing their levels to fall as much as 34 centimetres. Even the conservative scenario for 2035 predicted consumption of 720 cubic metres per second. This would decrease the flow of the St. Lawrence River by 8.6 per cent and drop the levels of Lake Michigan, Lake Huron and Lake Erie by 23 centimetres.

In a final report on the issue in 1985 the I.J.C. did not accept the long-term projections, because it felt that no one could make accurate predictions that far ahead. But the commission did say that a drop of several centimetres could cost hundreds of millions of dollars a year to industry alone on both sides of the border. And the I.J.C. was so concerned about the growing consumption of Great Lakes water by both countries and the possibility of diversions to the west that it issued an unusually strong warning. The commission declared that there is a "potential for dispute and conflict" over the right to Great Lakes water in the future. It said, "there is no 'surplus' resource but rather competition among users. If demands on the resource increase, the competition...will do likewise." The commission recommended that Canada and the United States should create a new, two-level watchdog body on water use. This would include a permanent committee to monitor existing and proposed consumption and diversions and a task force that would make periodic recommendations to governments about demands for water.

A 1985 Environment Canada analysis pointed out that the greenhouse effect is predicted to substantially reduce the amount of water in the Great Lakes over the next few decades. This would mean that the combined effect of human consumption and climate change could lead to a reduction of as much as 28 per cent in the flow of the St. Lawrence and a drop in its level of as much as one metre. The report did not even try to calculate the economic effects but they would be measured in the many hundreds of millions of dollars at the very least.

Canada and the United States have yet to attack the problem of unequal water consumption but provincial and state governments have started their own approach to this potentially divisive issue. In early 1985 Ontario, Quebec and the eight Great Lakes states— Minnesota, Wisconsin, Illinois, Indiana, Michigan, Ohio, Pennsylvania and New York—signed a document called the Great Lakes Charter. It is not a legal treaty but the charter pledges the governments to regulate all large water withdrawals within their boundaries and at least consult with the other governments over mammoth withdrawals. Although this language does not prevent any province or state from unilaterally approving another Chicago Diversion, it is seen as a statement of intent that they will not move in this direction. More significantly for Canada, it gives this country direct contact with the U.S. water planners who will control the future levels of the Great Lakes. The question is, when it comes to increasing water consumption, will the opinions of Ontario and Quebec have any influence on states like Illinois, Michigan or New York?

Another party has entered the debate over rights to water with increased vigor in recent years. Some native groups are launching claims to water resources, usually as part of land claims. The most successful, in dollar terms, has been that of about 12 000 Cree and Inuit who were compensated for loss of some water rights, among other losses, caused by the James Bay power project. In the western United States there is a backlog of over 50 lawsuits by native groups trying to enforce treaty rights to water. In the last century the natives were given water rights but often they have been unable to actually get at that water and use it for such purposes as irrigation.

The picture of water ownership and water rights that emerges from even such a cursory look as this poses more questions than it answers. If water, a basic part of our environment, is a common inheritance,

The future of our water resources is at a turning point. Will we use more and more of them for industrial expansion? How much water will we preserve for recreation and enjoyment?
(ENVIRONMENT CANADA)

how is it that some people are allowed to pollute it, rendering it unfit for others to drink? And why do polluters who destroy whole rivers receive relatively small fines, while citizens are sent to jail for stealing a few hundred dollars? In addition to polluting a river, should a company have the right to take it over for its own purposes? For example, should Inco Limited, the giant metals company, be allowed to build another power dam on the Spanish River in northern Ontario, making it a less attractive place for the public to canoe? Should the Great Northern Paper Company have the right to build a dam on the west branch of the Penobscot River in Maine, flooding out some fine whitewater used for recreational rafting? What are the rights of fishermen whose catch is inedible because of pollution, or whose lakes have been rendered lifeless because of acid rain? And what of the fish themselves? In its final report the federal water inquiry concluded that we do not even really know what minimum flows are required to maintain life in rivers. This is becoming an important question in the west, where rivers are being dropped to record low levels by the demands of farmers and industry.

Governments, traditionally seen as the protectors of the public interest, will be forced into making more clearcut choices as there are more and more claimants for our waters.

CHAPTER THIRTEEN

IS ANYONE DOING ANYTHING?

INTO THE UNRELENTING TORRENT of evidence that our environment is in serious trouble, it is useful to throw at least one small stick of hope to which we can cling. That stick, if we use it wisely, can be the basis of a dam with which we can some day stop the flood of pollution before it destroys our water resources and us with them. That stick is the news that sprinkled among the horror stories of more pollution, there are important victories.

Two decades ago Lake Erie was turning into a giant bowl of pea soup. Today its waters are clearer than they have been for a long time. Many dangerous chemicals have been controlled and whole species of birds on Lake Ontario are no longer being poisoned out of existence. Growing numbers of industries have installed costly pollution controls and sharply reduced the amount of poisonous discharges from their sewers and chimneys. Governments are showing signs that they are going to pass tougher and more comprehensive anti-pollution laws to close some of the existing loopholes. More and more farmers are learning to plough in ways that will reduce erosion and thus pollution, are seeking to minimize pesticide and fertilizer use and are adopting or experimenting with water conservation measures when they irrigate.

If we are to understand what has been done so far and what is going to happen in the future, it is crucial to know who the decision-makers are.

In any environmental discussion business is labelled as the polluter, the villain in the piece. Businesses, whether they be giant petro-chemical complexes, small metal-finishing shops, corner garages or even farms, are directly and indirectly the physical source of most of our problems. For many years it was ignorance of the effects of

chemical discharges, sometimes a deliberate ignoring of the possibili-
ties, which has driven us into one crisis after another. Now there is
little innocence left. If a company does not know whether its
discharges are hazardous it is because the owners have decided not to
do the requisite testing. Business is also the source of the solutions to
the problems because this is where much of the expertise about our
pollutants was first created. Companies have learned to assemble
complex chemical structures and they have the ability to find ways to
disassemble them back into harmless forms. Many companies have
spent very large sums on pollution control and a growing number of
corporate officers have developed an environmental awareness. It is
their job to convince all players in the business community to clean up
before the environment collapses under them.

On the side of environmental protection the most obvious players
are the politicians, for it is the federal and provincial governments that
set most of the rules. They also do or pay for much of the environmental research, put up much of the money for clean-ups and set or fail to
set a climate of public opinion about environment issues. Unfortunately we have had very few "professional" environment ministers,
that is ministers who understood the issues before they took the
portfolio, who sought the post and had a clear sense of what needed to
be done. In most jurisdictions environment is still treated as a junior
portfolio. Sometimes it is a way station for ministers on the way down,
sometimes a testing ground for bright prospects hoping for higher
posts and sometimes just a grey area with little clear definition. Some
ministers who were plunged into the inevitable crises which come with
the job have done well. They stayed up late learning the complex
jargon of toxicology and grappled with such elusive issues as drinking-water safety. Others failed miserably and brought disgrace on
their governments. Because of both success and failure, ministers
have changed posts and as a result complex policies, such as waste
management, get delayed again while a new minister is briefed.

In addition to the minister, the political forum includes the opposition environment critics and their research staff. If the critics are good
they can be extremely effective watchdogs, forcing governments to
speak publicly on touchy issues. While it is the federal and provincial
governments which have environment ministries, the municipal
governments play a major role in environmental issues. It is the
municipalities that rule on housing and development plans that will
affect water use and pollution. Local taxpayers foot most of the bill for

sewage treatment plants and sometimes it is local officials, often health agencies, that investigate environmental issues.

The second government component is the civil service, ranging from the technician in the field to the deputy minister of environment. Here there is expertise and a wide range of attitudes. Within the ranks you find everything from the true environmentalist who wants to eliminate the problems, to the professional problem managers who try to handle issues in ways that will make the minister look good. It is the government scientists and technical experts who have the largest budgets and usually the best-equipped research laboratories to carry out costly and time-consuming studies of pollution. As a result governments are the key source of information about what is going on in the environment. There are many struggles for access to that information by people outside government, and many attempts to control or sometimes even suppress controversial findings by nervous bureaucrats and politicians.

There is a third category which can be loosely grouped under the government umbrella. This includes the government-appointed bodies that advise on and sometimes regulate environmental activities. A prime example is the International Joint Commission, which is appointed by the prime minister of Canada and the president of the United States to report on boundary water issues. Other government-appointed bodies act as advisors to environment ministers, hold hearings on pesticides and even build waste treatment centres.

Second only to government in importance in the battle to save our water are the environment groups. Often maligned by polluters and incompetent politicians who were the victims of their criticisms, the groups are the least understood and most undervalued environmental protectors. This is not to say that they are saints, that they do not indulge in power plays or do not sometimes get their facts wrong. But in the aggregate of their work they play a vital role in our knowledge of and concern about environmental issues. They do little original scientific research because their budgets are tiny. In fact they rely heavily on volunteer labor or work done at low wages. Their role is more to take the data prepared by others and interpret it in ways that often shed new light on problems. This allows them to prepare the devastating critiques about the state of our environment which are the bane of polluting companies and are the accusing fingers pointed at environment departments. They have been called the commandoes of the environment.

In recent years more and more environment ministers have decided that the groups are better treated as allies than as foes and there are more attempts by politicians to work cooperatively. In some jurisdictions the environment groups effectively have replaced environment ministries which have remained silent on key issues. In other cases the groups have represented Canada in political or legal actions in the United States when the federal and provincial governments chose for political or diplomatic reasons not to act. While the first role of the environment groups is that of watchdog on environmental quality, the groups have a vital secondary role: offering advice on how to avoid problems in the first place. A number of groups have mounted demonstration projects on energy conservation and waste prevention and have even published anti-pollution handbooks for use by business.

The education system is another player but it remains behind the scenes more than the environment groups. Academic research is second only to that of government in defining and trying to solve our environmental problems. It was academics who did much of the key work on alerting us to the dangers of acid rain. The universities are not only the source of much information, but the training ground for many of the people who play important roles in other fields. For example, some leave academe to work for government or industry on pollution research and control. The schools and universities can play one of the most important roles of all—that of educating the next generation to be more environmentally aware than the last. To some degree they do this in environment courses but these are limited to a small number of students who will become specialists. What is needed is much more broadly based environmental education so that everyone who leaves school, whether they will become a truck driver hauling hazardous cargo or the chairman of a chemical company, has a basic understanding of the issues.

The news media are also key players in the environment debates, for it is in the newspapers and magazines and on the airwaves that most of the information about the state of the environment is disseminated. News stories inform the public, which then reacts, sending signals to politicians to devote more effort to environmental protection, and to companies to clean up their pollution to protect their corporate images. It is through the media that the politicians send their message to the public that they are trying to do something, and that the business community offers its explanations, excuses and proposed solutions. Of course it is through news media that the environment groups operate most effectively, since a story in a newspaper will have far more impact on an environment minister than will a stack of briefs. Although the news media carry an increasing number of environment stories, most are written by general assignment reporters. There are still very few full-time, experienced environment reporters, so many of the stories are limited to repeating what other people say rather than analyzing the importance of what they say and pointing out trends to the public.

And finally there is the public, you, the citizen, who, in the final analysis, is the most important player of all. It is you as an individual who will decide whether or not to recycle cans and bottles instead of throwing them into the garbage, whether or not to use fewer toxic chemicals and dispose of them more safely. It is you who will write or phone your elected officials to express your opinion about environment issues. And it is through your demands and patterns of consumption that business will get the strongest signal about what kind of a job it is doing.

What has been done by all these players? There is a growing list of success stories, including the major effort to reduce the sewage going into the Great Lakes. By the 1960s many people thought Lake Erie was dead or dying and that Lake Ontario was next. It turned out that Erie was just gravely wounded and some strong action has nursed it back to at least better if not perfect health. There are far fewer complaints abouts mats of rotting algae on the beaches and foul-tasting drinking water each summer. The Great Lakes clean-up has received probably the greatest sustained infusion of money and attention of any pollution control project on the continent, if not the world. One set of widely used figures states that between 1971 and 1984 Canada and the United States spent $8.851 billion on sewage control around the lakes. This breaks down to $6.846 billion on the U.S. side and $2.005 billion in Canada. But some people estimate that when one counts the spending on sewage treatment by local governments, that estimate could double. Over 200 communities in the Great Lakes basin have made improvements to their sewage treatment, including the installation of 142 new treatment plants.

Other actions to protect the Great Lakes are harder to quantify in dollar terms. In order to help control phosphorus pollution which was over-fertilizing the lakes, most governments limited the amount of phosphate in detergents. Ontario cut the amount in laundry detergents to 2.2 per cent while Minnesota, Wisconsin, Michigan, Illinois,

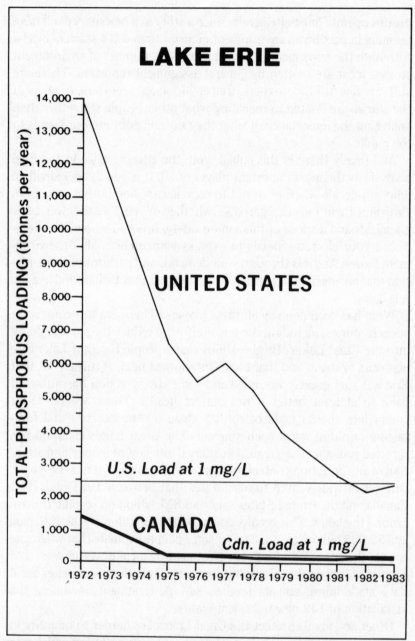

LAKE ERIE

TOTAL PHOSPHORUS LOADING (tonnes per year)

14,000
13,000
12,000
11,000
10,000
9,000
8,000
7,000
6,000
5,000
4,000
3,000
2,000
1,000
0

UNITED STATES

U.S. Load at 1 mg/L

CANADA

Cdn. Load at 1 mg/L

1972 1973 1974 1975 1976 1977 1978 1979 1980 1981 1982 1983

This chart, based on information from the International Joint Commission, shows the dramatic drop in phosphorus pollution once Canada and the United States agreed to save Lake Erie from eutrophication. In the 1960s and 1970s Lake Erie was said to be dying from excess pollution.   (BERNARD BENNELL)

Indiana and New York all restricted it to one-half of one per cent. Only Pennsylvania and Ohio have failed to impose controls.

The Great Lakes are a world-class success story and a symbol of efforts being made in many countries to stop the destruction of our fresh waters. Lake Baikal, the world's largest lake by volume, contains more water than even the Great Lakes system, but the water quality of this huge reservoir has been endangered by timbering and industrial development. In an effort to protect water quality and fish such as the omul (a type of salmon), the Soviet government banned timber drives in the tributary rivers and imposed stringent controls on pulp and paper factories on the shores of the lake. A railway was rerouted away from the north shore in a further effort to protect the lake's ecosystem.

In Europe the Rhine has been terribly polluted for decades but in recent years Switzerland, Germany and France have instituted pollution controls and the toxic tide is being reduced. Across the channel the restoration of the Thames to the point that salmon have returned is another positive sign. Closer to home a number of industrial rivers in North America run cleaner than they have in many years. By 1960 salmon were virtually wiped out of the St. Croix River, which forms part of the boundary between New Brunswick and Maine. After pollution controls in both countries improved the water quality and fish ladders were installed around dams, salmon once again swam in from the sea. To the north the Saint John River, which also forms part of the international boundary, has undergone a similar improvement.

There are many other important ways to fight pollution. Government agencies are cracking down with tighter pollution controls. Industries are responding with more anti-pollution equipment and with research into ways of avoiding pollution in the first place. William Neff of the Canadian Chemical Producers' Association estimates that 10 to 15 per cent of the money spent in changing chemical processing goes into pollution controls. R. G. Denning, general manager of the Lambton Industrial Society, which represents industries along the St. Clair River, said that they spent $135 million on environmental projects between 1980 and 1985. In a 1984 statement Ontario's environment ministry estimated the pollution control spending in the province from 1967 to 1982 by three major sectors—petroleum refiners, steel mills and pulp and paper mills—at $500 million. The ministry said that similar expenditures had been made in other industrial sectors, such as petrochemical, metal finishing and fabrication, and food processing.

Another victory in the battle against pollution is the banning or severe limitation of specific toxic chemicals. One of the early major moves was against DDT, which was regulated to low limits, although not totally outlawed, by Canada and the United States between 1969 and 1971. Mercury was found to be a serious health hazard in fish from some parts of Canada, particularly downstream of Sarnia. Since controls were imposed in 1970, mercury discharges have been reduced to low levels and commercial fishing has resumed in the western basin on Lake Erie and, for some species, in Lake St. Clair. The production of PCBs was voluntarily limited in 1971 by its prime North American manufacturer and stopped in 1978. However, the chemical is still widely used in electrical equipment. Other toxic substances which have come under very strict controls include: Aldrin, Chlordane, dibromochloropropane (DBCP), Dieldrin, Endrin, ethylene dibromide (EDB), Heptachlor, Kepone, Lindane, Mirex, Silvex, strychnine, 2,4,5-T and Toxaphene. Alachlor, the most widely used pesticide in the United States, is coming under stronger controls, as are two major wood preservatives, pentachlorophenol and creosote. Both countries are reducing the use of lead as a gasoline additive and there are signs that it may eventually be eliminated.

Air pollution controls are vitally important for water quality, as was discussed in Chapter 5. In many ways our air is cleaner now, a fact that is obvious if we look at photographs taken early in this century which show cities almost obscured by their own smoke. This improvement was partly the result of using cleaner heating fuels, such as oil, gas and electricity instead of coal, and the introduction of controls on car exhausts. But one of the "cures," tall smokestacks to disperse pollution, alleviated local air problems and created a water problem by spreading the fallout far and wide over lakes and rivers.

Most of the discussion of controls on toxic fallout has focussed on acid rain because this is the part of the problem which has been most studied. In the case of sulphuric acid rain, the bulk of the pollution comes from relatively few sources. In Canada a dozen major smelters and power plants produce most of the sulphur air pollution. Action to reduce acid rain has been slow but there are agreements which will take effect over the next decade. For example the Economic Commission for Europe, part of the United Nations, prepared the 1979 Convention on Long-Range Transport of Air Pollutants. It pledges nations to "limit and, as far as possible, gradually reduce and prevent air pollution" that is affecting their neighbors. In 1985 Canada and 19 member nations signed a protocol, a specific commitment under that agreement, to reduce their sulphur dioxide pollution by 30 per cent by 1993. (The United States and Great Britain did not sign that protocol.) Canada in fact has pledged to make a 50-per-cent cut by 1994 and several other nations are making a reduction greater than one-third.

In 1980 Canada and the United States signed a Memorandum of Intent to negotiate a clean air agreement, but negotiations were stalled in 1982 when the United States rejected the Canadian proposal for specific reductions in sulphur dioxide pollution. At a regional level eastern Canadian premiers and eastern U.S. governors pledged in 1985 that they would reduce sulphur dioxide emissions by 32 per cent by 1994, an important step but not one that can reach the major polluters in the U.S. midwest.

The most important acid rain control actions have been taken in Canada under a landmark agreement between the federal and provincial governments to reduce sulphur dioxide pollution in eastern Canada by half by 1994. It took years of long and hard negotiating for Ottawa and the five eastern provinces involved in major cuts—Manitoba, Ontario, Quebec, New Brunswick and Nova Scotia—to hammer out an accord. The provinces will be responsible for ordering controls on the polluters and for paying for the clean-up of power plants. Environment Canada estimates the 50-per-cent clean-up will cost about $500 million a year over 20 years, with half of that for the nickel and copper smelting industry. The federal government will contribute up to $150 million towards the clean-up of polluting smelters but the rest of the estimated $750-million cost will come from the companies and possibly the provinces. In 1980 Ontario froze the emissions of the Sudbury smelter of Inco Limited, the continent's biggest source of sulphur dioxide. The next year the province ordered Ontario Hydro, its electric utility, to start reducing sulphur pollution by 1986. In 1985 the province ordered a dramatic new round of cuts for the province's four big polluters in order to reduce their pollution by 67 per cent in nine years. Inco and Ontario Hydro are to make further substantial reductions and new cuts were imposed on Falconbridge Limited, in Sudbury, and The Algoma Steel Corporation Limited in Wawa, north of Sault Ste. Marie, Ontario. In 1985 Quebec passed strong regulations ordering the Noranda Incorporated smelter, Canada's second-largest source of sulphur dioxide, to reduce its pollution by half by 1990.

The United States has always argued that it reduced its sulphur dioxide pollution steadily during the 1970s and in fact this is true. However, it is far from enough. Much of the reduction was due to a set of regulations called New Source Performance Standards, which required new coal-burning power plants to capture most of the sulphur dioxide before it went up their smokestacks. This still leaves dozens of big, old power plants that do not have to conform to the standards and that may keep on spewing out millions of tonnes of pollution for decades before they finally fall apart. So although the United States has 90 anti-pollution scrubbers on its power plants, as many as 200 more are needed to choke off the acid rain. Worse, a 1985 report to the E.P.A. predicted that pollution levels are likely to start rising again. The United States has long led Canada in one field, that of regulating car pollution. In particular it has cracked down on nitrogen oxides which lead to nitric acid rain and ozone pollution, and on the gasoline additive tetraethyl lead, which is a neurotoxin. Canadian lawmakers are just catching up with U.S. standards but there are signs that the United States will again move ahead with even tighter controls.

The disposal of hazardous waste is one of the most topical pollution issues. It involves such high-profile areas as Love Canal and hundreds of other old toxic dump sites around the continent, in addition to the ongoing discharges from industries. For years most of the hazardous wastes not pumped into lakes and rivers simply have been dumped into great holes in the ground where it was assumed that they would stay. Over the last couple of decades we have found out that all dumps leak, though at varying speeds, and there is a desperate search for alternative disposal methods. Industry has failed to cope with the amount and variety of waste for a number of reasons. One of the most important reasons is a set of laws which made it cheaper to dump the stuff than treat it. Private treatment firms handle some wastes but governments are stepping in more and more to take over at least part of the disposal role.

Alberta and Ontario are the two provinces most advanced in developing major waste treatment and disposal sites, although other provinces are showing interest in creating their own high-technology treatment centres. Alberta formed the Special Wastes Management Corporation, to supervise the construction and operation of a waste treatment centre by private industry. The site is near Swan Hills, 180 kilometres northwest of Edmonton, and the government wants to see it start operation by 1987. After several abortive tries by the government and industry to set up waste treatment centres in Ontario, the province created the Ontario Waste Management Corporation in 1981. This Crown corporation was ordered to build and operate a top-quality waste treatment centre for the province's hazardous wastes. The O.W.M.C. stated that its aim was to stop the dumping of raw chemical wastes into sewers and the ground and to chemically or physically treat wastes, solidify them, neutralize acids and alkalies and incinerate the most dangerous chemicals. The residues of these processes would be buried in a specially lined and monitored pit in the ground. In 1985 the O.W.M.C. announced a "preferred" disposal site on the heavy clay lands of southern Ontario south of St. Catharines. With the time needed for further testing and public hearings over the suitability of the site and the proposed technology, no waste treatment is likely until late in this decade.

The United States instituted a major change in waste disposal in November, 1985, with new regulations by the U.S. Environmental Protection Agency. These required that landfill dumps used for hazardous wastes be fitted with equipment to prevent them from leaking, be monitored for leakage and be covered by heavy liability insurance in case of leaks. Within days of the rules taking effect, more than two-thirds of the toxic waste dumps said that they could not meet the new requirements and would probably have to close.

Nuclear waste disposal has been the most intractable long-term disposal issue. In the case of chemical and metal wastes there are accepted techniques to destroy them. But no one has yet found an acceptable way to destroy nuclear waste and various radioisotopes can remain dangerous for centuries, even millennia. Most of the waste from nuclear power plants around the continent is now stored in water tanks which are like huge swimming pools, where the radioactive material glows with an eerie blue light. The research for waste disposal sites is now focussing on deep underground entombment in granite rock, such as that in the Precambrian Shield. Ontario, which operates most of the nuclear power stations in Canada, is focussing on sites in northwestern Ontario, while the United States is looking at a number of sites. The U.S. government is getting involved in a Canadian study of that concept. Researchers have been boring deep into granite near Lac du Bonnet, Manitoba, to find out how solid deep granite really is and what dangers there would be of underground water dissolving stored wastes and carrying them to the surface. In late 1985 Atomic Energy of Canada Limited, which is conducting the studies, said evidence so far shows there is little chance of rapid leakage. An agency official stated that if radioactive waste is buried in corrosion-resistant containers 500 to 1 000 metres deep it will not seep to the surface for tens of thousands of years. A final report on the research is due in 1988 and the first Canadian disposal site is not expected before 2010. The United States wants a solution to its nuclear waste disposal problems by 2006.

The biggest problem facing most waste disposal projects is not technical but social. The repeated failure of governments and industries in the past to protect or even warn the public adequately about hazardous waste has created a climate of fear and suspicion of anything linked to the issue. In recent years governments in both Canada and the United States have had an increasingly difficult time getting any area to accept a hazardous waste treatment site, even a very modern one with low risks. The public reaction to and rejection of such sites has been dubbed the Not In My Backyard (NIMBY) Syndrome. It can be so severe that the O.W.M.C. is taking the better part of a decade to find and get approval for a site and its technology, even though every day that is lost adds to the pollution in the environment. O.W.M.C. head Donald Chant, a prominent Canadian environmentalist and founder of the Pollution Probe organization, has said that the only way to win public confidence is by proceeding slowly and in full view every step of the way.

What about not creating the problems in the first place? Environment Canada estimates that 80 per cent of the toxic contamination we must dispose of need not have even been made. The solution to this part of the problem lies within the grasp of industry and so far there are signs that companies are trying to reduce their toxic discharges, but there is no clear picture emerging about the net effect. What about recycling? An obvious question but one that, curiously enough, does not seem to have been pursued with much vigor by industry or governments. A number of environment experts believe that governments suffer from a psychology which considers it more interesting to build large edifices, such as sewage treatment plants, than to quietly nick away at the problem at the source. Laws and pricing policies for years have made dumping the cheapest alternative to industry, even though it is far more costly to society in the long run. The result is predictable: a 1981 U.S. study said that industry recycled only about 4 per cent of its toxic wastes. Indications are that Canada did little better. Ontario created a waste exchange to foster the trading of industrial materials that are wastes to one company, yet can be usable products to another; but the project has had only a minor effect on waste quantities. Some municipalities, such as Kitchener, Ontario, and Victoriaville, Quebec, have taken the initiative by distributing special garbage containers to each household. The containers are divided into compartments for such reusable materials as paper, glass and cans, which are sold to recycling companies rather then being dumped or burned, two processes which turn garbage into pollution. Recycling also cuts water use. For example a tonne of aluminum made from scrap rather than raw ore can reduce the volume of water required in manufacturing by 97 per cent. Recycling newspapers not only saves 20 mature softwood trees for every tonne of newsprint but also prevents a lot of water pollution caused during the harvesting and processing of those trees in the first place.

Environmental groups have often spearheaded recycling projects. Pollution Probe in Toronto even wrote a book about waste reduction and reclamation, called *Profit from Pollution Prevention*, a major study of how businesses have reduced waste, saved money and protected the environment at the same time. Quebec environmentalists who operate a number of programs claim that most municipalities fail to see the benefits of recycling because setting up the projects has more immediate operating costs, even though it reduces the long-term expense of creating and caring for big dumps.

There are signs that governments recognize that the current ways of protecting the environment are simply not good enough. For example Ontario Environment Minister James Bradley said in 1985 that he plans to put a limit on the amount of hazardous pollution that each company can discharge into the lakes and rivers. This is a revolutionary departure from the historic method of telling companies that they could discharge a certain concentration of a chemical. The old law put no limit on the amount of chemical dumped as long as it was diluted with enough water in a big pipe to soften its impact immediately downstream from the factory. Mr. Bradley said that his aim is the elimination of the discharge of persistent toxic substances into Ontario's waters by the year 2000.

And there are new technological wrinkles which hold promise. For example experiments are being conducted to find newer and cheaper ways to make old smelters and power plants cleaner. There are even attempts to bury pollution artificially in the sediments. An ingenious technique being studied in Montreal may cover up the polluted muds on the bottom of the historic Lachine Canal. Environment Canada is conducting tests to see if a polyester or polyester-like membrane can be spread across the bottom of the canal to trap pollution, then be covered with sand and gravel to speed up the natural process of sedimentation, which buries pollution over a long period of time.

The second half of the water equation is quantity, and in dry areas efforts to reduce water wastage are no less important than pollution control. A number of major industries which use water intensively are starting to recycle the water instead of using the "once-through" procedure that demands a constant supply. While Ontario builds its nuclear power plants on the Great Lakes so they can use gigantic amounts of cooling water, the Palo Verde nuclear station has been built on the desert outside Phoenix. It has no nearby water bodies but instead will take treated wastewater from local communities and reuse it 15 times. Alberta's Sundance power station, which burns coal, recycles North Saskatchewan river water 70 times. A number of municipalities have mandated water meters, often cutting household demand in half.

But the big water user is agriculture and it is on the farm fields that the major battles to conserve water will be won or lost. In the Prairies 72 per cent of the water consumed is for irrigation and that goes to 1 per cent of the land under cultivation. The success or failure of policies and techniques to reduce agricultural water consumption are crucial. They may mean the difference between major water diversions or sustained agriculture with local water reserves. Sandra Postel, in one of her water reports for Worldwatch, a Washington-based organization, points out the amounts involved. Ms Postel writes that by raising irrigation efficiency worldwide by just 10 per cent, we could save enough water to supply all global residential uses.

For millennia farmers have irrigated their land simply by pouring water into furrows which run between rows of crops, but as much as half the water fails to get to the plants. It seeps through unlined canals into the ground, it is evaporated away by sunshine and wind or it runs right past the plants and off the field. In recent years a new type of irrigation system has been introduced to get more water onto the fields—a system similar in some ways to garden sprinklers. It is based on the centre pivot irrigators that use pipes mounted on wheels to roll over the fields delivering water. They can be 70 per cent efficient with current designs but even this is not good enough when vast amounts of water are involved. Researchers in Texas are modifying the

In an effort to sharply reduce the waste of water in farming, researchers are finding ways to apply irrigation water more directly to the plants. This will extend the lifespan of underground water supplies. (MICHAEL KEATING)

sprinklers so that instead of spraying their water high into the air, where it can be evaporated by the wind and sun, they drop it straight onto the crops with delivery rates as high 98 per cent. Possibly the most efficient system yet is drip irrigation, highly developed in water-short Israel, where parts of the Negev Desert have been turned into gardens with a minimum of water usage. The system involves laying or burying pipes or tubing on the ground and trickling out small amounts of water from little holes, one beside each plant. Unfortunately, it is also expensive to install, prone to plugging with dirt and unsuitable for some types of crops. But it will certainly become more common as the cost of water rises.

Other techniques hold great promise. Water which runs down furrows past the plants is being collected and pumped back to the top of the fields. Water-demand forecasting is being geared to real crop needs and to weather conditions to maximize water use and minimize evaporation. New ways are being developed to mine water from dry wells. Researchers in dry north Texas are driving compressed air into the ground in an attempt to break the bond between capillary water and soil particles. They hope that the water in effect will be shaken out of the soil and will collect in depleted underground aquifers where pumps can get at it.

And Canadian forest biologist Melvin Tyree is developing a system which can tell when plants need water, based on the sounds they make when they get thirsty. Ultra-sensitive microphones are stuck in the ground to pick up the high-pitched popping noise of plants' water delivery systems cracking when they get too dry. With such devices farmers might be able to listen to plants when they need water, thus avoiding wasteful over-watering.

High technology and common sense are being combined now in the battle to stop pollution and water waste. Sadly, we held back our ingenuity until much damage had been already done.

CHAPTER FOURTEEN

SAVING THE WATER: WHAT YOU CAN DO

THE PIONEERS, who had to carry their water by the bucketful, probably got by with about 20 litres a day each. Today Canadians are the world's second-largest users of water. On average we each "use" a bit more than 4 100 litres of water per day, while the U.S. demand runs at 6 300 litres a head. Of course that figure has little to do with what the normal person runs down their drain. It represents the water an industrial society uses on our behalf. Vast amounts of water flow through our factories, steel mills and power plants to cool giant furnaces, provide our electricity, operate equipment and process the very food we eat. The average Canadian personally uses an average of 285 litres per day at home, for drinking, cooking, washing and sanitation. That national average varies from 90 to 320 litres a person, depending upon whether you draw from a limited supply in a rural well or have a powerful city supply and water a large lawn.

By comparison with most countries we are water profligates. In Sweden and the United Kingdom the average use is 200 litres per person per day, in West Germany and France about 150 litres, in Beijing, 145, in Israel 135 and in Latin America it ranges from 75 to 100 litres. In parts of the world where people have to draw water from a communal tap or an open fire hydrant, water use drops to the 20–70-litre range. The use plummets in arid regions, such as parts of Africa, where people must walk long distances just to bring home one container of water. Here people often get by with 2–5 litres a day, close to the biological minimum.

Where does the water go in an average Canadian home? Every day we use water with gay abandon for everything from long, luxurious showers to intensive lawn watering. About half the average person's daily water supply is flushed away and about one-third goes down the sink or bathtub drain after washing. Our lawns are planted with grasses imported from wet climates and we insist on having green lawns everywhere, even in the desert.

In fact our actual need for water is only an average of 1 to 2 litres each to drink and we need about the same amount from our food. The rest is used and disposed of by our machines. For example:

A flush toilet uses 20 litres.
A shower uses about 25 litres a minute.
A bathtub holds about 130 litres.
A dishwasher uses about 65 litres.
A clothes washer uses about 230 litres.
A garden hose uses 1 500 litres or more an hour.

A dripping tap wastes from 30 to 100 litres a day and, on average, water leaks account for 5 to 10 per cent of the water use in North American homes.

Our lifestyle accounts for the other 3 800 litres per day used on our behalf. For example, it takes as much water to fill a backyard swimming pool as it does to produce enough food for a single meal for a family of four.

Here are some examples of the amount of water used in the production of everyday items.

One tonne of high-quality books uses 770 000 litres of water.
One tonne of steel requires up to 250 000 litres.
A steak takes 13 200 litres.
One large weekend newspaper takes 570 litres of water.
One egg requires 450 litres.
One litre of high-grade whiskey requires 140 litres of water.
One litre of gasoline takes 10 litres of water.

Most of the water is not literally in the product but it was used in its production, for example in the feed used for the animals.

It is not just the water use which is important, but what is added to the water after it passes through the entrails of industries. "Our lifestyle depends on production which results in harmful agricultural runoff, toxic waste dump sites and concentrated industrial pollution adjacent to highly populated areas on major water supplies,' says the U.S. National Water Alliance. It is not just industries which are fouling the lakes and rivers with their sewage. Most households have enough chemicals in them to start a small but lethal laboratory. We are bombarded with commercials encouraging us to pour cleansers and drain cleaners into our water. These chemicals should not be put in our drinking water and many of them are clearly labelled as hazardous. In addition to human sewage we dump a vast amount of other wastes into our drains, including some nasty chemicals like paint wastes and pesticides. Sewage treatment plants are not equipped to cope with most of these chemicals and as a result they go into our sources of drinking water and into our fish.

Now we are going to have to think about reducing, even rationing, water use in some heavily populated areas. And we are going to have to be a lot more careful about what we put into our water. Why bother in a country which has so much water? In dry areas, which include most of the Prairies, the Okanagan Valley and inland towns and cities in regions like southern Ontario, there are already limits to the water supply. If the population keeps growing, each person will be forced to cut back his or her personal use or face periodic rationing. There is also a monetary reason. Money can be saved by reducing the amount of water which has to be treated and the amount of equipment needed to purify and deliver it. A reduction in water consumption will be reflected in the tax bills because less money will be spent to deliver water and to treat sewage flows. It will also be reflected in indirect but important ways, such as the reduction in energy required to pump and to heat water. Reducing energy demand reduces pollution too, such as the amount of coal burned and acid rain produced. Most of us could reduce our water use by one-third by using a few simple techniques and some inexpensive equipment.

"Save water. Shower with a friend," was the New York slogan during the water shortage of the 1960s. Robert McEwen, U.S. co-chairman of the International Joint Commission on Canada-U.S. boundary waters, does not take group showers but he does boast, "I turn off the shower while I lather with soap." The easiest way to do this is to install a small water shutoff valve, costing a few dollars, behind the showerhead. When you are soaping up you can reach up and turn the handle to reduce the water flow to a dribble without affecting the water temperature. In addition you can install a small water flow reducer which allows less water volume through the showerhead but maintains the water pressure. The equipment can be bought in hardware stores and most people install it themselves. All you need is an adjustable wrench and some Teflon tape to waterproof the joints.

North American toilets, with their 20-litre tanks, are wasteful by European standards. Most West German toilets use as little as 9 litres per flush, while those routinely installed in Scandinavia since 1975 get by with as little as 6 litres. There are high efficiency toilets on the market that can get the job done with as little as 2–4 litres, sometimes by using a jet of air along with the water. The efficiency of the flush depends not just on the amount of water used but on the force with which it is delivered. A number of water-saving devices can be installed in most North American toilets, including a $5 gizmo which forces the water delivery flapper to close partway through the flush. If you want a long flush, just hold down the toilet handle until the tank empties. When it comes to dishwashers and washing machines the main rule is to make certain they are full before using them. When you buy water-saving equipment you should invest in a small water shutoff for the nozzle end of your garden hose as well. That way you will be less tempted to leave it running while you are washing the car.

Lawn watering can consume vast quantities of water and nothing looks sillier than to see a sprinkler on during a rainstorm. Many people put more water than necessary on their lawns and could save water by following the instructions in a gardening booklet. There are other ways to deal with thirsty lawns. William Andrews, former president of the Conservation Council of Ontario, lets natural wildflowers and weeds grow in his country property and finds them so adapted to the climate that they never need watering. A number of stores now sell a wildflower mix which can replace grass. In the southwestern United States individual water demand can skyrocket to 1 000 litres per person per day mainly because of lawn watering. A booklet of advice to California residents recommends testing your lawn to see if it really needs watering. If the grass springs back after you step on it the lawn does not yet need water, according to the pamphlet. A number of western cities, such as Tucson, Denver, and Austin, as well as the state of California are actively promoting water-conserving landscaping, using plants that do not demand large amounts of water.

Cities play an important role in water conservation. Water metering is one of the most effective ways of cutting demand because it forces people to think about water as they pay for it. It encourages conservation because you are billed on your own use, not some city-wide average. Edmonton homes have meters and use about one-half as much water as those in Calgary, which are unmetered. Kitchener,

Ontario, made it civic policy to have new homes built with water-saving devices and so far has avoided the necessity of importing water from the Great Lakes via an expensive pipeline. The city is still getting by with water from local wells and rivers and it may be a model for other cities. Across the continent conservation laws which require water-efficient appliances and restrict lawn watering have reduced household consumption by 20–40 per cent in some municipalities. If we are going to stop poisoning the water it is crucial to reduce the amount of pollution going down the drain. Governments are still wrestling with the problem of industrial waste but average citizens would do well to look at their daily 1.4 kilograms of garbage each. If there is a municipal recycling program, use it. Many cities pick up newspapers separately and some are now collecting bottles and cans. This is just a start. Ideally we should all have compartmentalized garbage containers with a space for plastics as well so they will not go into incinerators, releasing partly burned compounds into the air. The most difficult products to dispose of are old cans of paints, pesticides and corrosive chemicals like oven cleaners, so think before you buy and use hazardous products. First, many paints, solvents and high-powered cleaners release unhealthy fumes into the air you breathe when you use them. Secondly, they create hazardous wastes during their production and thirdly, they create more dangerous waste when you dispose of them.

Oven cleaners are potent grease removers but many of them release a cloud of fumes into the air. It may not be quite as fast, but a mixture of baking soda and water is a safe, cheap alternative. For stubborn grease you can apply some ammonia and let it work on the grease overnight, although this chemical does release some strong odors. Household drain cleaners often contain hazardous chemicals. Such potent materials are rarely needed and can often be replaced by a little work with a plunger, by pouring boiling water down a drain or by using baking soda followed by a small amount of vinegar for a balky drain. Wire cables called plumber's snakes can be bought in a hardware store and they will sometimes dislodge a blockage. Most drains will not plug in the first place if they are protected by small strainers and if you do not pour grease down them.

If you do buy a hazardous product it is better to use it up, following all safety instructions, rather than to dump it. And if you do have to dispose of a hazardous substance check with your municipal sanitation department to see if they have special facilities. Some cities have "special waste days" with depots to collect hazardous products.

British Columbia has the most extensive system, with eight special waste storage centres where citizens can bring their problem garbage. As a last alternative to pouring chemical wastes down the drain, it is usually better to dispose of them in the regular garbage—but they should be in well-sealed containers and heavily wrapped in paper and plastic.

The car is a major polluter of our environment. To reduce that toll keep your car properly tuned and its tires inflated so that it does not waste fuel. If you are buying a car, consider purchasing one that runs on unleaded gasoline, natural gas or propane. If your car runs on unleaded fuel do not use leaded gasoline just to save a few pennies on a fill-up. First of all it is illegal, secondly, it may cost you more in maintenance and repairs and thirdly, it is helping to pollute the atmosphere and water both by requiring the manufacture of lead and by spewing it into the environment from the exhaust pipe. If you are a home mechanic do not pour the oil down the drain but take it to a recycling depot.

Information about how the individual can reduce waste and substitute less toxic products is becoming more commonly available but still requires tracking down. Sometimes provincial environment departments or municipal offices can help but the best sources are often local environment groups.

One of the major problems facing cities today is coping with the amount of sewage that must be treated. And the problem of sewage treatment plants being flooded out by storm sewers during rainstorms has caused governments to spend tens of millions of dollars separating storm and sanitary lines. Now cities are realizing that the storm water is polluted with wastes washed off the streets, so some municipalities are building giant holding tanks to catch storm water so it can be run through treatment plants during dry spells. Barry Adams and Henry Regier of the University of Toronto suggest that one way to reduce the problem would be for people to disconnect the downspouts from their eavestroughs from the storm sewer systems and direct the water onto their lawns. This would eliminate huge amounts of basically clean water from the amount of liquid that has to pass through sewage plants. It would also water the lawns more thoroughly, they say.

The fact is that information about how an individual can control pollution exists but it is not well disseminated. As a result citizens and politicians are often ill informed about the means, often inexpensive ones, to reduce water wastage and pollution. The education process may be the most important part of the battle to save our waters.

CHAPTER FIFTEEN

WHERE DO WE GO FROM HERE?

THE SPREADING SCOURGE of pollution has done more than poison the well. Along with the threat of global nuclear war it has destroyed the myth of sanctuary which all previous generations enjoyed. Until recently we could at least dream of a Shangri-la, some place on the planet where one could escape war, famine and pestilence. Now we know that even those people living in the mountains and the polar reaches carry traces of pesticides and industrial chemicals in their body fat. And in one city, one industrial and one farming region after another, water supplies are dwindling. We cannot run away from our water problems. Even if we packed up and headed to the northern wilds airborne pollution would catch up with us. We have to stand and fight.

So far we have attacked our water problems with half-measures and partial solutions. Our society has given itself a free ride by treating water as something which did not have to be protected. In moments of panic we have banned some chemicals and controlled others, thus slowing the rate of environmental degradation. But chemical production is now at record levels, so our waters will be under even more pressure unless pollution controls somehow manage to outpace production quotas. We are now starting to pay the price for quick and dirty disposal practices as old chemical dumps start to leak into our drinking water. To compound the problems even the chlorination of drinking water is under close scrutiny because of the hazardous byproducts it creates in tap water.

The whole toxics issue has become so complex that it defies clear understanding. We don't know the real safety of much of our drinking water and we face the possibility of multi-million-dollar bills for advanced drinking water treatment in some areas. In the meantime we continue to buy millions of litres of bottled water, sometimes containing other trace contaminants, and to install home water filters which health authorities warn are difficult for most people to maintain.

As for water quantity, our society is even less aware of the existing and incipient shortages that are going to define the way a lot of us live and eat. Farmers in parts of the Canadian west are taxing local rivers to the limit and in parts of the U.S. west they are pumping their wells down to the point that they are becoming unusable. Again the water supplies being used up are treated as a virtually free good with no price tag.

These problems of quality and quantity are being repeated around the world. The situation is becoming so serious that it threatens to bog down our economies as we spend more and more time and money just trying to rectify the problems that we are still creating. They are becoming grave enough to threaten an increasing degree of entropy, which is the tendency of a system towards increasing disorder and inertness.

Can we turn the toxic tide and stop the drying up of whole regions? We can, but only if we adopt a fundamental change in our thinking about the problems and their solutions. In some cases it simply means paying attention to what was said years ago.

In 1962 Rachel Carson warned us of the dangers of widespread chemical pollution in the web of life when she wrote in *Silent Spring* that the excessive use of pesticides was destroying whole species. Ten years later the Club of Rome, a gathering of world scientists, educators, economists, humanists, industrialists and civil servants, issued a report whose title has become a definition of the global situation. *The Limits to Growth* said that such physical resources as fresh water, arable land, metals, forests and the oceans are "the ultimate determinants of the limits to growth on this earth." They warned that "there is an upper limit to the fresh water runoff from the land areas of the earth each year and there is also an exponentially increasing demand for that water."

The following year another important phrase entered the world's environmental lexicon. "Canadians as individuals, and their governments, institutions and industries, [must] begin the transition from a consumer society preoccupied with resource exploitation to a conserver society engaged in more constructive endeavors." That prescient statement, which included the first use of the phrase "conserver society," was published by the Science Council in January, 1973. By then it was abundantly clear that many of the already serious environmental problems were the result of the destruction and waste of natural resources. These resources were being reduced to garbage, often toxic waste. In 1977 major leakage of toxic chemicals from Love Canal revealed the full fury of wastes. About the same time, acid rain was recognized as a major pollution problem in North America. The 1970s was also the decade of the poisoned fish as one chemical after another led to a seemingly endless series of bans and warnings across the continent about eating fish.

The warnings created a stir but no fundamental change. Those who preferred the status quo did their best to discredit the predictions of the Club of Rome by looking for errors in specific facts. They mocked the idea of a conserver society and dubbed its proponents as "eco-freaks" who were on the fringe of "normal" society. Acid rain was not a real problem, they said, and even if it was we could not afford to control it. They suggested that any systematic attempt to attack pollution and excessive consumption of natural resources would rip apart the fabric of our comfortable lifestyle and plunge us into privation and economic chaos. Such propaganda has staved off coherent and coordinated action. It encouraged governments sometimes to ignore their own rules governing hazardous chemicals and to allow many to be used freely until they were proven harmful and had to be removed as a result of public outcries.

Only the discovery of chemical poisons in our drinking water and actual water shortages followed by rationing have succeeded in scaring people into realizing what rational arguments could not accomplish. We had to walk to the precipice and look over. Until we found our own toxic wastes coming out of our taps we could not understand that we are part of the environment, not apart from it. There is no "out there" and if we pollute the environment we pollute ourselves.

Now we are at a turning point in our understanding of our place in the environment. Until now we have dealt with problems by reacting to them, but it is time to move beyond crisis management to reach a comprehensive understanding of how the environment works and how we must behave if we want to continue enjoying a comfortable lifestyle. On a personal level we must become aware of the limits to water usage and water wastage. We simply will have to learn to conserve water and stop fouling it. As a society we will have to make some long-term changes, including some choices which will be difficult in the short term. We have to find ways to reduce pollution and the use of hazardous chemicals without derailing our economic system overnight. Chemical waste treatment centres must be built to get rid of existing wastes and at the same time they must stop simply producing more problems. In the dry farming regions we will have to reduce wastage of water and at some finite point decide if we want more irrigated crops and hydro-electric projects at the cost of losing some of the remaining wild and natural northern rivers.

Any serious change in our approach to the use and abuse of water must involve a number of key players, including governments, environment groups, industry, agriculture and the education system.

Since governments set many of the rules they are the most visible of the actors, though not necessarily the most important in the long run. What they should offer is environmental planning of a calibre rarely seen so far. If governments are going to provide advice and produce regulations that really protect and conserve the environment they are going to have to get their acts together, both individually and collectively. Environmental responsibilities are now fragmented within and between governments. As a result we are living with a basketful of policies which catch some polluters and water wasters but not others—the equivalent of one bureaucratic finger trying to plug a dyke full of holes.

For example, there are 11 federal, provincial and state governments plus the Canada-U.S. International Joint Commission involved in monitoring, using and protecting the Great Lakes. There are also dozens of regional and municipal governments making important decisions. But there is no coordinating body.

In Canada the responsibility for water is carved up between levels of government. The provinces have most of the responsibility because water is listed as a natural resource, but Ottawa has some powers governing fisheries, navigation, pollution and boundary waters. Within governments the fragmentation continues. The federal government has 22 departments and agencies, each with a significant interest in water but often with a different perspective. For example, pesticides are a major threat to water quality but they are regulated by Agriculture Canada, which has shown more interest in maximizing crop production than in minimizing risks. Car and truck exhausts produce nitric acid rain but the responsibility for imposing tighter emission controls rests with Transport Canada, which has done so only with great reluctance. To understand the significance of much pollution one has to explain the health risks but this task is jealously guarded by

Health and Welfare. Within the provinces the story is repeated. Natural resources, forestry and agriculture departments, for example, often make the decisions relating to the use of pesticides.

The fact that Canada has federal and provincial environment departments is not entirely bad; it provides a valuable set of checks and balances with one agency often keeping watch on the other. And despite the fragmentation of responsibilities between and within governments there have been some notable cases of cooperation. Canadian environment ministers were able to sign an accord pledging them to spend billions of dollars fighting acid rain. The federal energy department did a key study on the costs of cleaning up the polluting smelters. The governments have also collaborated on programs to improve sewage treatment, reduce pollution from the pulp and paper industry and search for abandoned hazardous dumpsites. Departments such as environment and health sometimes do collaborate on researching the effects of toxic chemicals and transport was dragged into car emission controls that would at least match those of the United States.

This is good but it is not good enough because it is based on ad hoc responses to problems, not a systematic approach to the environment. The present system of governance is neither structured nor administered in a way which can develop the complex environment policy changes needed for the future. The environment portfolio has too often been treated as a junior posting or a revolving door. For example, Ontario had 12 environment ministers in 14 years. Canada has left as many as two of its three seats on the International Joint Commission vacant for months at a time, then sometimes appointed people who were not familiar with the highly complex issues.

Premiers, prime ministers and their cabinets are going to have to understand that the environment is not something which can be dealt with in neat little packages. Political leaders are going to have to have the guts to offend senior ministers and transfer some of their responsibilities into environment departments.

Environmentalists are often most effective when they act as shadow environment departments, analyzing the claims of governments and industries, then reacting from the viewpoint of a public affected by those actions. This means that it is not enough for public interest groups just to understand the workings of the environment, the green side of the equation. The successful ones also understand how governments and bureaucracies work and why some things happen and others do not. They must also understand what drives business, in order to comprehend why perfectly nice people can pollute whole rivers and skies. Governments and industry are not monolithic and environmentalists on the outside know that those bureaucracies include people who are trying to reform the system and who can become allies. And since the only effective message is one that is heard, the groups must understand the communications media and how to use them most effectively.

The attitude of business is crucial. The business world has been painted as the bad guy because it is the segment of society which actually produces the hazardous waste. But any successful business must be adaptable and these days a wise business leader realizes that the economy and the environment can no longer be treated as two solitudes. Environmental blackmail is no longer acceptable and people will not bow to the threat that a company will pick up its multi-million dollar factory and move to another country in the face of pollution controls. They are no longer willing to trade a clean environment for jobs. They were able to pay for cleaner cars and they expect business to clean up its act and keep functioning. One poll after another has shown that people are willing to pay higher prices for goods and services if necessary, in order to have clean production. The first thing that a business does is to try to stay in business and to make a profit. Until now that has often been done by wasting water and by dumping chemical garbage into the nearest river, lake or hole in the ground. Now there is a small but growing number of senior business leaders who understand that we cannot have a healthy economy in a degraded environment. It is up to them to spread this awareness and put it to work and it is up to government to provide the framework of regulations to prevent cheating. After all, if a factory can put a hazardous chemical together it can take it apart afterwards.

Agriculture, like business, holds some of the most important keys to the future of our waters and lands. The illusion that farming means being part of nature is a dearly held but inaccurate notion. There are still a few farmers who work the land with horses and natural fertilizers but modern farming is generally highly mechanized, depends heavily on a wide variety of chemicals, many of them quite toxic, and is often carried out by large corporations rather than small families. As discussed earlier, the agricultural use of chemicals delivers a one-two punch to the environment. The first blow comes when the chemicals are fabricated and their wastes dumped. The second comes when pesticides and fertilizers are used.

There is a growing recognition of the need for less intensive use of chemicals, not only because they are risky but because they are expensive and drive up the costs of producing food. The alternative to the growing use of synthetic pesticides is something called integrated pest management, a catchy term for the concept of using natural means of pest control as much as possible, and reserving hazardous chemicals for true emergencies, such as outbreaks of insect infestation. Farmers also have a major responsibility to protect soil from erosion and prevent the reduction of water resources caused either by too much irrigation or by the drainage of too many wetlands, which are natural reservoirs. It is up to farm organizations and agricultural departments and colleges to reorient their education programs towards presenting the true value of fresh water to the farmer and explaining the risks inherent in the present system of water management.

More and more important decisions will have to be made across the country and around the world on irrigation, power development, industrial consumption, pollution, farming practices, industrial clean-up, sewer works, and improved and advanced water purification and supply systems. Only if the key players in the environment field understand the problems and are willing to act will we be able to make truly rational decisions and avoid increasing conflicts over rights to diminishing water supplies. The driving forces behind the problems are going to make the choices even more difficult.

And this means one more group, the education system, must assume a far more important role in the environment. This field of study can no longer be treated as a "frill" course. Everyone who goes to school must be taught at least the environmental basics if our society is going to be truly successful in stopping the juggernaut of pollution and consumption which threatens our basic resources and therefore our well-being.

Population growth will increase both the demand for water and the load of wastes. This will be compounded by increasing mechanization of the world, which will raise the per capita consumption of water and increase the amount of industrial waste. The time frame for action is shrinking. Historically, water problems have arisen when the amount withdrawn from a water system approached half the stable minimum supply of water. That minimum is usually considered to be the amount of water in the rivers during the driest year in a decade. Using this criterion two Swedish hydrologists, Malin Flakenmark and Gunnar Lindh, predicted several years ago that Africa, Asia and Europe will surpass the benchmark early in the next century.

The industrialized world faces a growing bill for its abuse and neglect of water resources. In Canada the cost of cleaning up toxic waste dumps has not yet been calculated because the dumps are still being discovered. However, we know that we must spend billions of dollars more just to provide adequate waterworks. The Pearse Report on Canada's waters says that we spend about $2.4 billion a year on providing and upgrading water and sewage works, "but this is clearly insufficient to provide and maintain the facilities needed." It notes that only 57 per cent of Canadians living in municipalities have any kind of sewage treatment. One study suggests that we should be spending about $4.1 billion a year on our water and sewage systems, both to keep up with growing demand and to keep the old pipes from falling apart.

The bills are even more horrendous in the United States. One estimate says that it will cost about $100 billion just to clean up the old toxic waste dumps. James Magner of the National Water Alliance estimated that cleaning up waste, repairing decaying waterworks and adding new water and sewage treatment poses a trillion-dollar bill for his nation.

Air pollution is clouding the future of global water resources and yet the toxic rain continues to fall unabated. Canada has promised a 50-per-cent cut in its sulphur acid air pollution but this will not be complete before 1994, according to current plans. The United States has not even started to impose new controls on its much larger acid rain problem. We are just beginning to grasp the seriousness of other forms of toxic rain, such as the long-range transport of pesticides and a wide variety of industrial chemicals including PCBs. An atmospheric greenhouse is silently being formed with the air pollution of every passing day and as more nations industrialize, burn fossil fuels and cut their forests, it will form even faster. It will bring coastal flooding and droughts in the interiors and affect the entire global waterworks, including the amount and quality of water in our pipes, our reservoirs and our power dams, just to mention a few of the effects. Whole farming regions may be reduced to marginal semi-deserts and new ones opened up. In the face of such a complex issue we must find every possible way to try to reduce the pollution and we must prepare to cope with great changes.

What new directions should our society take? Our water crises are "fundamentally a problem of mismanagement of an adequate resource," says Brent Blackwelder of the Environmental Policy Institute in Washington. Even in the dry west "we have plenty of water if we could use it wisely." What Mr. Blackwelder and others, such as Sandra Postel of Worldwatch Institute, are saying in ever more detailed studies is that there are solutions to the excessive use of water.

Water and oil do not mix but they do have a lot in common. Following the embargo on oil shipments by members of the Organization of Petroleum Exporting Countries in 1973–74 we learned to conserve oil. Since then our cars have become 70 per cent more fuel efficient. We must apply the same ingenuity to water conservation; environment experts claim that we can become 90 per cent more water efficient. No matter what, water is going to be scarcer and more expensive. How much more it will cost depends on how fast we stop abusing it. If we consume and pollute a lot there will be less left and it will cost more. It is that simple.

In order to undertake change we need better information about the most important problems to attack and the alternative solutions from which to choose. That means we need proper state-of-the-environment reports with true audits of the change in water resources, not just a hodge-podge of unrelated findings which arouse great concern on our part about the state of our water but do not give us a coherent picture so we know where to direct limited resources.

Once we have a more detailed picture of water use and pollution we can start developing rational water plans. We need such plans quickly because important development proposals for our remaining rivers are already coming forward or are waiting in the wings. Each is presented as a discrete package of benefits, ignoring the overall impact on the environment and society. We will have to deal with the pros and cons of major hydro developments, such as the second half of the James Bay power project, and with plans for hydro projects across the north.

Agricultural demand for water will be fanned by each new drought and finally brought to a head by the greenhouse effect. Already there are heated debates about the amount of money invested in local diversions for irrigation, compared to the value of the crops produced. There are even greater concerns that the drainage of wetlands is destroying some of the most valuable wildlife habitats in the country and drying up natural reservoirs which meter our water during dry spells. Many drainage laws are now archaic and better suited to a pioneer society. The present laws support a rich and powerful industry that makes millions of dollars a year digging ditches and installing drainage tiles but has no incentive to maintain a healthy environment. Even greater questions loom in the future as one farming area after another runs up against the limits to water in the west. For years there have been calls for water diversions from the north. Now is the time to see what the true cost would be.

While many questions about water remain to be answered, we do know enough about the problems and the realities of human behavior to start imposing a realistic price on water right now. It is basic economic theory that when something is cheap that is a signal to use a lot of it but if it is expensive that means it is valuable and should be conserved. So far water has been treated as a free good and is delivered to your tap for no more than the price of purification and pumping. In some cases people are even charged water rates which decline as consumption increases. It is no wonder we have wasted it. There would be a two-fold benefit from a price on water. First, it would be an incentive for conservation and secondly, it could create a fund to help pay for improvements to sewage treatment, industrial clean-ups and the provision of safe drinking water everywhere. How much should we pay? Joseph Rossillon, president of the Minnesota-based Freshwater Society, says it takes 5 000 litres of water to put a restaurant meal of meat, potatoes and a soft drink on the table. He suggests that a $3 surcharge on such a meal would be a realistic value for the water used in producing and delivering it.

Once we establish a price on water, then severe fines for polluting it will be a logical move. The Law Reform Commission of Canada recommended that cases of wanton pollution should be treated as "crimes against the environment" and the heads of offending companies should be tossed into jail. In fact wasting and polluting water, our most valuable resource, are among the gravest crimes against society but the punishment has rarely fit the offence. Political leaders have been slow to recognize not only the public interest but the public desire. A major U.S. public opinion survey conducted by the Louis Harris organization found that 85 per cent of 10 000 people polled favored strict enforcement of existing clean air and clean water statutes while 66 per cent wanted even tougher laws. Ontario Premier

David Peterson summed up the situation, saying that historically penalties have been so "grossly inadequate" they amount to a "licence to pollute."

If we are going to control pollution we need the right tools. The Pearse Report noted that despite years of study, Environment Canada has yet to produce a toxic substances control law which defines hazardous substances, and says where they are, what risks they pose and what controls are needed. A number of toxic chemical experts hold that it is lack of organization, not knowledge, that is the greatest handicap. They point for example to the list of the Dirty Dozen pollutants which pose the greatest threat to the Great Lakes, and they maintain that if you control these hazards you will simultaneously control dozens if not hundreds of substances which come from the same industrial sources.

We must tackle the Hydra-headed issue of chemical dumps that litter our landscape, threatening to pollute our water indefinitely. Techniques exist to treat all the toxic substances but governments have been slow to provide or encourage the creation of safe and effective detoxification centres for our industries. The big factories have started reducing many forms of pollution over the years but they are still only dealing with a fraction of the problem. New plants are adding to the total burden and some old sources still do not meet government regulations.

Water conservation techniques range from fixing leaky taps with a 10-cent washer to spending hundreds of thousands of dollars lining irrigation canals so they will not leak. Industries are just starting to seriously improve their plumbing systems and manufacturing techniques to recycle more and more water before discharging it. Farming can and must become far more efficient not only by improving irrigation systems but by applying water to crops only when weather and plant growth dictate and by metering out only what is needed. Our society as a whole will have to recycle more water, especially in the dry regions. For example Israel, a country with little water but plenty of ingenuity, is now using about 30 per cent of its treated municipal sewage water, mainly for irrigation, and this may go as high as 80 per cent by the year 2000.

The use of treated sewage water is limited in many areas by the amount of pollution which remains after conventional sewage treatment, a process that is not geared to removing toxic chemicals and heavy metals. Sewage treatment will have to become more sophisticated, both in what it removes from the water and in how it copes with many and varied discharges. For example the polluted runoff from urban streets now often bypasses the sewage plants and goes directly into rivers and lakes.

It is already too late to save the drinking water in some areas and we will lose more before we stop pollution. Environment and health officials are now wrestling with the very controversial issues of advanced water treatment systems to remove chemicals. In some parts of the world these special filters are a fact of life. We may have to introduce systems like granular activated carbon in parts of Canada to cope with excessive pollution. If this happens it should be regarded as a wartime-type measure, a temporary, emergency installation not to be continued any longer than necessary. Chemical filters should never be regarded as a final solution to our pollution problems or we will end up repeating the mistakes of chlorination made nearly a century ago. After two or three generations we have forgotten that chlorine in our drinking water is no more natural than gasoline fumes in our air. If we had truly effective sewage treatment we would need little if any chlorination, let alone carbon filtration, on most water, particularly that from large lakes.

While it is necessary for Canada to clean up its own pollution and not waste its water reserves, we have seen that no country can manage its environment in isolation from the rest of the world. Half the acid rain falling on Canada comes from the United States, while the air pollution creating the greenhouse effect comes from all nations and will affect the entire globe. Environmental protection has become part of our foreign policy and it will be even more important in the future. At the present rate the prevention of major environmental problems will rank second only to the prevention of war in maintaining stability in international politics. The devastation of the Sahel region by drought and the resulting starvation is just one example of what can happen to a whole region. If pollution and excessive water consumption continue unabated the global summits will have to deal with them just to prevent a collapse of normal economic patterns and social stability.

On the international scene there are some encouraging responses to environmental crises. The 1972 Stockholm convention pledged nations not to pollute one another and this promise is being reinforced by the 1979 agreement of the Economic Commission for Europe to control long-range air pollution. The agreement got some clout from a protocol in which Canada and a number of European nations promised to reduce sulphur emissions by 30 per cent. These are important first steps but what is really needed is a truly effective international environment agency. Such an agency would collect and constantly update information on the state of the global environment and particularly on the balance of water resources. With such information nations would be much better able to make rational decisions. Secondly, the global agency would propose solutions for the water problems we face, taking into account the social and economic conditions of various nations and possibly seeking international funding. The United Nations Environment Program could be the basis for such an agency if it were given adequate funding and clear direction to undertake such tasks.

"Whether lifestyles will be diminished in the face of growing water demands or whether a continued increase in enjoyment and productivity can be sustained will depend upon how we manage this essential resource," the Canada West Foundation told the federal water inquiry.

In recent decades a process called the Green Revolution changed agriculture in the Far East. Improved farming techniques dramatically improved crop yields, allowing more and more people to feed them-

What kind of an environment will we leave to the next generation? (MICHAEL KEATING)

selves instead of starving or having to depend on imported food. What we need now, on a global scale, is a Blue Revolution, which will teach the world the techniques needed to protect water from pollution and unnecessary demands.

The decisions we make now are not just for our own benefit but will form the most important part of the heritage we leave to our children. Even if we started digging up old chemical dumps tomorrow the job would not be finished for several years, and chemicals seeping through the rocks will continue to pollute our waters for an unknown period. Chemicals like PCBs will not break down in the environment for decades, possibly centuries, so what is loose out there now will continue to circulate until it is gradually decayed by sunlight and microbes or buried by natural sedimentation. "If we make the controls work now, it is my children's children who will not be exposed to chemicals," says Douglas Hallett a scientist and father of two.

In Canada we can still enjoy wilderness canoe trips where one can dip a cup into the water and drink it straight and relatively clean. Such trips will become even more precious. From the viewpoint of the canoeist we should return once more to that of the astronaut. Living in a space capsule or space station the astronaut drinks water that is recycled and purified—and looks down and wonders when the inhabitants of space station Earth will realize that they too drink recycled water and so must protect its purity.

As British author William Golding, winner of the Nobel Prize for Literature, once said: "It is the only planet we have got, after all."

APPENDIX ONE

METRIC CONVERSION CHART

Metric to Imperial Measure (approximate figures)

LENGTH

1 centimetre = 0.39 inches
1 metre = 3.28 feet
1 kilometre = 0.62 miles

AREA

1 hectare (10 000 square metres) = 2.47 acres
1 square kilometre (100 hectares) = 0.38 square miles

WEIGHT

1 gram = 0.035 ounces
1 kilogram = 2.2 pounds
1 tonne = 1.102 tons

VOLUME

1 litre = 0.22 Imperial gallons (0.26 U.S. gallons)
1 cubic metre = 1 000 litres
1 cubic kilometre = 0.24 cubic miles
1 cubic kilometre = 1 billion cubic metres = 1 trillion litres

APPENDIX TWO

GLOBAL AND CANADIAN WATER RESOURCES

As DISCUSSED IN CHAPTER ONE, most of the world's 1.35 billion cubic kilometres of water are salt seas and therefore not available for human use. Much of the fresh water that exists, about 29 million cubic kilometres of it,* is frozen in glaciers and polar ice caps. Over history the world's ice cover has fluctuated greatly and there is evidence that at one time glaciers covered as much as 30 per cent of the earth, including 97 per cent of Canada.

About 8 million cubic kilometres more of the fresh water supply lie underground but much of that is so deep or far from settlement that it is very expensive to reach. When underground water is drawn up by wells it is replaced by nature, but at far slower rates than surface water. In many areas the rate of replenishment is so small that except for minor withdrawals, such as household wells, underground water must be considered a nonrenewable resource within an average human lifetime.

This leaves only about 1/100 of 1 per cent of the world's water, or 180 000 cubic kilometres, readily available to sustain life. Of that, 125 000 cubic kilometres are in the lakes. There are about 60 000 cubic kilometres in the soil, 13 000 cubic kilometres in the sky, where we often see it as clouds or rain and snow, and only 1 250 cubic kilometres in the rivers at any one time.

In total the Great Lakes contain 22 800 cubic kilometres of water or about 18 per cent of the fresh water on the planet's surface.

---

*Note: Some figures in this section may not match exactly because they were drawn from different sources or years.

238

The world's 10 largest lakes by volume contain 70 per cent of the world's fresh surface water.

WORLD'S LARGEST LAKES

NAME AND LOCATION	VOLUME (cubic kilometres)	AREA (square kilometres)	MAXIMUM DEPTH (metres)
Baikal, USSR	23 000	31 500	1 741
Tanganyika, E. Africa	18 940	34 000	1 470
Superior, Canada-U.S.A.	12 000	83 300	307
Nyasa, E. Africa	8 400	30 800	706
Michigan, U.S.A.	5 760	57 850	265
Huron, Canada-U.S.A.	4 600	59 500	223
Great Slave, Canada	4 000	30 000	614
Great Bear, Canada	4 000	29 500	137
Winnipeg, Canada	3 110	24 530	19
Victoria, E. Africa	2 700	68 800	79

SOURCE: Global Environmental Monitoring System, United Nations Environment Program.

Lakes are important as reservoirs for drinking water, as wildlife habitats, and for commercial, recreational and aesthetic reasons. But it is the water in the rivers and in the air which is most important for keeping those lakes full and for supplying water to animals and crops and to life along and within the rivers.

The water flowing in the rivers and in the air is in dynamic motion, supplying our needs for drinking and industry and watering our crops as, in the form of rain and snow, it falls, runs off and is evaporated back into the sky. There are about 500 000 cubic kilometres of water on the move each year, lifted by the sun's energy through the process of evaporation to fall again as rain and snow or to condense as dew and frost. About 71 500 cubic kilometres are evaporated from land, while 110 300 cubic kilometres fall on land. This means that 38 000 cubic kilometres of water per year are distilled from the oceans by the sun and fall on the land. Some of this water is taken up immediately by plants but much becomes runoff in the rivers, making its way towards the sea and providing us with a constant supply of fresh water. Sandra Postel of Worldwatch Institute in Washington wrote that in 1983 world river flows provided an average of 8 300 cubic metres (8.3 million litres) of water per person per year.

The average annual runoff per capita varies greatly from country to country, ranging for example from 90 cubic metres in Egypt to 10 000 in the United States and 110 000 in Canada. What is disturbing is that as population increases, the amount of available water in runoff per person will decline by an estimated 24 per cent worldwide between the early 1980s and 2000. In fact that estimate of 8 300 cubic metres per person represents the maximum amount of water theoretically available in 1983. In real terms much less is usable on a steady basis because about two-thirds of the annual runoff rushes past us in floods, often causing destruction, before reaching the seas. Ms. Postel notes that the stable, reliable flow for such needs as drinking water and irrigating crops or for use by industry year-round is only about 14 000 cubic kilometres or 3 000 cubic metres per person. That figure is projected to drop to 2 280 by the end of the century. To make calculations more difficult we must remember that not only do some regions have much less runoff than others, but periodic climate fluctuations, notably drought, make that base flow even less reliable, on a year-to-year basis, particularly in areas like the North American West and large parts of Africa and Asia.

MAJOR RIVERS OF THE WORLD

NAME AND LOCATION	LENGTH (*kilometres*)
Nile, Africa	6 690
Amazon, S. America	6 296
Mississippi-Missouri, U.S.A.	6 020
Chang Jiang (Yangtze), China	5 797
Ob, USSR	5 567
Huang Ho (Yellow), China	4 667
Yenisei, USSR	4 506
Paraná, S. America	4 498
Irtish, USSR	4 438
Congo, Africa	4 371

SOURCE: *The 1986 Information Please Almanac*

While the global water supply remains relatively stable, over the centuries the human demand for that water use has been growing at a dramatic rate. In 1900, as the industrial age and population growth began to accelerate sharply, the world demand for water for all uses was an estimated 400 billion cubic metres, or 242 cubic metres per person each year. By 1940 the demand had doubled, although the population had increased only 40 per cent. The demand rose even more rapidly in the era of postwar population and industrial growth. By 1970 the annual per capita withdrawal had reached 700 cubic metres, an increase of 60 per cent over 1950. Water demand is now over 800 cubic metres a person and rising steadily.

Today we use about 10 per cent of the total renewable supply and about one-quarter of the stable supply and Ms. Postel projects that we will be using one-half the stable supply by the year 2000. While this leaves a large margin of safety globally, she points out that meeting demands in the Middle East and North Africa will require virtually all the usable fresh water supplies in these regions. Southern and eastern Europe and central and southern Asia will also come close to the limits of reliable water supplies, she writes.

The following table shows the withdrawal of water per person per year for 22 nations, measured in cubic metres (thousand litres). This includes withdrawals for all uses, including the cooling of power plants and irrigation.

How Much Water Do We Use?

United States	2 306	Germany	686
Canada	1 509	Turkey	669
Australia	1 281	France	663
Portugal	1 062	Norway	489
Spain	1 016	Sweden	479
Netherlands	997	Yugoslavia	392
Italy	985	New Zealand	383
Japan	923	Austria	298
Belgium	917	Denmark	239
Finland	775	United Kingdom	226
Greece	720	Switzerland	108

For comparison: it would take about seven average-sized bathtubs to hold one cubic metre of water. That amount of water weighs one tonne.

SOURCE: Organization for Economic Co-Operation and Development, 1980.

CANADA

Canada is a huge land and has the world's largest share of fresh water. With a surface area of 9 922 335 square kilometres, it is second in land mass only to the Soviet Union, with its 22 402 000 square kilometres. Canada's territory stretches 4 634 kilometres from Cape Columbia on Ellesmere Island in the high Arctic to Middle Island in temperate Lake Erie, and 5 514 kilometres from Cape Spear, Newfoundland, to the Yukon boundary with Alaska. Canada has 9 167 170 square kilometres of land and 755 165 square kilometres of water, about 7.6 per cent of its surface area. The water area rises to 20 per cent when wetlands are included. Canada has the world's largest collection of freshwater lakes. They hold about 17 500 cubic kilometres, or 14 per cent of the world's fresh water, for only 6.7 per cent of the world's land area and 0.5 per cent of the population. Canada also shares the Great Lakes system, which contains close to one-fifth of the fresh water on the planet's surface. The country has or shares with the United States seven of the world's largest lakes.

Canada's rivers discharge to the oceans, on average, 105 135 cubic metres of water per second, or 9 per cent of the world's renewable water supply of 1.13 million cubic metres per second. This puts Canada behind the Soviet Union and Brazil but ahead of China, the United States and India in river flow. Canada's minimum reliable discharge 19 years out of 20, which is the safe supply limit for the creation of steady demands such as farming, towns and industries, is 75 856 cubic metres per second.

Some water figures on Canada:

- The longest river is the Mackenzie at 4 241 kilometres.
- The deepest lake is Great Slave, 614 metres to the bottom.
- The largest lake entirely in Canada is Great Bear Lake, which, covers 31 328 square kilometres.
- The highest lake is Chilco, in British Columbia, at an altitude of 1 171 metres.
- The highest waterfall is Takakkaw Falls, British Columbia, which, at 503 metres high, is the sixth-highest in the world.
- Niagara Falls, with a flow of 5 365 cubic metres per second, is shared with the United States.
- The highest dam is Mica Dam on the Columbia River in British Columbia, at 244 metres.

Rain and snowfall are the crucial factors in setting the amount of water in the rivers. The driest region of Canada is not the Prairies, which get around 300 millimetres a year even in the dry zones, but the high Arctic, which gets a meagre 100 millimetres per year. By contrast the lush Pacific coast, whose mountains rake water out of ocean winds, gets 3 000–7 500 millimetres of precipitation a year, producing temperate rainforests and some of the tallest trees in the world. The populated areas in eastern and central Canada typically get 750 to 1 000 millimetres a year. Not all this water goes into the rivers because, on average, about half the precipitation is evaporated from the land and water surfaces or transpired from the surface of plants back into the air.

The average water supply is 360 cubic metres (360 000 litres) per person per day, although that fluctuates immensely depending on where you live. For example, on average, people living on the major southern Prairie rivers have less than 2–5 cubic metres per day.

A comparison of river flows by province and territory helps to illustrate the regional water disparities caused by climate and geography. The figures, from A. H. Laycock at the University of Alberta, are in cubic kilometres per year.*

RIVER FLOWS IN CANADA

Yukon	170
Northwest Territories	900
British Columbia	900
Alberta	72
Saskatchewan	58
Manitoba	98
Ontario	335
Quebec	800
New Brunswick	46
Nova Scotia	45
Prince Edward Island	3.5
Newfoundland and Labrador	322.5
CANADA TOTAL	3 750

Canadians use more water than anyone except U.S. citizens. Our average demand is over 4 000 litres per person per day. Canada's water use in 1981 was 37.8 billion cubic metres per year with about 10 per cent of that being consumed, that is, not returned directly to the adjacent waterway.

The underground water that flows to the surface in springs or is captured in wells accounts for only about four per cent of the amount of water we use but it plays a vital role in water supply. This resource, technically referred to as ground water, is the source of all household water for 6.3 million people, more than one-quarter of the population. Over 80 per cent of the rural population uses this as its sole source. In addition 984 municipalities rely on ground water. In Prince Edward Island 100 per cent of the residents use ground water and the figure is 64 per cent in New Brunswick, 54 per cent in Saskatchewan and 45 per cent in Nova Scotia.

*1 cubic kilometre = 1 billion metres or 1 trillion litres.

APPENDIX THREE

POPULATION
STATISTICS

To UNDERSTAND THE FUTURE of the world's water
resources one must look not only at the amount of water in
the lakes and rivers but at the increasing population which must share
that fixed resource. Over the previous millennia the world's population increased very, very slowly. According to one study by Professor
Arthur H. Westing of Hampshire College in Amherst, Massachusetts,
there were about 3 million people during the Mesolithic ages some
40 000 years ago. By the dawn of agriculture, about 8000 B.C., the
population had only crept up to about 5 million. At the birth of Christ
it was probably 200 million, a figure accepted by a number of studies.

After that the rate of population increase began to slope ever more
sharply upwards, reaching an estimated 500 million by the year 1650,
1 billion around 1830, 2 billion by 1930 and 4 billion by 1975. What
this means is that the population took more than 1 600 years to
double from A.D.1, 200 years to double that number, 100 years to
double again and only 45 years to double once more. This is a
geometric rate of progression which means ever-accelerating growth.
In 1986 the world population reached an estimated 4.92 billion and it
will break the 5-billion mark during 1987. By the year 2000 the global
population will likely be 6.12 billion, considered an accurate estimate
because of the short time period involved.

Where will it go from there? We know it will go up and the only
question is how fast. The rate of growth has levelled off a bit in the last
few years and was at 1.67 per cent per annum in 1985, but that still
added 80 million people a year, more than three times Canada's
population, to the face of the globe. It will continue at a high level for

some time because of the large numbers of young people entering their reproductive years.

One set of long-term projections concludes that the planetary population will reach 8.2 billion by 2025 and 10 billion by 2050, the time when today's children will be retiring. Estimates of when the population will finally stabilize range from predictions of an actual decline to 8 billion by 2080, to a high estimate of 14.2 billion by 2130 and a middle estimate of 10.5 billion by 2110. The United Nations Environment Program calculates that 10 billion is the maximum level the planet can reasonably support.

The rate of growth will not be even around the world. Canada is still one of the most underpopulated regions and is likely to stay that way. We passed the 25-million mark in early 1985, up from 3.4 million at Confederation, but our birthrate is slowing dramatically. There are only 3 Canadians per square kilometre of land, compared to 26 in the United States, 322 in Japan and 353 in the Netherlands.

There have been marked declines in population growth rates in east Asia, southeast Asia, Central America and the Caribbean. China, with over 1 billion people, has cut its growth rate in half over the past decade but India still has a high rate of increase. India's population is now about three-quarters that of China, but India is likely to become the world's most populous nation by 2025 because it is still growing, while China's population is stabilizing. Much of Africa still has very high rates of population growth and 19 of its nations face a doubling of their population every 23 years or less. This is on a continent that has not been able to feed itself since 1971 and where large areas have been in the grip of a devastating drought for much of that time. In 1984 the World Bank reported that sub-Saharan Africa is the only region in the world where fertility has not begun to fall and where growth is expected to accelerate in the next decade. It expects the region's population to double by the year 2005 and perhaps triple in the next three decades. That paints a frightening image of increased privation and even starvation in an area which has been suffering from water shortages for years.

On a global basis the United Nations estimates that when the population passes 6 billion in the year 2000 we will need 50–60 per cent more agricultural output than in 1980. The demand for agricultural products will double in developing countries and in many cases they are the nations with the poorest water supplies, both in terms of available water and in piping, water and sewage treatment to supply clean water to their people.

APPENDIX FOUR

WHOM TO WRITE TO FOR INFORMATION AND ACTION ON WATER ISSUES

INTERNATIONAL

United Nations Environment Program, Room A-3630, United Nations, New York, N.Y., 10017, U.S.A.

International Joint Commission
This group, formed as a result of the 1909 Boundary Waters Treaty between Canada and the United States, is composed of six members, half appointed by the head of each nation, plus a staff of officials. The I.J.C. researches and advises the governments on a wide range of boundary water issues ranging from diversions and pollution to water levels. It has three offices:

Canadian Section, 100 Metcalfe St., 18th Floor, Ottawa, Ont. K1P 5M1

United States Section, 1717 H Street N.W., Suite 203, Washington, D.C. 20440

Great Lakes Regional Office, 100 Ouellette Ave., 8th Floor, Windsor, Ont. N9A 6T3

CANADA

In Canada jurisdiction over natural resources lies mainly with the provinces. However, the federal government has several direct and indirect powers governing the state of our environment and the quality of our waters. Environment Canada has little regulatory power but it can play an important role in setting the agenda on environmental issues in the country through its research, and grants for research by others, and by subsidies for pollution cleanups. The fisheries department is responsible for protecting fish from pollution and this has a direct bearing on water quality. The health department is the lead agency in advising Canadians about risks from pollution and in setting drinking water guidelines. Agriculture Canada is responsible for choosing which pesticides may or may not be used in this country. The provinces may shorten the list within their boundaries by not allowing some federally registered pesticides to be used. Indian Affairs and Northern Development is responsible for a number of water-related issues in the far north.

Federal Government
All the ministers can be contacted through House of Commons, Ottawa, Ont. K1A 0A6

Prime Minister's Office
Minister of the Environment
Minister of Fisheries and Oceans
Minister of Health
Minister of Agriculture
Minister of Indian Affairs and Northern Development

Environment Canada has a series of regional offices, each with an information section, which can provide useful information on water issues.

Atlantic Provinces
Information Office, Environment Canada, 45 Alderney Dr., 5th Floor, Dartmouth, N.S. B2Y 2N6

Quebec
Information Office, Environment Canada, Box 10 000, Ste-Foy, Que. G1V 4H5

Ontario
Information Office, Environment Canada, 25 St. Clair Ave. E., 6th Floor, Toronto, Ont. M4T 1M2

Prairie Provinces and Northwest Territories
Information Office, Environment Canada, Twin Attria 2, 4999 - 98th St., Edmonton, Alta. T5K 2J5

British Columbia and the Yukon
Information Office, Environment Canada, Box 1540, 800 Burrard St., Vancouver, B.C. V6Z 2J7

Provinces
The Canadian Council of Resource and Environment Ministers, 60 Bloor St. West, Suite 701, Toronto, Ont. M4W 3B8, provides information for the provincial ministers responsible for the environment and natural resources.

In addition you can contact the ministers directly.

British Columbia
Minister of the Environment, Parliament Buildings, Victoria, B.C. V8V 1X5

Alberta
Minister of the Environment, 132 Legislative Building, Edmonton, Alta. T5K 2B6

Saskatchewan
Minister of the Environment, Legislative Building, Regina, Sask. S4S 0B3

Manitoba
Minister of the Environment, Legislative Building, Winnipeg, Man. R3C 0V8

Ontario
Minister of the Environment, 135 St. Clair Ave. E., Toronto, Ont. M4V 1P5

Quebec
Ministre de l'environnement, 4900, rue Marly, Ste-Foy, Que. G1X 4E4

New Brunswick
Minister of the Environment, Box 6000, Fredericton, N.B. E3B 5H1

Prince Edward Island
Minister of Community and Cultural Affairs, Box 2000, Charlottetown, P.E.I. C1A 7N8

Nova Scotia
Minister of the Environment, Box 2107, Halifax, N.S. B3J 3B7

Newfoundland
Minister of the Environment, Box 4750, St. John's, Nfld. A1C 5T7

Yukon
Minister of Renewable Resources, Whitehorse, Yukon Y1A 2C6

Northwest Territories
Minister of Renewable Resources, Yellowknife, NWT. X1A 2L9

Municipal
A growing number of municipalities have environment committees
and groups responsible for everything from the planning of waste
disposal sites to recycling. Contact your municipal government,
including the politicians, waterworks section and health department,
for information on what they are doing to protect local water
resources.

Non-Government Organizations
The environment groups play a vital role in alerting Canadians to the
state of pollution and their value cannot be overestimated. Usually
running on a financial shoestring and using volunteer labor much of
the time they have publicized countless incidents of environmental
abuse and pushed, prodded, shamed and even worked co-operatively
with governments in an effort to rectify the situation. For example the
Canadian Coalition on Acid Rain represents more than 1.5 million
Canadians who belong to several dozen groups representing many
interests, all of which are worried about the state of the environment.
The coalition has goaded domestic governments when they were
dragging their feet on acid rain clean-ups. It has also lobbied forcefully
in the United States, where it has encouraged action by U.S. groups
and politicians.

Pollution Probe, based in Toronto, has done more than any other
single environment group to put the question of drinking water safety
on the public agenda in Canada. Starting several years ago it released
a report, *Toxics on Tap*, which polarized the growing public concern
about what was in tap water, and this forced governments to deal

publicly with the difficult issue. Pollution Probe has also helped to arouse public concern about leaking toxic chemical dumps along the Niagara River and has even mounted court challenges in the United States in an effort to get them removed. In Quebec the Société pour vaincre la Pollution (SVP) has played a similar role to that of Pollution Probe. Possibly its greatest work is a pollution map, "Toxic St. Lawrence River," the first document to graphically point out who the polluters are, and how badly the river is fouled.

Among groups which deal with water issues are the following:

A court d'eau, 184 rue Notre-Dame, bureau 101, Repentigny, Que. J6A 2P9

Action Committee Against Garrison, 245 Thompson St., Riverton, Man. R0C 2R0

Alberta Canoe Association, Box 4571, S. Edmonton Post Office, Edmonton, Alta. T6E 2H6

Alberta Fish and Game Association, 6024–103 St., Edmonton, Alta. T6H 2H6

Alberta Wilderness Association, Box 6398, Station D, Calgary, Alta. T2P 2E1

Association des biologistes du Quebec, 45 rue Jarry Est, Montreal, Que. H2P 1S9

Association québécoise de lutte contre les pluies acides, 307 boulevard Henri-Bourassa Est, Montreal, Que. H3L 1C2

Association québécoise des techniques de l'eau, 6290 rue Périneault, bureau 2, Montreal, Que. H4K 1K5

Birken Clean Air and Water Committee, Attn: Debra Whitman, General Delivery, D'Arcy, B.C. V0N 1L0

Canadian Coalition on Acid Rain, 112 St. Clair Ave., W., Suite 504, Toronto, Ont. M4V 2Y3

Canadian Environmental Law Association, 243 Queen St. W., 4th Floor, Toronto, Ont. M5V 1Z4

Canadian Environmental Law Research Foundation, 243 Queen St. W., 4th Floor, Toronto, Ont. M5V 1Z4

Canadian Nature Federation, 75 Albert St., Suite 203, Ottawa, Ont. K1L 8B9

Centre for the Great Lakes, 3 Church St., Suite 500, Toronto, Ont. M5E 1M2

Churchill Naturalists Society, Box 85, Churchill, Man. R0B 0E0

Conservation Council of New Brunswick, 180 St. John St., Fredericton, N.B. E3B 4A9

Conservation Council of Ontario, 74 Victoria St., Suite 202, Toronto, Ont. M5C 2A5

Dene Nation, Box 5307, Whitehorse, Yukon Y1A 4Z2

Ducks Unlimited, Box 1160, Stonewall, Man. R0L 2Z0

Energy Probe, 100 College St., Toronto, Ont. M5G 1L4

Environmental Law Centre, Suite 202, 10110–124 St., Edmonton, Alta. T2N 1P6

Environmental Resource Centre, 10511 Saskatchewan Dr., Edmonton, Alta. T6E 4S1

Federation of Alberta Naturalists, Box 1472, Edmonton, Alta. T5J 2N5

Federation of Ontario Naturalists, 355 Lesmill Rd., Don Mills, Ont. M3B 2W8

Fédération pour la protection de l'environnement des lacs, 4545 avenue Pierre-de-Coubertin, C.P. 1000, succursale M, Montreal, Que. H1V 3R2

Fraser River Coalition, Attn: Wendy Turner, 3831 W. 50th Ave., Vancouver, B.C. V6N 3V4

Friends of the Earth, 53 Queen St., Suite 53, Ottawa, Ont. K1P 5C5

Friends of the Stikine, 1405 Doran Rd., North Vancouver, B.C. V7K 1N1

Garrison Focus Office, Box 47, 1495 St. James St., Winnipeg, Man. R3H 0W9

Greenpeace, 427 Bloor St. W., Toronto, Ont. M5S 1X7

Island Nature Trust, Box 265, Charlottetown, P.E.I. C1A 7K4

Lake Windermere Naturalists, Box 511, Invermere, B.C. V0A 1K0

Lethbridge Naturalist Society, 2314–22 St. S., Lethbridge, Alta. T1K 2K2

Manitoba Action on Garrison, Box 490, Portage la Prairie, Man. R1A 3E2

Manitoba Fly Fishing Association, 9–607 Gertrude Ave., Winnipeg, Man. R3M 0H6

Manitoba Naturalist Society, Suite 214, 190 Rupert Ave., Winnipeg, Man. R2B 0N2

Manitoba Wildlife Federation Inc., 1770 Notre Dame, Winnipeg, Man. R3E 3K2

National Capital Pollution Probe, 54-53 Queen St., Ottawa, Ont. K1P 5C5

National Survival Institute, 53 Queen St., Suite 27, Ottawa, Ont. K1P 5C5

Nechako-Neyenkut Society, Louise Kaneen and Bruce Kanary, Box 1834, Vanderhoof, B.C. V0J 3S1

Offshore Alliance, Box 132, Nanaimo, B.C. V9R 5K4

Operation Clean Niagara, 83 Gage St., Niagara-on-the-Lake, Ont. L0S 1J0

Pincher Creek Area Environmental Association, Pincher Creek, Alta. T0K 1W0

Ploughshares Saskatoon, Box 823, Saskatoon, Sask. S7K 3L2

Pollution Probe, 12 Madison Ave., Toronto, Ont. M5R 2S1

Red Deer River Naturalist Society, Box 785, Red Deer, Alta. T4N 5H2

Residents for a Free Flowing Stikine, Attn: Joe Murphy, Telegraph Creek, B.C. V2C 5L2

Save Our Streams Inc., 17 Mill St., Willowdale, Ont. M2P 1B3

Sechelt Marsh Protective Society, Box 543, Sechelt, B.C. V0N 3A0

Sierra Club of Ontario, 191 College St., Toronto, Ont. M5T 1P9

Sierra Club of Western Canada (Alberta Group), Box 342, Station G, Calgary, Alta. T3A 2G3

Sierra Club of Western Canada (Saskatchewan Group), 863 N. Athlone Dr., Regina, Sask. S4X 2G7

Skeena Protection Coalition, Attn: Earl Hamilton, Box 954, Terrace, B.C. V8G 4R2

Slave River Coalition, Box 930, Fort Smith, N.W.T. X0E 0P0

Slocan Valley Watershed Alliance, Box 139, Winlaw, B.C. V0G 2J0

Société pour vaincre la Pollution, C.P. 65, succursale Place d'Armes, Montreal, Que. H2Y 3E9

Southern Alberta Environmental Group, 1203 Stafford Dr. N., Lethbridge, Alta. T1H 2B9

Squamish Estuary Nature Centre, Ad Hoc Committee, Box 396, Garibaldi Highlands, B.C. V0N 1T0

Steelhead Society of B.C., Box 33947, Station D, Vancouver, B.C. V6J 4L7

STOP, 1910 boulevard de Maisonneuve ouest, Montreal, Que., H3H 1K2

Temiskaming Environmental Action Committee, Terry Graves, General Delivery, New Liskeard, Ont. P0J 1P0

United Canadian-American Anti-Garrison Lobby, 705–195 Young St., Winnipeg, Man. R3C 3S8

Wildlife Society, Manitoba Chapter, 190 Rupert Ave., Winnipeg, Man. R3B 0N2

Yukon Conservation Society, Box 4163, Whitehorse, Yukon, Y1A 3T3

UNITED STATES

Environmental Protection Agency, Office of the Administrator, Washington, D.C. 20460

Each state has its own range of environment and natural resource agencies.

U.S. Non-Government Organizations
Centre for the Great Lakes, 435 N. Michigan Ave., Suite 1773, Chicago, Ill. 60611

Environmental Policy Institute, 218 D Street S.E., Washington, D.C. 20003

Freshwater Society, 2500 Shadywood Rd., Navarre, Minn. 55392

Great Lakes United, 24 Agassiz Circle, Buffalo, N.Y. 14214

National Water Alliance, 50 E Street S.E., Washington, D.C. 20003

Natural Resources Defense Council, 1350 New York Ave. N.W., Washington, D.C. 20005

World Resources Institute, 1735 New York Ave. N.W., Washington, D.C. 20006

Worldwatch Institute, 1776 Massachusetts Ave. N.W., Washington, D.C. 20036

SELECTED REFERENCES

Allen, Robert. *How to Save the World: A Strategy for World Conservation*. London: Kogan Page, 1981.

Attenborough, David. *Life on Earth*. Toronto: Little, Brown, 1979.

————. *The Living Planet*. Toronto: Collins, 1984.

Barney, Gerald O., and Associates, Inc. *Global 2000: Implications for Canada*. Toronto: Pergamon Press, 1981.

Bocking, Richard C. *Canada's Water: For Sale?* Toronto: James Lewis & Samuel, 1972.

Bourassa, Robert. *Power from the North*. Scarborough: Prentice-Hall, 1985.

Brown, Lester, et al. *State of the World, 1985*. Markham: Penguin Canada, 1985.

Brown, Michael. *Laying Waste: The Poisoning of America by Toxic Chemicals*. New York: Washington Square Press, 1981.

Campbell, Monica E., and Glenn, William M. *Profit from Pollution Prevention: A Guide to Industrial Waste Reduction and Recyling*. Toronto: Pollution Probe Foundation, 1982.

Canadian Geographic, "A New View Canada," August–September. Ottawa, 1985.

Carroll, John E. *Environmental Diplomacy*. Ann Arbor: University of Michigan Press, 1983.

Carson, Rachel. *Silent Spring*. New York: Fawcett Crest, 1962.

Foster, Harold D., and Sewell, W. R. Derrick. *Water: The Emerging Crisis in Canada*. Toronto: James Lorimer and Co. in association with the Canadian Institute for Economic Policy, 1981.

Furon, Raymond. *The Problem of Water: A World Study*. London: Faber and Faber Ltd., 1967.

Garrod, S., et al. *The Regulation of Toxic and Oxidant Air Pollution in North America*. Toronto: CCH, 1986.

Golubev, Genady, and Biswas, Asit K. *Large Scale Water Transfers: Emerging Environmental and Social Experiences*. Riverton, N.J.: Tycooly, 1985.

Health and Welfare Canada. *Guidelines for Canadian Drinking Water Quality, 1978*. Ottawa: Canadian Government Publishing Centre, 1978.

Howard, Ross, and Perley, Michael. *Acid Rain: The North American Forecast*. Toronto: Anansi, 1980.

Irwin, Ronald, et al. *Still Waters: The Chilling Reality of Acid Rain*. Ottawa: Canadian Government Publishing Centre, 1981.

————. *Time Lost: A Demand for Action on Acid Rain*. Ottawa: Canadian Government Publishing Centre, 1984.

Jackson, John, and Weller, Phil, and the Waterloo Public Interest Research Group. *Chemical Nightmare*. Toronto: Between the Lines Press, 1982.

Marsh, James H., ed. *The Canadian Encyclopedia.* Edmonton: Hurtig Publishers Ltd., 1985.

Meadows, Donella, et al. *The Limits of Growth.* New York: Signet, 1972.

Ministry of the Environment, Ministry of Natural Resources. *Guide to Eating Ontario Sport Fish* (updated annually). Ontario Ministry of the Environment.

Myers, Norman, gen. ed. Gaia: *An Atlas of Planetary Management.* Garden City, N.Y.: Anchor/Doubleday, 1984.

Nriagu, Jerome O., and Simmons, Milagros S., eds. *Toxic Contaminants in the Great Lakes.* Toronto: John Wiley and Sons, 1984.

Office of Technology Assessment. *Protecting the Nation's Groundwater from Contamination.* Washington: U.S. Congress Office of Technology Assessment, 1984.

Pearse, Peter H., MacLaren, James W., and Bertrand, Françoise. *Currents of Change: Final Report of the Inquiry on Federal Water Policy.* Ottawa: Environment Canada, 1985. (Note: There are two discussion papers and 22 research papers produced by the inquiry.)

Postel, Sandra. *Water: Rethinking Management in an Age of Scarcity, Worldwatch Paper 62.* Washington: Worldwatch Institute, 1984.

————. *Conserving Water: The Untapped Alternative, Worldwatch Paper 67.* Washington: Worldwatch Institute, 1985.

Royal Society of Canada and National Research Council of the United States. *The Great Lakes Water Quality Agreement: An Evolving Instrument for Ecosystem Management.* Royal Society, Ottawa, and National Research Council, Washington, 1985.

Sadler, Barry, ed. *Water Policy for Western Canada: The Issues of the Eighties.* Calgary: University of Calgary Press, 1983.

Sheaffer, John R., and Stevens, Leonard A. *Future Water.* New York: Morrow, 1983.

Vallentyne, John R. *The Algal Bowl.* Ottawa: Environment Canada, 1974.

INDEX